The Master Musicians S

SCHUBERT

Series edited by
Stanley Sadie

THE MASTER MUSICIANS SERIES

SCHUBERT

by
Arthur Hutchings

Formerly Professor of Music in the University of Durham
Professor Emeritus of the University of Exeter

With eight pages of plates
and music examples in the text

J. M. DENT & SONS LTD
London, Melbourne and Toronto

Printed in Great Britain
by Biddles Ltd, Guildford, Surrey
and bound at the Aldine Press, Letchworth, Herts
for
J. M. DENT & SONS LTD
Aldine House, Welbeck Street, London
First published 1945
Revised edition 1973
Paperback edition 1976
Last reprinted 1979

Hardback ISBN: 0 460 03139 2
Paperback ISBN: 0 460 02111 7

CONTENTS

NOTE TO THE FOURTH EDITION

THE enlarged edition of O. E. Deutsch's *Schubert: The Documents of his Life and Work* was issued two years later than the first edition of this book; but through the late Dr Eric Blom, then General Editor of the Master Musicians, I secured not only carbon copies of Deutsch's monumental work but its author's generous permission to use their contents with only general acknowledgment. This surely prevented extensive revisions in later editions of my book, but I have been forced to make a few in deference to more recent work by other scholars. Some of them show my indebtedness to Maurice J. E. Brown's *Schubert: A Critical Biography* and to his articles on Schubert's unpublished music, the chronology of his piano sonatas, etc. I have had also to give some account of Professor Gerald Abraham's work on what can now be the 'Unfinished Symphony' only by popular misnomer. Although during the past few years Schubert's works for the stage have elicited both performances and valuable writings I have resisted the temptation to expand the very short commentary upon them. They contain items of vintage Schubert but still show no likelihood of entering the repertory; their full discussion still strikes me as belonging to a musicological review and not to this book.

A. H.

ILLUSTRATIONS

Between pages 122 and 123

SCHUBERT
(*from a Lithograph by Josef Teltscher, 1826*)

VIENNA, VIEW FROM THE UPPER BELVEDERE
(*from a Coloured Engraving by F. C. Zoller, c. 1800*)

JOHANN BAPTIST JENGER, ANSELM HÜTTENBRENNER AND SCHUBERT
(*from a Coloured Drawing by Josef Teltscher, c. 1827*)

SCHUBERT EVENING AT JOSEF VON SPAUN'S HOUSE
(*from an Oil Sketch by Moritz von Schwind, c. 1870*)

SCHUBERT
(*from a Water-colour by Wilhelm August Rieder, 1825*)

THE UNFINISHED SYMPHONY. THE OPENING OF THE FIRST
MOVEMENT

COURT AND GARDEN OF SCHUBERT'S BIRTHPLACE WITH THE
'TROUT' WELL ON THE RIGHT

'TO MUSIC'. AS WRITTEN IN THE ALBUM OF ALBERT SOWINSKI

vi

CHAPTER I

SCHUBERT AND VIENNA

AMONG the lives of the master musicians Schubert's is the shortest: it is also the least meteoric, the least romantic in the Byronic sense. Though the admired centre of his own circle, he cut no public figure as performer, publicist or impresario, and whatever his faults he was the most modest of men, to whom it can never have occurred that his was the next name in the apostolic succession of musical pontiffs to follow that of Beethoven. Some of his greatest music is easy-going; some of his weakest is flabby; and only his idolaters could imagine his having what is usually meant by a strong character.

In the year of his death at the age of thirty-one, his reputation was spreading, not from any push on his part but because his work came in on the flood-tide of the new lyric verse, and because gatherings of the 'Schubertiad' type were increasingly popular with the humbler citizens and tradesfolk as with the artistic bohemian bourgeoisie. The atmosphere of these Viennese musical evenings is for ever enshrined for us in Schubert's *Moments musicaux*, in the *Impromptus*, the vast pile of sociable piano duets, the waltzes of days before the Strausses (more hearty and less heart-felt than theirs) and above all in the songs which poured almost ceaselessly from his pen. Publishers were discovering the commercial value of this music with middle-class home musicians, for whom one of the new pianofortes not only enhanced the social amenity and status of the drawing-room, but also placed that apartment on the direct road to the land where the pale citrons grow.

From these middle classes Schubert came; for their immediate emotional demands he wrote; the picturesqueness of the verses they loved was his inspiration, and their hospitable homes were as much his evening resort as were the coffee-house and theatre; with him bohemianism was no revolt from a class, but from a routine. None of the misconceptions concerning him is more false than that which supposes he was unhappy or without honour in his own city. Was he so very poor or ill-used?[1] Are business terms in sheet-music more generous to-day? With our trusts, scholarships, gramophone societies and broadcasting committees, which may help a few whose talents have been seen early and by the right people, are not most of our young composers beholden to parents or, as was Schubert, to friends (though they more often to him)? Are not most of our more promising youngsters forced to strum, scribble or teach to buy the food and lodging used while composing? And what academy would engage a young Schubert?

If Schubert's hand-to-mouth life was one of poverty, the iron did not enter his soul, as it must have entered Mozart's or Wolf's in Vienna. True, he applied for a *Capellmeister's* post, but he was more anxious for the success of his operatic ventures. Apart from his teaching in the Esterházy household there was no evidence that he did a single piece of work which he did not wish to do; his life was his art and nothing else, and though that art includes creations which impress with their magnificence, his most typical work is like himself—spontaneous, endearing, heartfelt, sincere. To us no more than to his contemporaries does he present a titanic figure after the style of Handel, Beethoven or Wagner—Nietzschean supermen with the will to be conquerors in their own world and ultimately to enjoy its tributes. As a critic has said, 'every work by Schubert is an early work,' and though he had his adult and magniloquent moods, the idealized Vienna of his fancy is a city of eternal youth with a countryside close at hand from which the blossom never fades.

It would be as easy to debunk Schubert's Vienna[2] as to debunk Schubert, its most vivid artistic representative. Congress Vienna was socially and morally lax. Her people, having been chastised with whips to pay for the war, were chastised with scorpions to pay for the lavish staging of larger and smaller acts in the Congress comedy. But the setting, the proscenium spectacle, was lovely

[1] Not all stories of publishers' rapacity are credible. Haslinger gave 300 florins to Ferdinand Schubert for the songs called *Schwanengesang*. Can we believe Grove's statement that the same man gave 10*d.* each for the *Winter Journey* songs?

[2] As late as in 1860, when Elizabeth, the young wife of the Emperor Francis Joseph, asked for a bathroom in the palace, the request caused consternation!

2

enough. During the prolific years of Schubert's artistic life Vienna was full of the sycophants, mistresses, lackeys and soldiery of a thousand foreign emissaries, and as Metternich's police and spies made it impossible for intelligent Vienna to think what it liked, or at least to mention what it thought, it needed little dissuading from thought; it gave itself up to *Gemütlichkeit*—to gaping at fireworks, at the fashionable worshippers in St. Stephen's or at the notabilities to be met in the streets and shops or in the Augarten (which had been transformed into a veritable fair-ground), to dancing and singing, to drinking or love-making, to coffee-house chat or, if not inclined for these common dissipations of the evening, to giving parties devoted to music and romantic verses—Schubertiads in fact. However unpleasant we know the real Vienna to have been, we must continue to accept the romanticized Vienna if we are to know the Schubertian *Zeitgeist*; for Schubert and his circle themselves escaped into this idealized Vienna. The imagery of their verses, sad or merry, is taken from an idealized countryside-and-city set between Atzenbrugg and the Danube, all of whose inhabitants are young and lovelorn; for in the flood-tide of the romantic movement those in love with love included every youthful male and female of Vienna who had not reached the desperation of threescore years and ten. We have no certain knowledge of any private enamourings of Schubert, but 'Schwammerl'[1] was beloved of all in the dream-world of a Schubertiad.

There is a poem in one of the modern anthologies dealing with the transfiguration of a drab street by a sudden flood of light from the setting sun; the sunlight which transformed old Vienna came from within the hearts of its young romantics, and how easy it was, even without the two hundred lamplighters employed nightly for the carnival in the Prater, to see Congress Vienna through an aura of romance! Michael Kelly, Mozart's friend and first Basilio in *Figaro*, speaks of 'waltzing from ten at night until seven in the morning.' The waltzes Kelly heard, the waltzes Schubert heard Lanner play, were not the succulent, fully scored waltzes of the ambitious Strausses, but the *Ländler* and German Dances which Mozart knew.

[1] Literally something like 'Spongy'; the translation of the *Schubert Documents*, edited by O. E. Deutsch, has 'Tubby.'

3

They passed through Schubert's hands on their way into the city from the countryside, which in those days touched the ramparts of the inner city in many districts; some of his waltzes are actually entitled *Atzenbrugg Dances*,[1] and dancing in his day was as popular in the open air as in taverns and indoor resorts. As Schubert's waltz was Mozart's waltz, so Schubert's Vienna was Mozart's Vienna—the old city, not to be confused with the 'Blue Danube' Vienna of musical comedy.

Circumstance made old Vienna—and for that matter later Vienna [2] —the loveliest of the European capitals to look upon, with more open spaces, green or cobbled, than could have existed in London when Kensington and Chelsea were villages. Quality promenaded on the glacis, the greensward that sloped outwards from the rampart enclosing the old city and which, later in the century, made possible the magnificent Ringstrasse, with its double rows of trees, when the rampart was pulled down. Whole districts between the fortifications and a second, outer ring were truly rural; where dwellings existed they were either the residences and gardens of the wealthy, or satellite villages to aristocratic palaces. Idyllic escape was easy, as Beethoven knew. But within the gates, the inner city where Haydn first lived on his return from Esterház, where Mozart and Constanze set up house, where Schubert had his various lodgings—this too, still as handsome a centre as any capital can boast, was full of sights to delight Congress visitors. There was no need to walk out to the Belvedere or to Schönbrunn; within a stone's throw of St. Stephen's in the very centre of the city was a beautiful palace associated with Beethoven's conquest of nobility—the Lobkowitz Palace; not far away was the Rasumovsky Palace, into which Tsar Alexander's residence

[1] The German Dances (called by the abbreviation *Deutsche*) formed the type on which the later waltz was most closely modelled; but as witness to the rusticity of popular dancing in Schubert's Vienna we may note that one of the favourite measures was the old 'Bolster Dance' (*Polstertanz*). Whether or not Schubert intended people to dance to his piano waltzes, they reflect the craze of *Biedermeier* Vienna and form a link between the rustic waltz and the tunes of the Lanner Quartet to which the crowd waltzed at the 'Bock' and other coffee-houses near the Prater.

[2] But unfortunately not modern Vienna.

brought the most lavish ball of the Congress. But the eye could delight in less exalted things—in the grand shops of the Graben, the houses in fine streets like the Kohlmarkt, with exorbitant rents on the lower floors, but with the chance of useful connections for the poor musician or artist living in the top rooms (a situation paralleled in the more expensive colleges of Oxford and Cambridge). There were nodal centres like the Michaelerplatz, with its church, Burg Theatre and Michaelerhaus facing from different angles, the fine market squares terminating in the façade of a church or theatre, or crowned with a magnificent fountain or monument.

This was the city known wherever German is spoken as *Bieder-meier* Vienna. *Biedermeier* was a later creation of the humorous journal *Fliegende Blätter,* a simple, good-natured, Philistine character, sup-posed contributor of the verses called *Biedermeierlieder*. His name is applied to the period between 1815 and mid-century in Vienna as precisely as we apply the words 'Regency' and 'Victorian' to English periods. We have already noted the musical distinction between the *Biedermeier* period and its successor in comparing the local colour of the Schubert-Lanner waltz with the cosmopolitan *allure* of the Strauss-Waldteufel waltz. The names of Strauss's most popular successes are well known; Lanner's titles show the *Biedermeier* touch —*Terpsichore, Flora, Schönbrunner,* etc. The holiday Mecca of *Bieder-meier* Vienna was Leopoldstadt, the northern outgrowth of the city towards the river; here, farther out than the Augarten, was the yet more democratic Prater, a popular pleasance which served the pur-poses of our Hyde Park, Richmond Park, Vauxhall Gardens and Hampstead Heath combined.

The traveller Count de la Garde writes describing the Prater:

It is crossed by glorious avenues and, as at Schönbrunn, one sees in-numerable deer and fawns wandering in the glades . . . one is also provided here with all the charming amenities of culture and art . . . numerous booths, cafés and social resorts, where the Viennese can indulge their love of music to their hearts' content . . . there are delights of all kinds to suit the taste of every age.

In the morning, here was Vienna's Rotten Row; quizzers had their eyeful of elegance on horseback or within carriages; later in the day there were swings, peep-shows, entertainments or music on portable stages, such as had been seen for years in the old city market-places, and had been the *bêtes noires* of pious Maria Theresa. There were merry-go-rounds, waxworks, a 'Gothic Tower' and course after dainty course at the 'Sleeping Beauty,' the 'Green Poplar' or the 'Whale'; in the evening there were fireworks and the seemingly eternal music and dancing. Great popular holidays, when streets were crowded with a throng moving towards the Augarten and Prater, occurred at regular intervals, notably on May Day and on St. Bridget's Day in July; at such times grandees had to become ordinary townsfolk or miss the fun.

This cloud-cuckoo-land was enjoyed by musicians, poets, artists, actors and intellectuals (if there were any—perhaps one should say '*salon* philosophers') as much as by the butchers, bakers and candle-stick-makers and their wives and children; but the *salon*-goers and Schubertiad-holders, when not listening to music, had two favourite topics—poetry and drama. Of all ironic choices, Beethoven's *Fidelio* was the first opera to be seen by the royal and exalted visitors, who might, however, have gone to one of Kotzebue's romantic melodramas at the Theater an der Wien, the beautiful playhouse built by Schikaneder, with a drop curtain showing figures from *The Magic Flute,* the pride of his old Theater auf der Wieden. The new stage was said to be the largest in German lands and had secured the first performance of *Fidelio* back in 1805. Those with superior literary tastes could betake themselves to the Burg Theatre to hear the grandiose language of Schiller, for Schreyvogel, the manager, had ideals not unlike those of Lilian Baylis at our own Old Vic, and the Burg Theatre during the *Biedermeier* period set out as a national theatre devoted to German plays and German translations; like our Old Vic, too, it taught actors new standards of teamwork and devotion to the playwright's intentions. Schreyvogel's greatest discovery was the young Grillparzer, a goodish pianist and later an ardent Schubertian. His *Ahnfrau* in 1816 was followed by the overwhelming success, *Sappho,* with Schröder, the great court actress, in the name-part. Grillparzer became the idol of the city and frequented the most celebrated of the artistic-intellectual *salons*— that of Karoline Pichler, the bluestocking novelist. The Kärntnertor Theatre, as also the Theater an der Wien, was wholly conquered during the *Biedermeier*-Schubert period by French and Italian opera. Spontini's spectacular *Vestale* followed *Fidelio* in 1814 at the Theater an der Wien, and after it came the Rossini operas *Tancredi*, *The Barber of Seville* and *Othello*, which were received even more enthusiastically than the pieces by Spontini and Cherubini. The Kärntnertor outdid its rival in one respect—ballet, with Taglioni and Elssler as leading dancers. Satire, comedy and pantomime naturally had their home in the Leopoldstadt Theatre nearer the Prater; the genius of this house, as much the local god of comedy as Grillparzer was of tragedy, was Ferdinand Raimund. Tremendously popular were his 'magic' farces, showing romantic affinities with *The Magic Flute* and *Der Freischütz* (it was the German folklore atmosphere of *Freischütz* which checked the Rossini craze; Bauernfeld's diary informs us that 'wreaths were thrown and poems spouted' at its performance for the benefit of the singer Schröder-Devrient). But Raimund appealed to the hearts of the poor; he mixed comedy with sentiment, himself taking parts like those of a pathetic old man with an extraordinary command of gesture. His chief ability was as an impersonator rather than as an actor. Every poor home in Vienna sang or hummed his song 'Brüderlein fein' from the play *The Girl from Fairyland ; or Cottager as Millionaire*.

All this was Schubert's Vienna, the material for conversation in taverns and coffee-houses or in artistic homes like those of Ignaz Sonnleithner, Grillparzer's uncle; Sonnleithner's son Leopold, of the same age as Grillparzer, was one of Schubert's friends; and Josef Sonnleithner, Ignaz's brother, was one of the founders of the Vienna Philharmonic Society. With the poetry discussed and recited in such homes and with the young men who wrote it we shall deal in the chapters about Schubert's songs. If little detail is given here of the specifically musical life of *Biedermeier* Vienna it is because that is the subject of this book; there never was a more musical city, and no man was ever more representative of his city and time than was Schubert.

There is no indication that Schubert's greatness, had he lived another fifty years, would have been more than musical greatness. He was not a mystic or visionary, like Beethoven, but a dreamer. His art is Apollonian rather than Dionysiac. When Liszt called him the 'most poetic of musicians,' he thought of the same kind of romantic, lyric poetry that appealed to Schubert. Schubert's life cannot therefore be so interesting as that of the visionary Beethoven or the introspective Mozart; yet an artist's biography may be interesting even when his reputation is local and his life suburban. The domestic circumstances, technical interests, religious outlook and inward growth of the recluse Bach are as fascinating as the external struggles and financial battlefields of the more public Handel, of whose private and inner life we know almost nothing. Musicians usually read biography to gain insight into the mentality of one whose music has expressed for them those emotions and experiences common to all sensitive humanity, and their reading can at least give the spice of adventure to subsequent hearings of the familiar music. This cannot be given by a biography of Schubert. Despite the marvellous vein of pathos in his greatest songs, or the magnificence of certain instrumental works, we cannot be sure that he would ever have developed a great inner artistic life which would have taken him apart from his companions or his beloved Vienna. His scanty and scrappy correspondence, whether tender, impulsive or strictly functional, is as spontaneous and disordered as his hand-to-mouth life. The diaries and letters of his friends, so carefully collected by Otto Erich Deutsch,[1] tell us that he has been seen with company at So-and-so's, was at this or that coffee-house or has been composing with unusual industry (if industry could ever be unusual with him). We still know little of the man. His body lived in the real, sordid Vienna; but his imagination inhabited the romantic *Biedermeier* city.

[1] English edition, augmented and furnished with a commentary, published by J. M. Dent & Sons, Ltd., as *Schubert: a Documentary Biography* (1946). Many of the quotations given here are taken from this edition. A *Thematic Catalogue* appeared under the same editorship (1951). The commentary and thematic catalogue, however, were not available for reference at the time of writing; but the author and editor are greatly indebted to Professor Deutsch for making a number of invaluable suggestions.

CHAPTER II

SCHUBERT AT HOME

FEW gardens are attached to houses as near the centre of Vienna as is No. 54 Nussdorferstrasse; but when it was inhabited by the Schuberts and known as No. 72 Himmelpfortgrund (Gate of Heaven), there was a pretty courtyard behind it, with a fountain, gardens to all the neighbouring houses and open fields close by. What is now a long and dullish road leading out of the city became a pleasant country lane in those days soon after one had passed the Schubert home, and brought one to the idyllic scenery of Beethoven's favourite retreat. The house itself, now one of an unattractive row of buildings, was more pleasant then, bearing its sign 'Zum roten Krebsen' (The Red Crayfish).

Schubert's modest birthplace was in the Liechtental district, known for its weavers and laundresses. Franz Theodor Schubert, the composer's father, was parish schoolmaster in a scheme of elementary education not unlike that of the church schools set up in Gladstone's England. Though the surname means 'shoemaker,' his ancestors had been forest labourers or small holders in Moravia until his own generation. The composer's mother, first wife of Franz Theodor, came of Silesian stock, and her folk had been locksmiths, gun-makers and innkeepers. In her girlhood the family saw bad days and moved to Vienna, where the orphaned girls went into domestic service, probably as cooks. However, Elisabeth Vietz married the schoolmaster Schubert, some years her junior. Deutsch comments: 'The Vietz family were of lighter blood than the Schuberts and more artistically gifted, even if only as craftsmen. The Schuberts were the pious and respectable part of the mixture.' A portrait of Franz Theodor Schubert in the Schubert Museum, by an unknown painter, shows spare and somewhat hard-set features befitting his profession. That he could be stern upon occasion is shown by his forbidding his son to come home when the wayward youngster decided to put music before academic study. But the reconciliation, and other glimpses we have of his character, do not point to a harsh nature.

Franz Peter Schubert, the composer, was the youngest of five children; five other children had died early. The father was to have yet another five children by the wife he married in 1813, after the death of Schubert's mother. The composer's two brothers, Ignaz and Ferdinand, both became schoolmasters, and the father intended that Franz, too, should follow that profession. Franz was born on 31st January 1797, and showed his musical talent while still an infant. It is well to point out, however, that he was not a child prodigy, like Mozart, and the father is not to be condemned too harshly for failing to see his son as a budding genius. Those who have taught boys for some time know that musical talent often shows very early, and in nearly every school is to be found at least one boy who can play a song or hymn-tune with fairly correct harmony, even though he has never received any instruction at the keyboard. The father outlived his gifted son by two years, and supplied the following account of the composer's infancy:

Before he was five I prepared him for elementary instruction and in his sixth year sent him to school, where he was always higher in class than his fellow-scholars. When he was eight I gave him preliminary instruction in violin playing, and proceeded far enough with him to enable him to play duets fairly well; then I sent him for singing lessons to Michael Holzer, the Liechtental choirmaster. Holzer often assured me, with tears in his eyes, that he had never had such a pupil. 'Whenever I set out to teach him something new,' he said, 'I find that he knows it already. In the end I did not give him any real instruction, but only listened to him in silent amazement.'

Franz similarly outstripped his elder brother Ferdinand, who taught him piano playing. Kreissle states that before going away to school (we do not know where he received his elementary education—not, apparently, at his father's school) the boy had written songs and instrumental pieces, including string quartets. Ferdinand Schubert mentions a Fantasy for four hands, written in 1810, and the song *Hagar's Lament* as the earliest compositions; but this seems unlikely.

The best education to be obtained in Vienna, whether for duke's son or cook's son, was at the Imperial 'Convict,' a seminary whose German name sounds grim to English ears, though its derivation is as simple as that of 'convent.' The school, in the University Square, was attached to the Court Chapel, for which it supplied choristers, just as the City of London School supplies choirboys for the Temple Church. With no intention that his son should turn professional musician, Schubert's father saw the youngster prepared in Latin and elements ready to enter for a choral scholarship at the Seminary; only the musical side of the examination seems to have been competitive, and here he was well grounded in harmony, organ playing and general musical knowledge by Michael Holzer, the Liechtental choirmaster, under whose direction he had played the violin for Sunday mass and attracted the admiration of parishioners by his fine treble voice. It is said that his homely appearance—the spectacles on his chubby face, the grey homespun clothing—suggested the nickname 'miller' and caused general amusement among the other little beasts who had assembled on 30th September 1808 to appear before the court examiners, Antonio Salieri and Josef Eybler. In his old parish choir little Schubert had played and sung the masses written by these two notables; they, in their turn, were now impressed by the boy's ability at sight-reading and by the quality of his voice. The three choral scholarships were granted to the trebles Schubert and Müllner and to an alto called Weisse.

The 'miller' clothing was replaced by the impressive uniform of a court chorister. Father Schubert had done wisely in sending his lad to the Seminary. Friendships with boys who were not members of the choral foundation but who came from more wealthy parents and paid fees lasted Schubert all his life. Conditions at the school may have been Spartan, unless a certain letter from Franz to his brother exaggerates emptiness of stomach and pocket as schoolboys' letters usually do; but the Seminary can have been no coarser or rougher than famous English public schools before the general reforms following Arnold's lead at Rugby. One thing is certain: had either snobbery or bullying existed, we may be sure they would have made a serious impression on so sensitive a child as Schubert, and everything points to his being happy with his fellows and popular in a way that would scarcely have found a parallel among the young

Philistines of Eton and Harrow. Though he had to rise early after a meagre supper to practise in a cold room, there *was* a practice room, and his music attracted school friends—Stadler, Senn, Holzapfel, etc.—above all his devoted friend and protector, Josef von Spaun, leader of the school orchestra. This youth, nine years older than Schubert, lived at the Seminary, which was open to some of the university students. He studied law, and his later history as a civil servant shows him to have been sensitive, yet of solid parts, the least bohemian of Schubert's circle. His portrait bears out this impression. Schubert confided to Spaun that he composed, and would do so a good deal more could he but afford the manuscript paper; not the least of Spaun's kindnesses was the provision of music paper sufficient to last even the prolific Schubert for a long while.

There is no evidence for the statement, made in one life of Schubert, that 'the discipline was frightful' at the Seminary, or that Innocenz Lang, the director, was 'a martinet who brooked no nonsense.' As well as the usual subjects studied in an English school, the curriculum included religious doctrine (taught by a resident professor), Latin, French, Italian[1] and, for the choral scholars at least, singing, piano and violin. In May 1809 the school buildings were pierced by a French howitzer grenade, and a report by Dr. Lang to the court music chamberlain written in the following October makes this interesting comment: 'The pianoforte master Ruczizka continued, even in this agitated year, with his usual commendable zeal, especially to instruct the boys during off-hours in the various branches of music.' Later on, the court chamberlain himself writes: 'Although Ruczizka is under no obligation to work at anything beyond the pianoforte, it does this man the more honour that, apart from this instrument, the Imperial Seminary is indebted to him for a tolerably well-organized band, including even wind instruments.' After Schubert's work on Sundays and saints' days in the imperial choir, it is clear that the most useful features of the Seminary were the piano practice room, where Spaun first found him playing a Mozart sonata, and the regular practices of the orchestra which played works by Méhul, Cherubini, Haydn, Mozart and even Beethoven. Schubert soon

[1] These two languages were not taken by Schubert, however, as his reports show.

rose to leadership of the little band. On Sundays, saints' days and other school holidays the boy had more music at home, and especially enjoyed taking part in a home quartet—brothers Ignaz and Ferdinand playing first and second violins, Franz the viola and the father cello.

Now for the seamy side. The well-known letter to Ferdinand is dated 24th November 1812, and is as follows:

I have long been thinking about my situation and found that, although satisfactory on the whole, it is not beyond improvement here and there. You know from experience that we all like to eat a roll and a few apples sometimes, the more so if after a middling lunch one may not look for a miserable evening meal for eight and a half hours. This wish, which has often become insistent, is now becoming more and more frequent, and I had willy-nilly to make a change. The few groats I receive from Father go to the deuce the very first days, and what am I to do for the rest of the time? 'Whosoever believeth on Him shall not be put to shame.'[1] I thought so too.—How if you were to let me have a few kreuzer a month? You would not so much as know it, while I in my cell should think myself lucky, and be content. I repeat, I lean upon the words of the Apostle Matthew, where he says: 'He that hath two coats, let him give one to the poor,' etc. Meanwhile I hope you will give ear to the voice that calls unceasingly to you to remember

Your loving, poor, hopeful,
and again poor
brother,
FRANZ.

But neither the poor school fare nor the cold of the practice room was the major trouble of Schubert's schooldays. Most people who are even slightly musical have been sensitive children, and know how amazingly hardy childhood can be as regards harsh physical conditions. The real hardship of Schubert's boyhood lay not in the meagre coarseness of school fare but in a deeper conflict of claims. His father had not sent him to one of the famous boarding-schools in the country in order that he might benefit only from the unusual

---

[1] Both scriptural references in this letter are incorrect. The texts Schubert had in mind are Romans, x. 11, and Luke, iii. 11. In his later examinations for qualification as a schoolmaster he passed well in all subjects except divinity!

musical provisions: as soon as Franz's voice broke, his choral scholar-ship would terminate, but a high standard in academic studies might make him eligible for one of the endowed free places. During his first year and a half at the Seminary, the preparation in class subjects that the child had received under the scrutiny of his father made it fairly easy for the lad to keep abreast of his fellows. Thereafter his terminal reports show a disparity between musical and academic progress. Lang, far from appearing in the character of a martinet and Philistine, lays stress on the fact that Schubert's musical ability is an asset to the school; but the governors, watching to see that their free places are not misused, point out that 'music and singing are but secondary accomplishments.'

So also thought Schubert the elder who, forbidding his boy to think of a musical career, thereby provided us with the one and only example of disciplinary harshness on his part that we know. But on 28th May 1812 his first wife, Franz's mother, died of typhus, and in their bereavement father and son came closer together. During the following twelvemonth the boy's voice broke, but the school authorities were willing to grant him a 'Meerfeld endowment' place so that he might proceed to higher studies, on condition that he worked during his vacation to reach the qualifying standard. As he left the Seminary in October 1813, he either could not or would not avail himself of the endowment, but his connection with the school was far from being severed and his memory of his life there cannot but have been happy. With Spaun or others (no doubt through their generosity and his obvious popularity) he had frequently been during his schooldays to the Kärntnertor theatre to hear such operas as Weigl's *The Orphanage* and *The Swiss Family*, Boïeldieu's *Jean de Paris*, Cherubini's *Medea* and Spontini's *La Vestale*, and more en-during things too; like Spaun, he went back to the Seminary to play with the orchestra, his first Symphony, in D major, being per-haps played on Lang's name-day in 1813. We do not know what concerts he attended, but he must have become familiar with Beet-hoven's biggest works, which filled him with awe, as he told Spaun. On 14th May 1814 (after leaving school) he heard *Fidelio*, and early in the next year was tremendously impressed by Gluck's *Iphigenia in Tauris*, for Bauernfeld states that the performance led Schubert to make a careful study of the newly published Gluck scores. Thus did his school friendships and occupations cover over any sharp dividing-line between his life at the Seminary and after. Another link made the change even less sudden: the court musical director, Salieri, had been one of the first to recognize the child's musical ability, and was responsible for seeing that Ruczizka gave him lessons in composition; when that teacher reported that 'the boy knows everything already; he has been taught by God,' Salieri himself took Schubert's lessons, and Schubert continued with Salieri after leaving the Seminary.

Salieri's tuition covers the five years 1813–17. Had he not bene-fited, Schubert would not have continued. Without any defiance, he would have become an absentee. He had written parts of masses, works for wind instruments, three or four string quartets, three fan-tasies for piano duet and a birthday ode for his father. He added to these works during his first year after leaving the Seminary, and Salieri saw the extraordinary fund of invention and copiousness; he is said to have been particularly impressed with the song *Hagar's Lament* in spite of its being in German and of a sprawling nature. Two more quartets followed in 1814, and Salieri deemed his pupil sufficiently advanced to attempt an opera. It is said that Schubert absented himself for a few lessons and then appeared with a complete score of *Des Teufels Lustschloss* (*The Devil's Pleasance*) to a libretto by Kotzebue.

On leaving school Schubert would normally be conscribed for a lengthy period of military service. From this schoolmasters were exempt—a consideration which may have helped him to put no ob-jection to his father's plan to make him an usher in the Liechtental parish school and so keep the salary in the family, where it was badly needed. (The elder Schubert was married again, to Anna Kleyen-böck, and Franz seems to have been on the happiest terms with his stepmother.) Accordingly the youth entered the training-college of St. Anna for the academic year 1813–14. There followed two years at an occupation which, even in these days of reasonable hours and small classes, is drudgery to any man who does not feel teaching to be vocational. To Schubert these days must have been more prison-like than those in the Seminary with plenty of young friends who shared his tastes. Had he not been so hopelessly ill adapted to schoolmastering, one could not forgive—one does not even now—a man of his sensibility for 'keeping his hands in practice on the children's ears,' as his sister tells us. According to one Schmidtler, Schubert's lack of natural ability as a disciplinarian, culminating in a smart box on the ear of a stupid girl, led to his dismissal.

But no other occupation could have provided so much spare time and holiday time. In his first year at the usher's desk he covered a prodigious amount of manuscript paper. His first public success as a composer was with 'the most remarkable first mass ever written.' The prominence into which this Mass in F brought him was largely due, no doubt, to Salieri's enthusiasm. The first performance, on 16th October 1814, marked the centenary dedication festival of the Liechtental parish church. Schubert directed, Holzer played the organ and Therese Grob, claimed by some to be Schubert's first sweetheart,[1] sang the soprano solos. Shortly afterwards Schubert, Holzer and, most probably, Therese took the same parts in a second performance at St. Augustine's court church, and this was the occasion of Salieri's demonstration of respect and affection for his pupil. In the following year the Masses in B flat major and G major were given at Schubert's old parish church.

Schubert the elder could not but have been convinced of the fact that his ugly duckling was no duck at all. All we know of his spoken or written thoughts shows tenderness and appreciation. His part in the home quartet also shows that he was not without musical ability, and when we find a professional musician like the elder Mozart trying to dissuade his son from the hand-to-mouth existence of a freelance, how are we to blame old Schubert? Leopold Mozart saw only one link between a musical vocation and a place in the world—the work of a paid and regular servant; Wolfgang was let off the parental leash to secure 'a famous capellmeistership'; he came home instead with a wife who was not approved. Father Schubert

[1] It may be made clear at once, and for the rest of this study, that nothing certain is known of Schubert's love affairs, nor even that he ever had any one great love. Ephemeral dalliance may or may not be interesting; it depends on its quality and that of those who dally. No single sporting with Amaryllis in the shade casts either light or shade upon Schubert's work.

saw only the same hope for a son determined to be a musician. The precise month and year in which he resigned himself to the spectacle of Franz's living under the roof of no protector-employer, but in the lodgings of this or that friend, cannot be ascertained. The ties which bound Franz to his father's home were first stretched, without parental disapproval it seems, when he was freely received into other houses whose occupiers were interested in music and poetry. The widow Grob, mother of Therese, for instance, owned a silk factory in Vienna; she herself was a cultured woman and her son Heinrich was a good cellist and pianist. Schubert often visited the Grobs.

Then came the bohemian friendships. At this time Schubert popped in and out of the Seminary for band rehearsals, concerts or just unofficial Schubertiads, but most of his first school friends were a few years older than he and more familiar with the young poets, painters and amateur musicians of Vienna. Either when visiting their old school, or else when Schubert called at their own homes or lodgings, they widened a circle of which, it is clear, Schubert—the modest, unsophisticated schoolmaster-apprentice — was always the centre. That fact is important since, to us who did not know him personally, Schubert the man does not seem particularly attractive. There was never a real Schubertiad without Schubert: that we gather from many a letter from one member of his circle to another.

While still supposedly a teacher, Schubert was becoming the focal point of a circle whose chief original members were Spaun, Schober and Mayrhofer. They were to remain among the composer's closest companions, and it may be well to give a brief account of each as he comes prominently into the Schubertian picture. Spaun, after various other appointments, became director of the State Lottery Company, concerning which he wrote: 'It was a strange fortune that put me, who had always been opposed to this gambling business and had never drawn a prize or even bought a ticket, at its head.' Spaun's importance for us lies in the fact that he made Schubert known in society and arranged musical parties at his mother's house. He even wrote to Goethe on 17th April 1816 to interest the poet in the first published volume of Schubert's songs, but his letter was unsuccessful. He had begun his legal studies at Linz, continued them in Vienna, went as probationer for the Ministry of Finance, left the post in 1821 to become a bank manager first at Linz, then at Lemberg (Lwów). Then he returned to Vienna as an official and finally director of the lottery.

Next comes Franz von Schober, a man of most attractive appearance and vivid personality, who let these qualities see him through a pleasant coffee-housing existence. His rooms were the first home of the inner Schubertian circle in the years following Schubert's break with schoolmastering. If Schubert was the centre, Schober was the leader of the group, into which he was brought through the good Spaun's acquainting him with Schubert's early songs, and through the ties of romantic friendship with the painter Moritz von Schwind. Schober's is one of the least stable characters in the Schubertian circle, being thus in strong contrast with Spaun's. Many writers regard Schober as Schubert's bad angel, leading the composer to give a false impression of his character by bravado, bad manners and lax morality. An extract from Bauernfeld's diary, October 1825, reads: 'Schubert is back; a drinking existence often till two or three in the morning—Schober is the worst offender. Of course he has nothing to do and does nothing, which Moritz is always telling him.' Yet Schober dabbled in all the arts—music, painting (some canvases are compositely Schwind and Schober), poetry (*To Music* is one of his pieces) and drama. Add to this that he had also been something of an actor, like Wilhelm Meister, and that he designed Schubert's memorial stone in the Währing Cemetery, and we have a man of parts. How great became Schubert's regard for him we may tell from the composer's letter of 30th November 1826: '. . . you, dear Schober, I shall never, never forget; what you have been to me nobody else can be.'

Schubert was the last man to value a friend for his money, and when one or other of the circle helped him through a difficult patch, there was no question of sponging. The passage quoted from the letter shows genuine personal affection, but that Schober's friendship was practical we may judge when we consider that he and Spaun together made it possible for Schubert to quit schoolmastering. Schober got to know Schubert's songs while on a visit to the Spauns at Linz in 1813; when he came up to Vienna to study law, he sought out the composer and found him correcting school exercises. With

his own mother's and Schubert's father's consent, Franz was taken
away and set up in Schober's rooms in the Landskrongasse. Then
when Schober's brother, an officer in the hussars, required the rooms
and had first claim upon them, Schubert went back home to the
school-house in the Rossau suburb; but Schober always kept a room
ready for Franz, and the two friends shared lodgings whenever the
owner was in town.

Of Schwind and his place among the Schubertians we shall speak
later; Mayrhofer is the next to be described here, since 'a friend,'
probably Spaun, gave Schubert Mayrhofer's *Am See (By the Lake)*
to set to music in 1814. Mayrhofer was erudite, sensitive and
gloomy: he was embittered by his occupation as one of the censor's
officials under the Metternich system. He confessed himself to be
a recluse by nature, and only his love of Schubert's muse brought him
into gay company. At Linz he had studied for the priesthood and
served a three years' novitiate in the monastery of St. Florian. He
was nearly ten years Schubert's senior, and his life remained stoically
self-disciplined even after he had given up his theological training.
The chief quality of his poems is a quiet, romantic melancholy in
the contemplation of nature, which he loves too sincerely to spell
with a capital 'N.' At Schubert's death he was deeply moved.
Eight years afterwards he took his own life. Mayrhofer writes:

The young friend brought Schubert into that very room which, five
years later, we were destined to share. It was in a dark, gloomy street.
House and furniture were the worse for wear; the ceiling was beginning
to bulge, the light obstructed by a large building opposite, and part of the
furniture was an old worn-out piano and a shabby bookstand. . . . I
shall never forget the room nor the hours we spent there. This depth of
sentiment and love for poetry and music drew our interests closer and
closer; I wrote verses, he saw what I wrote, and to these joint efforts many of
his melodies owed their beginning, completion and popularity in the world.

Since forty-seven of Schubert's songs, including some of the best,
are set to Mayrhofer's verses, and since the libretti of two theatrical
works of 1815—*Adrast* and *The Friends of Salamanca*—are by Mayrhofer, his influence on Schubert must have been considerable.

It may well be said that Schubert 'found' himself as a composer
during the distasteful two years of schoolmastering. Apart from

the operatic works mentioned, there were cantatas for name-days or birthdays, masses for Liechtental church, quartets for the home players, symphonies and overtures, but above all the first great and truly Schubertian songs, for among all his six hundred and six none is more perfect in achievement of its artistic aim than is *Margaret at the Spinning-wheel* from Goethe's *Faust,* written in 1814, or the famous Goethe ballad *Erl King,* written very early in the following year. Other songs, such as the setting of Mayrhofer's *By the Lake,* mentioned above, are less striking only by comparison with the two supreme Goethe settings. *Erl King* was sung on the day of its composition in the old Seminary practice room, the first singer being either the composer or Randhartinger or Holzapfel: all three took a turn. It was repeated several times by Randhartinger for the en-thusiastic audience that had collected from within the school walls, and Schubert's right hand was exhausted by the repeating triplets. It is amusing to note that Ruczizka was at pains to 'explain' the jarring minor seconds at the words 'Mein Vater, mein Vater!' Randhartinger was given the manuscript for his efforts and later passed it on to Clara Schumann. The song was not printed until 1821, when the great baritone, Michael Vogl, first popularized it.

A way out of elementary teaching which might satisfy his father presented itself to Schubert in April 1816 by his application for the post of director of the music school at Laibach (Ljubljana), near Trieste. It was a government post and, for those days, better paid than most teaching appointments. The application was backed by a testimonial from Salieri, and so was that of one Jakob Schaufl, but neither was the successful candidate. Nevertheless in the following month Schubert joined other pupils of Salieri's in homage to the old musician at his jubilee. Tributes by Hummel, Moscheles and others took the form of works to be performed after the singing of a mass by Salieri and the presenting of a gold medal, chain and illuminated address. Schubert wrote a cantata to his own words: the little work comprises a chorus, an aria and a three-voice canon.

An entry in Schubert's diary for 17th June 1816 shows that the votive-cantata custom was of commercial value to musicians, for he writes: 'To-day for the first time I composed for money. Namely, a cantata for the name-day of Professor Watteroth, to words by

Dräxler.' This cantata, entitled *Prometheus,* was sung in the professor's garden by some of the law students, whose names include
those of Leopold Sonnleithner, Stadler and Anton Müllner. Another
cantata, produced in September of the same year, is what that age
would have called 'affecting in the extreme.' The work is for
soloists, chorus and orchestra, and bears the title *Expressions of
Gratitude on the part of t he Institute of Teachers' Widows at Vienna to the
Founder and Principal of the same.* This functionary was one Josef
Spendou, chief inspector of schools. Beginning with the words:
'There he lies, struck down by Death,' the work passes from the
spectacle of a dead schoolmaster-father to that of the orphans and
widows, who all dry their tears in a final panegyric of their founder
and protector.

Schubert's life at every point seems to be one of drift, not of clearly
marked-off periods brought about by a resolution to live here or live
there, to do this or do that. The music poured from him—in 1815
alone he had written over a hundred and fifty songs—and any change
in his place or manner of living was but an adjustment to avoid
interruption in music-making, as he might have shifted his body in a
chair because it became cramped in a certain position. Just as his
leaving school made no clear break in his life, and indeed was not a
complete leaving at all, so his leaving home to live with Schober was
what officialdom calls 'the regularizing of a position which had
arisen some time previously.' During the two years in his father's
school he gradually stretched the strings which held him to his
home and its attitude to music; the strings broke only as a boy's
voice breaks. The more his artistic circle grew, the more he belonged
to that artistic world and the less to the static and circumspect king-
dom of a parish schoolmaster. Yet his father hoped that a year's
semi-vagrancy as a musician trying to live by his art would bring
Franz back to school with new resolutions; at least he obtained a
year's grace from the educational authorities to allow his son to develop
his musical studies. Franz was free: he could not dig; to beg he
was ashamed. More precisely, he turned for a time to giving music
lessons, but it seems to have been a very short time, and he was not a
sponger, whatever else we may think to his discredit. Schober's
lodgings provided bed and roof.

CHAPTER III

SCHUBERT AND HIS FRIENDS

WHAT Schubert did and where he went during this or that period of his life is of little importance, and the aim of his biographers must be to show what he was rather than what he did, except compose. The mirrors of what he was are chiefly his friends: we shall glean remarks and opinions from their letters when separated and draw a pen portrait of each new one as he arrives. The brightest star to swim into Schubert's sky after he had ceased to live with his family was the great baritone, Michael Vogl.

Like Shaliapin in our own day, Vogl had a powerful personality and a commanding presence. In him was a rare combination of fine voice and fine musical intelligence. His upbringing had been monastic and one of his chief interests was moral philosophy; the Bible, Epictetus and Thomas à Kempis were his favourite mental pabulum, and he translated doctrinal works into German. He was a consistent diary-keeper and penned the following tribute to Schubert: 'Nothing could show more clearly the need for a practical school of singing (in German) than the songs of Schubert. . . . How many have learnt how the most beautiful words of our finest poets can be not only translated into music, but exalted and enhanced in the process.' This entry dates from some years after his first acquaintance with the composer, for Vogl had by that time retired from the theatre and specialized as a singer of songs. When Schober and Spaun first introduced him to Schubert, Vogl was the adored baritone of the Kärntnertor Theatre, where his recommendation interested certain other great artists among his colleagues in Schubert and his songs. We anticipate in mentioning one of them, Anna Milder, as one of the Schubertian group; our story has reached only the year 1817, but letters from Anna Milder-Hauptmann, as she became, telling the composer of the enthusiasm when she sang some of his songs in Berlin, were among the last Schubert received before his death. Milder had been Beethoven's first Leonora, and it was at her request to write an opera for Berlin that Schubert set to work on Bauernfeld's libretto *The Count of Gleichen*. He finished no more than the sketch.

At his first meeting with Vogl, Spaun tells us, the composer 'entered with shuffling gait and incoherent speech.' Vogl was not greatly impressed till he looked over the songs *Ganymede* and *The Shepherd's Lament*. On leaving, he tapped Schubert on the shoulder and said: 'There is some stuff in you, but you are too little of an actor, too little of a charlatan. You squander your fine thoughts instead of developing them.' But he soon returned and called regularly upon the composer, who was some thirty years his junior. The two men became close friends, and Schubert visited Vogl almost daily to try over new songs and to hear the singer declaiming verses for new settings. Vogl's literary taste must have influenced the younger man considerably, and it is generally supposed that the difficult range of some of Schubert's songs is attributable to the abnormal compass of Vogl's voice. *Mennon, Erl King, Wanderer* and *Postilion Chronos* are among the fine songs first popularized by Vogl before the last famous song cycles.

There are no important movements to be recorded for the year 1817. Friends called, Schubert called on the friends, they all called and had a musical party at a new friend's, or they went to the opera and waxed enthusiastic over Rossini, as did the rest of Vienna just at this time. The *Overtures in the Italian Style* reflect the fashion of the year. After a performance of *Tancredi*, the party being loud in its praises of Italian opera, particularly of the Rossinian overtures, Schubert dashed off the score of the D major Overture to show that the Italian fashionable style was easily imitated. Schubert's natural development veered away from Italian traditions towards the German *Singspiel*, melodrama and *Lied*. This alone would be enough to account for the parting of Schubert and old Salieri; after 1817 the court musician's name no longer appears in collected Schubertiana, except in a song-dedication, but there seems to be no foundation to the story of a violent personal quarrel supposedly following Salieri's correction of passages in the younger man's B flat major Mass.

One document of 1817 is amusingly comparable with the trade

notices of firms who wish to make it clear that they have no connection whatever with rivals of similar name. An esteemed musical
practitioner of Dresden, called Franz Schubert, was sent by mistake
the manuscript of *Erl King*, and penned the following document to
Breitkopf & Härtel, the Leipzig publishers:

I have further to inform you that some ten days ago I received a valued
letter from you in which you enclosed the manuscript of Goethe's *Erl King*
alleged to be set by me. With the greatest astonishment I beg to state that
this cantata was never composed by me. I shall retain the same in my
possession in order to learn, if possible, who sent you that sort of trash in
such an impolite manner, and also to discover the fellow who has thus
misused my name.

The greater Franz Schubert was still unknown outside his circle,
for he was not a public performer, nor a *Capellmeister,* nor had he
produced a successful opera. He was still without a salaried em-
ployment or any regular source of income.

In the summer of 1818 the opportunity was given to live comfortably, with a small salary and time to compose, at Castle Zseliz,
the country seat of Count Johann Esterházy. The father of Caroline
Unger, the singer, successfully recommended Schubert as music
tutor to the two Esterházy girls, and off the composer went to Hungary. A great deal of nonsense has been talked of Schubert's
wretched treatment by the Esterházys, who, even if they were not
such lavish patrons of music as had been their kinsfolk in Haydn's
time, behaved (to a young man of whom they knew little) no worse,
and probably a good deal better, than was customary in country
households. Within the city itself Beethoven had won the right
to disregard social disparity; Haydn knew his place even when, full
of years and honours, he conversed with Esterházy and his friends
on terms of familiarity, and his position when first brought into the
household was that of a superior servant, just as Schubert was
regarded. Moreover Schubert was without the social sensitivity of
Mozart and, in a way inconceivable in Mozart, Schubert's first
descriptions of personalities in the Esterházy household do not concern
the chief figures therein, but the denizens of the kitchen:

Not a soul here has any feeling for true art, or at most the countess now and again. . . . So I am alone with my beloved and have to hide her in my room, in my pianoforte and in my bosom. Although this often makes me sad, on the other hand it elevates me the more.[1] . . . Our castle is not one of the largest, but very neatly built. It is surrounded by a most beautiful garden. I live at the inspectorate. It is fairly quiet, save for some forty geese, which at times cackle so lustily together that one cannot hear oneself speak. Good people around me, all of them. It must be rare for a count's retinue to fit so well together as these do. The inspector, a Slavonian, is a good fellow, and has a great opinion of his former musical talents. He still blows two German dances in 3–4 time on the lute [!], with great virtuosity. His son studies philosophy, is here on holiday just now, and I hope I shall take to him. His wife is a woman like all women who want to be ladies. The steward fits his office perfectly: a man with extraordinary insight into pockets and bags. The doctor, who is really accomplished, ails like an old lady at the age of twenty-four. Very unnatural. The surgeon, whom I like best, is a venerable old man of seventy-five, always cheerful and happy. May God give every one so happy an old age! . . . A companion of the count, a merry old fellow and a capable musician, often keeps me company. The cook, the lady's-maid, the chambermaid, the nurse, the porter etc. and two grooms are all good folk. The cook rather a rake; the lady's-maid thirty years of age; the chambermaid very pretty and often my companion; the nurse a good old thing; the porter my rival. The two grooms are more fit for traffic with horses than with human beings. The count is rather rough, the countess haughty but more sensitive; the little countesses are nice children. So far I have been spared dining with the family. . . . I hit it off quite well with all these people.

As Schubert was by no means a prolific letter-writer, the correspondence with friends and family consequent upon his first parting with Vienna must be regarded as an abnormally fine crop. During the summer he tells every one that he 'lives and composes like a god,'

[1] To use space in refutation of the supposition that Schubert is here referring to a person, the younger of his pupils, who was only in her thirteenth year, and not to his muse is almost as fatuous as to support it. Romantic poets and musicians of the period proclaimed frequently the accommodation of their bosoms, but even Schubert would have had difficulty in an attempt to 'hide' any young woman in his breast pocket. Similarly ridiculous is the story that at his second stay at Zseliz Schubert's admiration for Caroline Esterházy reached the dimensions of an *affaire du cœur*.

but in the August he longs for his beloved gay Vienna which he has no prospect of visiting before November. Schubert did a little versifying now and again and might have made no poorer a poet or painter in the picturesque style than did some of his bohemian friends; the stay in Hungary must at least have enlarged his emotional experience. Some letters of this period between the Schubert brothers are evidence of the affection between members of the family. Ignaz writes to Franz in the October of this year:

How enviable is your lot . . . while the likes of us wretched scholastic beasts of burden are abandoned to all the roughnesses of wild youngsters and exposed to a host of abuses, not to mention that we are further humiliatingly subjected to an ungrateful public and a lot of dunderheaded bigwigs. You will be surprised when I tell you that it has got to such a pitch in our house that they no longer even dare to laugh when I tell them a funny yarn about superstition in the Scripture class. . . . I am often seized with a secret anger, and am acquainted with liberty only in name. . . . Our papa's name-day was solemnly celebrated. The whole Rossau [1] school staff with their wives, brother Ferdinand and his wife, together with our little aunt and Lenchen and the whole Gumpendorf crew, were invited to an evening party . . . before the repast we played quartets, but keenly regretted not to have our master Franz in our midst; so we soon put an end to it.

The next day, the feast of our holy patron-saint Franciscus Seraphicus, was kept with great solemnity. All the scholars had to be taken to confession, and the bigger ones had to gather at three o'clock in the afternoon before the saint's image; an altar had been erected, and two school banners were displayed right and left; a short sermon was preached which several times reiterated that it is needful to learn to 'decide' between good and evil and that much gratitude was due to the 'troublesome' teacher. Also, a litany was addressed to the saint—a litany the oddity of which astonished me not a little. At the end there was singing, and a relic of the saint was given to all present to kiss, whereupon I noticed that several of the grown-ups crept out at the door, having no desire, perhaps, to share in this privilege.

A postscript reads: 'If you want to write to papa and me at the same time, do not touch upon any religious matters.'

It seems pretty plain that the brothers had exchanged pleasantries concerning religious instructors and the type of cleric who is also

[1] Schubert the elder had been promoted from the headship of the Liechtental school to that of the larger school in the Rossau suburb.

pedagogue; what schoolmaster cannot recall incredible fatuities practised in the name of moral instruction for the young? Old Schubert was obviously of the 'old school,' and therefore his tolerance of his son and the son's friends is a tribute to his kindness of heart.

Father tells me that even your little sisters inquire every day 'When is Franz coming at last?' . . . Papa let Mayrhofer read your last letter, and the secret that Schober is devoting himself to landscape painting is kept no longer. . . . Father asks me to warn you not to send money without keeping a receipt.

The same letter (from Ferdinand) asks Franz to name a price for his piano. Franz replies: 'Do take my fortepiano; I shall be delighted. . . . I hate your always talking about payment, reward and thanks—to a brother, fie, for shame!' He then returns in kind Ignaz's account of school ecclesiastics:

Your implacable hatred of the whole tribe of bigwigs does you credit. But you have no conception what a gang the priesthood is here: bigoted as mucky old cattle, stupid as arch-donkeys and boorish as bisons. You may hear sermons here to which our most venerated Pater Nepomucene can't hold a candle. They chuck about blackguards, riffraff, etc., from the pulpit, something lovely; they put a death's head on the pulpit and say: 'Look here, you pock-pitted mugs, that's how you will look one day.' Or else: 'There, a fellow takes a slut into the pub; they dance all night, then they go to bed tight, and when they get up there are three of 'em,' etc. etc.

In November the Esterházys came to town and Schubert with them, though there is no evidence that he continued as music tutor to the countesses. Nor does any correspondence repeat conversations which must have taken place between Schubert and his father; the latter intended that Franz should go back to school or to some musical post of a permanent nature involving teaching. But the young man did not live at home and never took up any permanent position with a fixed salary, teaching or otherwise. He went to live with Mayrhofer in the Wipplingerstrasse. Concerning his relationship with his father we must draw our own conclusions; he continued in affectionate correspondence with his brothers.

Drab though his quarters were under Mayrhofer's roof, Schubert could never have been more satisfied. For the first time in his life he had an empty house—Mayrhofer was away at his office in working hours—an instrument and the time to compose. He had freedom and the necessities of existence. As might be expected, he composed all morning, and visited whom he would after midday unless a special access of inspiration kept him in later. The evenings were given to conviviality—the favoured tavern at this time being 'Zur ungarischen Krone' (The Crown of Hungary)—or to musical gatherings. It is therefore expedient at this point to give an account of one or two friends who, though not new personalities in Schubert's life, became visitors and visited during this period, and were found in coffee-house or musical party.

A constant visitor was Anselm Hüttenbrenner, who came from Graz and had also been a pupil of Salieri when Schubert was taking lessons from the old master. His compositions, now forgotten, were numerous; his nature was sunny and versatile; his reminiscences are a valuable source of information on the habits of the circle. He formed a male-voice quartet which included himself and Schubert, and on Thursday nights it met to perform, with other pieces, a composition written during the week by each of its members; sometimes Schubert's was not written until he arrived for the performance! The two also played piano duets, using the medium of four hands to read full scores, including those of Handel, which Schubert much admired. Anselm had two brothers, Josef and Heinrich, who were ardent Schubertians, and the Hüttenbrenner family formed quite a cell of Schubert propaganda at Graz. Josef settled later in Vienna, and we are much indebted to him for his good work in collecting and preserving products of the composer's pen which Schubert's own carelessness would have lost for us. Anselm says in his reminiscences:

Often Schubert could not remember to whom he had lent a song, and did not know where it had gone. My brother Josef resolved to collect all the scattered copies, in which task he largely succeeded after much labour and research. I found one day that my brother had more than a hundred of Schubert's songs carefully sorted and docketed in his drawer.

This good Josef, having commercial astuteness which the composer notoriously lacked, was responsible for liaison with publishers

and theatrical agents as well as for the preparation of several manuscripts for the press.

Then there was Johann Jenger who, like Hüttenbrenner, had
known Beethoven personally. Jenger held high position in Viennese upper middle-class circles as an official in the War Chan-
cellery. Amongst others to whom Schubert was introduced by
Jenger were the actress Sophie Müller, the surgeon Dr. Menz
and the Pachlers at Graz, of whom we shall hear more later. Of
more interest, however, than his social standing was his taste and
ability as a musician. He was a splendid accompanist of Schubert's
songs, especially when the singer at a Schubertiad was Baron von
Schönstein. The baron first came to know Schubert when visiting
the Esterházys in Hungary; his attitude to social distinctions between
musicians is plain from his companionship with the composer
during walks in the Zseliz countryside. His singing of Schubert's
songs was no less inspired than Vogl's, though we may suppose that
Vogl had the bigger voice. (We are not actually told so.) However, Schönstein was a powerful amateur baritone to whom the
Mill Cycle was dedicated, and it was his singing of Schubert's
songs that deeply moved Liszt, causing him to use, in a description
of the baron's singing, the famous remark about Schubert's being
'le musicien le plus poète que jamais . . .' a remark which is true
enough if we understand what Liszt implied by the word 'poet.'
if we allow the words their usual modern meaning, we must declare
that, whatever Schubert's understanding of contemporary verse, he
was the most purely musical of musicians.

The friendship with Vogl had deepened to such an extent that
the singer, double the composer's age, proposed a summer tour of
the Austrian Alps with him. They set off to make their first stop
at Vogl's birthplace, Steyr, being assured of friends and of the enthusiastic attention to Schubert's compositions and playing and to
Vogl's singing. A letter to Ferdinand written from Steyr on 13th
July 1819, describes the countryside round that city as 'inconceivably
lovely,' though equal space is devoted to the attractions of eight young
female inhabitants of his host's house. A cantata was composed for
Vogl's birthday early in August, the words being written by Albert
Stadler, an old 'Convicter,' not the only school friend with whom

Schubert was to renew acquaintance during this dream-summer. Stadler was a government official at Steyr; he had a charming sister who, like himself, was a lively amateur musician. So also was Silvester Paumgartner, leading burgess of Steyr, in acknowledgment of whose large hospitality and cello playing Schubert composed the 'Trout' Quintet. The two tourists went on to Linz, where one of the first families to be visited was, of course, that of Schubert's good friend Spaun. Kathi Stadler's album informs us that the return to Vienna was dated 14th September, though we do not know why the tour stopped at Linz without proceeding to Salzburg, birthplace of Schubert's beloved Mozart, as first projected.

Schubert rarely wrote long reflective descriptions in epistolary form, but the summer tour of 1819 must have been of great importance in his romantic education. Good food and good living, happiness among friends and whole families who loved him for what he was and did not want him to be otherwise, plenty of walking in the healthiest air of Europe—these things must have done much for a body that for some time had fed neither daintily nor regularly and had huddled short-sightedly over music paper too long and too often; a tremendous expansion of the imagination must have followed the experience of the blue lakes, the hills, the climbing roads, the castles, monasteries and romantic old towns of Upper Austria.

Back in Vienna, Schubert's chief hopes were on an operatic enterprise. After all, he had no intention of being other than a musician, and no intention of being a pedagogue-musician or a *Capellmeister*; the only other musicians who seemed financially sound were successful opera composers like Rossini. Moreover Schubert was not known to the general concert- or theatre-going public. The only public performances of any Schubert works so far had been those of the F major Mass in 1814, of an Overture for eight hands played at a concert given in Vienna in March 1818, in which the composer played one of the parts, and of the song *The Shepherd's Lament* sung by one Jäger at one of Jaell's popular concerts —though these performances were well received by the musical press. It has often been said that Schubert tried to interest Goethe in his music again in 1819, despite the poet's failure to acknowledge Spaun's previous application on his friend's behalf, and the incident is mentioned here in order to make it plain once and for all that it belongs, not to 1819, but to 1825. The songs enclosed with Schubert's letter were *Postilion Chronos, To Mignon* and *Ganymede,* but in all Goethe's correspondence with Zelter there is no mention of the man without whom millions would never have known the poet. The letter was not answered.

The operetta *Die Zwillingsbrüder (The Twin Brothers),* though written in January 1819, did not get produced at the Kärntnertor Theatre, which had commissioned it at Vogl's instigation, until June 1820. It had only six performances, though it was most enthusiastically received and the composer was called for. Anselm Hüttenbrenner says that Schubert was with him in the gallery, but was too bashful to appear in front of the curtain in his shabby overcoat, and that the manager made him laugh by his declaration to the audience that the composer was not in the house. The press commended the little work, though one critic said that the music was that of a man who would excel in a more serious vein. A powerful testimony to the fact that *The Twin Brothers* at least attracted the notice of connoisseurs is the request for another piece by Schubert from the rival Theater an der Wien, which suggested to him *The Magic Harp,* a work written by Hofmann, whose translation from the French had formed the libretto of *The Twin Brothers.* The overture is the well-known one now called *Rosamunde,* the re-naming having been done by Schubert when he published it as a piano duet in 1828. *The Magic Harp* got several sporadic performances; nothing remains known to us but the overture, and the work cannot be called a success. Critical opinion now somewhat patronizingly suggested that Schubert's ability was more suited to an idyllic subject. The choruses were declared 'vapid and weak,' the harmonies harsh and the instrumentation overloaded. An exceptional review was that by the Schubert admirer, Baron Schlechta, who, after detailing the excellences of the piece, expressed the wish that Schubert might 'often repeat his efforts to awaken us from the stupor into which we have sunk in these degenerate days by giving us melody on the stage from the endless riches of his genius.' The opera *Sakuntala,* which was to be his next essay for the theatre, was not finished; nor, unfortunately, was another work of 1820—the C minor string Quartet which marks Schubert's full maturity as an instrumental composer; and it is plain that the Symphony in E minor belonging to the following year, of which only the sketch was done, was to have been on the grand scale of the last Symphony.

A small work written in the last month of 1820 bears witness to an important friendship. It is a setting, for two sopranos and two contraltos, with pianoforte accompaniment, of Moses Mendelssohn's German version of the twenty-third Psalm, 'The Lord is my Shepherd.' But the singers for whom it was written were the pupils of Anna Fröhlich, one of four sisters as delectable as their name. Their household was what the Pickwickians might have called 'an abode of the Muses and Graces'; Grillparzer was a frequent visitor, was later to become a resident and died under the same roof as the four sisters, though it was not the roof under which Schubert first found himself in 1820. The girls had been well-to-do, and impoverishment had made them seek an income from their considerable talents—Anna and Josefine as professional singers and teachers of singing in the new Vienna Conservatorium, Betty (Barbara) as a painter and Kathi, the most fascinating, as—well, we do not quite know. She ruled both the household and Grillparzer's heart, though he did not marry her. She was devoted to music. Through the Fröhlich girls Schubert came to set poems by Grillparzer, and at their house he met a whole crowd of artistic and literary lions and jackals.

He was brought to the Fröhlich *ménage* through the Sonnleithners. Ignaz, the father, held musical gatherings at his home at which a civil servant with a good tenor voice, one August von Gymnich, sang Schubert songs, *Erl King* being the favourite as usual. The son, Leopold Sonnleithner, was a lawyer and good amateur musician, who brought a number of original manuscripts of Schubert's works for Kathi Fröhlich to try over, and the ladies were anxious that the composer himself should visit them with yet more songs. Asked why the songs were not published, Schubert explained that no publisher would accept them, whereupon Sonnleithner, Josef Hüttenbrenner, Johann Schönauer and Johann Schönpichler clubbed together to publish them privately, bringing the newly printed copies to musical evenings and selling them on the spot. In 1821 these sheets included

The Fröhlich Sisters—First Published Songs

Erl King, Margaret at the Spinning-wheel, Shepherd's Lament, Little Hedgerose, The Wanderer, The King in Thule, Memnon, Anselmo's Tomb, Death and the Maiden and others of no smaller value . . . what a list! Suddenly the privately subscribed publications cease and the crafty Diabelli begins to deal directly with Schubert, buying up manuscripts for small sums cash down. It does not seem to have occurred to the composer that he should have insisted on some sort of arrangement similar to the royalty system, which, it is true, did not then exist in Austria and Germany: he thought, no doubt, that whenever he wanted money he could pour out more songs.

Testimonials written by Dietrichstein and Vogl in January 1821 show that Schubert had the passing intention of seeking some salaried post. But passing it was. Of greater importance is the appearance of his songs in programmes of the Society of Noble Ladies for the Furtherance of the Good and the Useful, Vogl's singing of *Erl King* being repeated in response to public demand. The year 1821 is of great importance to students of Schubert's nature, especially to those who would consider him to have had a raw deal. For it is clear that, had he so chosen, he could have become lionized by the wealthy and cultured grandees of Vienna. The dedicatees of these first published songs include Count Dietrichstein, Count Fries, Count Széchényi, Ladislaus Pyrker, Patriarch of Venice, Salieri and Ignaz von Mosel. But he never aspired to the more famous *salons*; he preferred the company of his own friends and visits to middle-class music-lovers like the Fröhlichs or the Bruchmanns.

This same year and those following saw considerable changes in his circle. Spaun left to take up his Linz appointment; then Schubert parted company with Mayrhofer, with no quarrel or immediate reason for the parting, though Mayrhofer said they were aware of temperamental differences. Anselm Hüttenbrenner went to Graz where he inherited his father's estate. Schober alone remained of the original group and he, of course, had his rooms at Schubert's disposal. It will be seen later that the formation of a deep romantic friendship with the painter Moritz von Schwind completely shifted the axis of Schubert's circle.

But for the moment Schubert had engaging enough company in the man with whom he lodged, and the gay pair set off in July

1821 for a visit to Atzenbrugg, between Vienna and St. Pölten, where Schober's uncle, the Bishop of St. Pölten, had his country seat, the romantic castle of Ochsenburg. They were handsomely housed and fêted by the local aristocracy, one Schubertiad including several countesses. The bishop was a connoisseur of the arts, so Schubert's quarters were furnished with a fine piano, and Schober declares that his friend did a great deal of work. The sketch of the E minor Symphony was set aside for concentration on their joint effort, the opera *Alfonso and Estrella*. This holiday with Schober marks the heyday of Schubert's hopes. The world was a promising place; he might be separated from his old friends for a time, but that might be a good thing, and there were other friends of fascinating personality whose minds he had yet to unravel.

So Schubert and Schober enjoyed the hills, woods and streams, the grand park of the castle and the little baroque town of St. Pölten; *Alfonso and Estrella* was going to set them up and 'make' them when they got back to Vienna. Meanwhile there were happy evenings of reading, pipe-smoking or music-making, and Schubertiads with the bishop, Baron Mink or one of the lady grandees near by. All was well in the best of possible worlds.

CHAPTER IV

BOHEMIAN DAYS

NEITHER its composer nor its librettist conquered Europe with *Alfonso and Estrella*: the piece did not receive so much as a single performance while they lived. Liszt first produced it at Weimar in 1854. But, to the day of his death, Schubert persisted in dramatic essays. At the rejection of *Alfonso and Estrella* he immediately set to work on a *Singspiel* written by a popular dialect versifier, Castelli. Into this little work, originally called *Die Verschworenen* (*The Conspirators*), though the official censor changed the title to *Der häusliche Krieg* (*Domestic Strife*), Schubert put some excellent music; but Domenico Barbaja, newly appointed manager both of the Theater an der Wien and of the Kärntnertor, was a supporter of the Italian fashion: the piece was not accepted. Again Schubert set to work on a new text, *Fierabras* [1] (*The Braggart*); but he was destined to see neither this work nor its predecessors staged.

Fierabras brings us, however, into the new circle of Schubert's friends—a circle better known and even more bohemian than the former one which included Schober, Spaun and Mayrhofer. We digress, perhaps, in mentioning the fact that the greatest musicians, unlike some of the greatest sculptors, poets, painters and dramatists, have rarely been bohemians, certainly not persistent bohemians. On the contrary, the dreams they have dreamt have been evident only in musical work; they have been shrewd, solitary men (even when married or lionized at their public appearances, they did their work in privacy), capable of long periods of immensely hard work. For the labour of writing out a score, full orchestral or merely vocal, at a time when the original inspiration may have to make room for a new germination, requires a degree of concentration not always recognized by the musical public. This capability of prolonged and arduous labour, admitted by Mozart, of all men, in connection with the seemingly spontaneous Quartets dedicated to Haydn, was possessed

[1] Schubert's 'Fierabras' is not the correct Spanish spelling.

as much by the exuberant Wagner as by the disciplined Bach or Brahms. Great musicians have rarely been gregarious during periods of what a wit has called 'partiturition'; even Schubert may have been capable of mental isolation among his gay company— of being temporarily with it yet not of it. Mayrhofer testifies to the long hours Schubert spent alone in their common lodging. What we can say for certain is that Schubert is unique among composers in that good music was actually written down by his hand while he was among a crowd. And what a butterfly crowd! Their hearts were on their sleeves, and their friendship had not the worth of Spaun's or Vogl's in his old circle. Schubert's poor earnings often paid the debts of this painting and versifying lot; their takings rarely paid his debts.

Our story brings us into their company, as was noted above, through the libretto of *Fierabras,* which was supplied by Josef Kupelwieser, brother of the painter Leopold Kupelwieser, who left drawings and water-colours of the Schubertian circle, one particularly famous example showing them all at a picnic. The axis of Schubert's newly developing company was his friendship with Moritz von Schwind, whose acquaintance with the composer dated from 1821, as did that of Leopold Kupelwieser who was for a time Schwind's teacher. Kupelwieser soon left the group to pursue his studies in Italy. There he stayed, leaving Schwind the unrivalled representative of romantic painting among the Schubertian circle. The other Kupelwieser remained in Vienna as a member of the tavern aristocracy. Exiles from the circle are of considerable value to us on account of their correspondence with their friends in Vienna. Sometimes the letters decrease in frequency and then cease, but they are usually by those interested only in the ephemeral conviviality of the home circle and unable yet to seek out midnight talkers and drinkers among the early bedders of the country town. Few readers can maintain interest in the sentimental recollections of happy nights here or there, or the replies from a friend who says he saw Schubert the other evening at this or that place—usually an inn —or who gives an opinion on one of those faction quarrels which loom temporarily large in the petty annals of a bohemian circle. (In a letter from Leopold Kupelwieser to his fiancée we read with amusement that the Schubert-Schwind camp cuts the Bruchmann camp dead when they meet in the street. The trouble seemed to be about Schober, the one important member of the old Schubert crowd to see the formation of the new artistic circle.) But the more musical exiles managed sooner or later to arrange provincial Schubertiads, like those at Linz or Graz. Such Schubertians really cannot be said to have left the group in Vienna, for their correspondence was pretty regular. Schubert still bound them firmly together, for his songs kept the provinces in touch with the sole fountain of further songs.

Apart from Schubert himself, the leading spirits of the group at headquarters were Schwind and Bauernfeld. Schubert's friendship with Schwind was the most remarkable of all the composer's attachments, and though it did not reach its closest manifestations till 1824 onwards, it was from the first sufficiently marked to be considered a dividing line in the composer's personal, though not artistic, history. Schwind was but a youth of seventeen when he sought Schubert's company in 1821, so it would be foolish to suppose that a man eight years the composer's junior could have been a great 'influence.' Rather was Schubert, an artist in triumphant command of his means of expression, an inspiration to the boy-painter who was passing through a period of storm and stress quite normal in so romantic a creature.

For Schwind was the almost perfect sample of romantic youth of that period; the type and the age need understanding, or we shall mistake the emotional outpourings in his letters to Schober, Schubert and other friends. Schwind's nature during his youth was impetuous and sentimental; his self-portrait—a fine piece of work—shows handsome and delicate, almost girlish features like those of Shelley, whom he much resembled mentally as well as physically. His slender beauty earned him the nickname 'Angel-face,' but a firmly tensed mouth belies the gentleness of other features. Schwind was not effeminate, unbalanced or sexually abnormal; on the contrary he was a determined and aggressively tireless artist whom we see, in our study of Schubert, during only one phase of his brilliant career. Ambitious, ardent and restless, he saw in these older Peter Pans, like Schober, people of sentiment who would talk the moon down and the sun up on the subjects nearest to his heart; they were apparently eternal youths (friend Schober was getting on in years to be excused as a play-boy, if excuse is sought) in love with life and in love with love. To such a man as Schober, Schwind could pour out his heart thus:

I do not want to die, but I am often conscious of the bliss of escaping from the shackles of the body. I long for existence, quiet and self-contained, and I am aflame with yearning and overflowing with love. Where is the heart, where are the arms which will open to soothe and free me?

Even in a much more sober period than that one, young men have felt as Schwind writes, though their race and time has not let them pen the words: 'Very often I cannot alight on a word, or a song fails me, and then I can somehow only express my feelings by opening wide my arms.' This is just the 'O altitudo!' the inarticulate 'Ah!' of Keats's poetry, the only expression, albeit a silly exclamation, possible to a youngster who has not forged a technique with which he can attempt to give his all-embracing love of life and things a permanent form. That is why young Schwind, just beginning to grapple with media whereby emotion is not so readily communicated as by music, saw in Schubert an artist who had gloriously achieved the realization of their common dreams.

Let us not, therefore, mock the letters which read like love-letters, nor consider Schubert's simple remark vulgar: 'He is my sweetheart, for he can penetrate the inmost recesses of my heart'; for that remark was kindly and unpatronizing, and whatever Schubert's faults, his spontaneous return of love wherever love was offered without other, more selfish intentions is entirely creditable. He would have no doubt achieved not a single work less had he never met Schwind, but the younger man cheered with his idealism and vitality what might have been wholly depressing days. Moreover Schwind, for all his poverty, had been well educated, had probably read more than Schubert, and was soaked in the atmosphere of chivalry and eldritchery. He lived in a mental world peopled by the personages of old ballads and took his ideas for painting from sources as varied as the Nibelung mythology, *The Marriage of Figaro*, Kleist's *Kätchen von Heilbronn* (a scene depicting her visit by the knight was exhibited in the Viennese Academy in 1826), *The Arabian Nights, The Magic Flute* (pictures of which were later to adorn the foyer of the Vienna Opera House), Goethe's ballads, including *Erl King* and *Postilion Chronos*, and other scenes from operas, amongst them a fine set from *Figaro*. Thus, as far as one art can be a close parallel to another, Schwind's painting and drawing was the counterpart of the music of Schubert's songs. It used the same scenic background, personages, imagery, and even when the objective elements in it were definite parts of the Viennese countryside—the party at Atzenbrugg for instance—the scene still belonged to the world of fantasy.

Naturally Schwind's best works, such as the murals at the Opera or the series of fairy-tale pictures from *The Fair Melusine*, were finished long after the Schubert period; but many of them had their first adumbration in sketches done in youth. He had a private collection which he called his 'unsalable gallery' containing some of his best impressions; these he did not show till his old age, when he declared that the handiwork of which he was most proud was the drawing of some music staves for Schubert, who had run out of manuscript paper. But in 1821 Schwind was as poor as his new musician-friend; while planning conceptions such as those just mentioned, he had to make money from the illumination of greeting-cards or illustrations to books—some of the latter constituting his most delicate work. It was because well-remunerated commissions were not forthcoming that he left Vienna for Munich in 1827 and, despite home-sickness for the city which he expressed in a letter to Bauernfeld, it was not until 1870, when he was aged sixty-six, that he was commissioned to execute the frescoes for the new Vienna Opera. His beloved Schubert died within a year of Schwind's leaving for Munich, and what that death meant to him is expressed, not in the old Schwindian gush, but in affectingly sober language, in letters to his fiancée, Netty Hönig, in whose home so many happy Schubertiads had been held, and in many a letter to Schober, Bauernfeld and others, both at the time of bereavement and for years afterwards.

If we would see Schubert and Schwind together, we could, of course, take ourselves in imagination to Bogner's café, the 'Green Anchor,' the 'Golden Partridge' or some other favourite coloured animal; but these were haunts of all the friends, and Schubert could have been found there before he met Schwind. The place above all which delighted their childlike feelings was the Moonshine House, Schwind's humble yet attractive home and place of work. The house was on the Wieden, and when Schubert moved outside the centre of the city to that suburb, he could pop round at all times of day and night. The family—Schwind, his mother and brothers— occupied only the second floor, where the dormer windows in the big sloping roof looked out over the buildings of the city to the glacis, across the Danube to the Leopoldsberg and the Alps. This Chelsea-ish little cul-de-sac was just the sort of place for a man of Schwind's temperament: a little courtyard, a row of trees and a wall enclosing a garden, belonging to the priest of the neighbouring Karlskirche, made this nook as attractive as some of the small Inns of Court gardens in London. On certain days the courtyard was used for a cattle market and the friends could look down at the goings-on. In the evenings they leaned out of the windows and smoked, watched the stars beyond the church dome and heard the organ booming. (Schubert's house on the Wieden was next door to the church.) Schober, Senn, Spaun, when in town, and Bauernfeld, to say nothing of satellites to the main sparks of the group, came in and out. Occa-sionally there was a house-party or a dance; here and elsewhere Schubert would play for the dancing without dancing himself— perhaps because he was plump and did not want to sweat. One of his nicknames from the friends was 'Schwammerl,' or 'Tubby'; others were 'Bertl' and 'Kanevas,' the latter on account of Schubert's favourite question when a new member was proposed for the circle: 'Kann er was?'[1] Spaun was known as 'Pepi Spaun,' and as well as 'Cherub,' Schwind had the appellation 'Giselher,' a name in the Nibelung saga, of which fun was often made at the Moonshine House, where, when there was money enough for 'gold dust,' as tobacco was called, there were long evenings of argument on matters arty, the spouting of poems, the trying over of new Schubert songs, readings from plays, each taking a part, dressings-up, fooling and horseplay with the Schwind boys, whether snowballing or a mock tournament in the yard. Men who were not poor like Schubert and

[1] The question implies 'What does he know?' as well as 'What can he do?'

Schwind recorded that a party at the Moonshine House was never to be forgotten.

It must be noted that the heyday of Schubertian frolics and serious-nesses at the Moonshine House was later than the period to which we have brought our life of Schubert (1821), but it is convenient not to interrupt the story of the composer by descriptions of occupations which were habitual during the whole of his last seven years—the seven years of his friendship with Schwind. Thus, one may as well introduce certain other of the Moonshine company even if, like Bauernfeld, they did not meet Schubert regularly until 1824 or so. Bauernfeld, on account of his diaries, is of the greatest value to Schubertian delvers. He must have been a charming fellow as well as a very intelligent one. We can tell that from his entry for 26th March 1826:

Schober is our superior in mind . . . that is in talk! But a great deal about him is artificial; his great gifts threaten to end in nothing. Schwind has a splendid, pure nature which is always in process of creating afresh, and bids fair to consume itself. Schubert has the right mixture of idealism and realism; the earth is all beauty to him. Mayrhofer is simple and natural. Schober maintains that he is a sort of good-natured *intrigant*. And I? Who knows his own character? Till I've done something worth doing I am a nobody.

Though a lawyer by education, Bauernfeld was a poet and amateur musician by vocation, having taken piano lessons from Schenk, one-time teacher of Beethoven.

In his memoirs Bauernfeld tells us that he was getting to grips with the Viennese edition of Shakespeare (for he had been a fairly diligent student before joining the Schubert gang) when Schwind brought in the composer and made him hear some of Bauernfeld's verse. 'Then we opened the piano, Schubert sang, and we played duets and then went to an inn till late in the night.' From that time, when Schubert and Schwind formed a trio instead of a duet, Bauernfeld was the third. The passage following that quoted above is worth repeating at some length:

We often wandered about town until three in the morning, and accom-panied each other home. As we were sometimes not in a condition to part, one of us not seldom slept the night in the rooms of another. We were not very particular about comfort in those days. Friend Moritz threw himself, wrapped only in a leather cover, on the bare floor, and once carved me a pipe, which article I had forgotten, out of Schubert's spectacle case. Whoever happened to be in funds paid the piper for us all. Some, times, however, it happened that two of us had no money and the third none. Of course it was usually Schubert who played Croesus among us; he swam in silver coins when he had sold a few songs or when Artaria had paid him five hundred gulden for the Walter Scott songs. . . . Then we spent right and left, and lived for the first few days like fighting-cocks, but before long had to economize again. Such was the ebb and flow of our fortunes.

It was due to a 'flow' that I heard Paganini. The five gulden this musical corsair wanted were unobtainable by me; needless to say, Schubert had heard him, but he refused to hear him again without me. He grew seriously angry when I would not accept the ticket from him. 'Don't be stupid,' he exclaimed, 'I've heard him once, and was annoyed that you were not with me. He is the devil of a player I tell you, and there will never be another like him.' We heard the most infernally sublime fiddler in existence, and were not less delighted with his perfect *adagio* than amazed at his antics on the strings, and amused at his incredibly diabolical, scare, crow figure, which resembles nothing so much as a black skeleton doll stretched on wires. After the concert I was entertained free at the inn, and a bottle extra was set before us. . . . Another time I went soon after dinner time to the coffee-house near the Kärntnertor Theatre and devoured half a dozen rolls. Soon Schubert joined me and did likewise. We congratulated each other on the good appetite we had acquired so soon after dinner. 'The fact is that I had nothing for my dinner,' my friend confided to me, shamefacedly. 'Neither had I,' said I, laughing.

A whole book could be written on Schubert's friends; yet not one of them, except Schwind and Grillparzer, was important as an artist. But they were all typical of their time and of their city. Their appreciation, their childlike imagination, their interest in all things artistic and romantic, their freedom from snobbery and capa, city for endless amusement made Schubert's life happy. For no account of Schubert is more false than that which makes him a pathetic figure, without honour in his country and generation. If you dislike him you can say he was as happy as a pig in muck; if you like him you can say with Rousseau: 'To live freely among equals, that is the true life,' and Schubert was happy in the mutual affection of equals in all but gifts; if you like him a great deal you can say that the only unhappy moments he knew were those which brought him down to earth as seen by non-musical, non-romantic folk, moments of pain or depression from an unpleasant disease; in all other moments he was happy in the fantastic world of romance, legend and *Biedermeier* Vienna. In the words of Bauernfeld quoted above: 'The earth was all beauty to him.' Whatever dark or sad thoughts sometimes came to him, he was a happy creature even in his last years. If we do not see him among the very 'top ten' of contemporary Viennese aristocracy, it is because, unlike Beethoven, he did not wish for their company or favour, even on his own terms. In any case, the top ten of *Biedermeier* days were not so intelligent or artistic as Beethoven's Lobkowitzes, Lichnowskys and Rasumovskys.

What is rather more surprising, though the matter is discussed in a more appropriate context, is that Schubert lived for a quarter of a century in the same city as the giant whom he held in such reverence, yet failed to establish with Beethoven the intimate contact he had made with Vogl or the Moonshine House friends. A few professional musicians, such as the players Schuppanzigh and Linke, can be numbered among friends to whom he was drawn because they were musicians, or rather because his music drew them; one cannot help thinking that he continued in their acquaintance, as he did in that of the actress Sophie Müller and some singers, because of temperamental understanding rather than from the musical ties. Instead of musical and socially exalted company, a large and increasing number of the prosperous bourgeoisie welcomed the opportunity to receive the man who turned a musical evening into a Schubertiad. If one gives an account of one of these friends one must do as much for fifty. Let mention be made, then, of the few whose names occur most frequently in letters and documents relating to the composer.

The Moonshiners might go to the Bruchmanns', for instance. The paterfamilias was a wealthy merchant whose son Franz was a school contemporary of Schubert's. Young Bruchmann, Senn, Schwind, Schober and the rest would declaim verse, read plays and for the evening give each other names taken from the Nibelung story. Josef von Gahy is a name to be remembered in connection with these evenings; he was a court official commended by Schubert for his accompaniment of the songs, and the composer liked to have him more than anybody as partner in a four-handed performance, playing treble to Gahy's bass. The elegant Baron von Schönstein was the singer at some parties; Vogl sang at others and was present when Schubert was introduced to the home of Matthäus von Collin, brother of the poet whom Beethoven honoured by writing the overture to his poetic drama *Coriolan*. Collin was a highly cultured man, and the company included Hammer-Purgstall, the orientalist, Karoline Pichler, the novelist and holder of the most 'elegant and distinguished' *salons* of the Congress period (she seems to have been a veritable Mrs. Leo Hunter, and managed to net both Grillparzer and Schubert), Count Dietrichstein and our old friend Pyrker, Patriarch of Venice, of whom we know more concerning his love of music and versifying than we do of his patriarchate.

Meetings at the house of one Frau von André seem to have been more specifically musical. Bauernfeld tells us that 'music was made until past midnight,' and the company included the tenors Barth and Binder, the baritone Rauscher from the Opera, Carl and Josef Czerny (of which brothers the first one needs no introduction to most aspiring pianists), the Giulianis, Linke the cellist and a number of others who formed a male-voice choir, one of the singers being Nestroy, the popular playwright and actor. Out on the Wieden, close to Schubert and the Moonshine House, lived one musical host who should have special honour. He was Carl Pinterics, a clerk who fastidiously collected as many of Schubert's songs as became available. Bauernfeld's diaries once more make good reading concerning Schubertian meetings at the home of the advocate Hönig in the Schulerstrasse; Bauernfeld himself was the means of introduction as he had been a school friend of the son of the house. There were the usual fun and games, with a little music. Schubert played duets with Netty Hönig, and Schwind fell in love with her. As she was his first love, and the lover was Schwind, there is no need to add that he fell in love well and truly. Now comes the Bauernfeld report:

Schwind won Netty's heart in a ragged frock-coat. All her relatives were summoned to the betrothal with drum and trumpet, a collection of

cousins, aunts, uncles and ancient Hofrats and such-like kin. . . . Friend
Moritz at first did not want to come, for he had no decent coat except his
painting-smock; a friend came to the rescue and lent his, but in the first
half hour he almost tore it off. His fiancée had the utmost difficulty in
keeping him there till ten. I awaited the happy bridegroom-to-be at a
coffee-house, with Schubert. He arrived all distracted and desperate,
and began comically to mimic the Philistine company. Schubert was so
delighted that he could not stop giggling. . . . The relatives shook their
Hofratish heads.

Other houses where the Schubertians were specially welcome were
those of the actor Heinrich Anschütz and of the composer Franz
Lachner, a Bavarian who came to Vienna for musical study, but
remained as organist at the Protestant church and, after 1826, as
conductor at the Kärntnertor. Later, like Schwind, he went for
better money as musical director to Munich, keeping up his friendship with the painter and with Bauernfeld after Schubert's death.
Randhartinger, who had sung *Erl King* in the school practice-room
at the Seminary, had become a musician of distinction and was not
only a singer, but also composed. He, too, was frequently one of a
Schubertiad.

So also was Senn before he had to leave Vienna. He came from the
Tyrol, and had hot blood in him. After his schooldays Senn studied
law at the University of Vienna, and often met the Schubert circle in
their evening drinkings. The heat of their discussions, whether on
matters aesthetic, or, when Senn was about, on wider issues, drew
interest from Metternich's Gestapo—the artist-student population
have always been victims of radical-hunters. It was just like the
Schubertian friends, on seeing a spy in their midst, to have a joke
and 'lead him on.' A rag seems to have taken place, and the secret
agent, having in the course of proceedings been forcibly ejected from
the inn, took his revenge by having them all arrested. Senn alone
was not at home, which made his case suspicious. The rest were
merely hauled out of their beds, examined and dismissed. But
among their papers was a letter from a friend which included the
passage: 'Senn is the only man I know capable of dying for a cause.'
At his arrest Senn made things worse for himself by challenging the
police on their right to arrest him: regarded as a dangerous character,

45

he was kept in prison for a short time and later banished to his native country. When Schwind left for Munich he visited Senn at Innsbruck. Two of Senn's poems were set by Schubert.

Yet other old 'Convicters' appear at the gatherings, having become civil servants, artists of one kind or another, or prosperous business men and dilettanti. Where does one end the list of houses to which the merry party could repair casually or to which they were specially requested to go for a Schubertiad? With old schoolfellows like Holzapfel or Stadler? With those to whom he was specially attached and who, like Mohn, Kenner or Schlechta, had a true insight into his most idiomatic expression? With artists of repute in their time and with honourable work still preserved, such as Rieder, later curator of the Imperial Art Gallery, Josef Kriehuber and Josef Teltscher, the fashionable portrait painters? Each of these three has left us likenesses of Schubert, and it is noteworthy that among the many portraits of the composer, or pictures and sketches which include his likeness in a group, only one was specially commissioned: every one of their artists he knew as a familiar friend and lover of his music.

There were Schubert parties indoors, Schubert parties in taverns or coffee-houses and also Schubert parties in the open air. Carriage excursions took the friends to the Wienerwald, to Döbling or, specially beloved spot, Atzenbrugg, where Schober's uncle was steward of the estate for the monastery of Klosterneuburg. A big three-day festival was yearly held in the park, and for one of these events—perhaps the one which is commemorated in Schwind's sketch of the outdoor fiddling and dancing, Schubert wrote his *Atzenbrugger Dances*. Flirting and a good drink supplemented more romantically styled pleasures; a good time was had by all. At Atzenbrugg, for the outing in September 1825, Bauernfeld informs us that he, Schubert and Schwind found a billet at the mill, where all three slept together in one big bed.

Such is the background of Schubert's life from 1821 till about a year before his death. The romantically minded may suppose it a good thing that Schubert died in the following year, for in the preceding twelvemonth Schwind had gone to Munich and the Moonshiners had married one after the other and settled down.

Bohemianism in normal, sensible artists belongs to youth. In their correspondence the friends might sigh for the Moonshine days, but to revive them artificially would have been insincere. A different background would have to have been painted for a biography of Schubert from 1827 onwards; the days of the *Winter Journey* cycle and of the great C major Symphony were more sober and solitary than those of the *Fair Maid of the Mill* songs and the jolly duets. It remains to finish the tale of Schubert's private musical life, so far as that is possible without constant reference to the Moonshiners and to good citizens who welcomed them to their rooms. In some years, e.g. 1823, we shall have to acknowledge the paradoxical parallel between the depression of illness combined with unusually small income and a tremendous access of creative energy. This could hardly be possible in a man without friends who appreciated him and without a nature fundamentally happy.

The year 1822 saw the composition of the B minor Symphony and the *Wanderer Fantasy*: both works were written in the late autumn. It was also the year in which Schubert came into contact with both Beethoven and Weber. I find it difficult to account for the fact that Beethoven and Schubert had not met before. True, these were the years of Beethoven's complete deafness and increased desire for soli' tude; and shyness, except among the Moonshine friends, was one of Schubert's chief traits. (His shyness at first meeting with so close a friend as Vogl has already been noted.) But there were several influential people in Vienna who knew both great men and must surely have mentioned the one to the other sufficiently to have made their mutual acquaintance a mere matter of time. One such friend, Schindler, gives the disappointing story of their meeting which is accepted by Grove. Schindler says:

In the year 1822 Franz Schubert set out with his Variations on a French Song (Op. 10), which he wished to present personally to the master he so greatly honoured. These variations, written in 1818, he had previously dedicated to Beethoven. In spite of Diabelli's accompanying him, and acting as spokesman and interpreter of Schubert's feelings, Schubert played a part in the interview that was anything but pleasant to him. His courage, which he managed to retain up to the very threshold of the house, forsook him entirely at the first glimpse he caught of the majestic artist, and when

Beethoven expressed a wish that Schubert should write the answers to his questions, he felt as if his hands and feet were tied and fettered. Beethoven ran through the presentation copy, and stumbled upon some inaccuracy of harmony. He then, in the kindest manner, drew the young man's attention to the fault, adding that it was no deadly sin. Meantime the result of this remark, intended to be kind, was utterly to disconcert the nervous visitor. It was not until he got outside the house that Schubert recovered his equanimity and rebuked himself unsparingly. This was the first and last meeting with Beethoven, for he never again had the courage to face him.

Kreissle, unlike Grove, will not accept this story, though he gives no other reason for his doubt than his opinion that the details seem to him improbable, and that Josef Hüttenbrenner was told by Schubert himself that Beethoven was not at home when he called and so the Variations were left with a servant. Naturally Schubert would refrain from passing on the humiliating account given by Schindler, true or not. Hüttenbrenner further adds that 'Schubert subsequently heard with great pleasure of Beethoven's enjoying the Variations and playing them frequently with his nephew Karl.'[1] Considering the disparity in the composers' ages and temperaments, the circles in which they were most happy and the fact that Beethoven was entirely deaf, one can surely accept Schindler's account of the formal meeting, of an approach on Schubert's part which must have seemed ambitious even if organized by others or prompted only by motives of hero-worship; one could accept it, moreover, even were it proved that the two had met unofficially before—say at the *Gasthaus*, as we are led to believe by Rochlitz, who had come to Vienna specially to make the acquaintance of Beethoven. He says:

I was just going to dinner when a young composer, Franz Schubert, an enthusiastic worshipper of Beethoven, met me. *Beethoven had spoken to him about me* [modern italics]. 'If you want to see him cheerful and unrestrained,' said Schubert, 'you ought to dine in the same room with him at the *Gasthaus*, where he always goes to dine.' He brought me to the house. Most of the places were taken; Beethoven sat surrounded by several of his friends, who were complete strangers to me.

---

[1] An entry by Karl in Beethoven's conversation book for August 1823 runs as follows : 'They praise Schubert highly, but he is said to hide himself.'

The dealings with Weber bade fair to be a worse fiasco, but the story ends happily, thanks to Weber's good nature. He came to Vienna to conduct that tremendous success *Der Freischütz,* and it is clear from remarks made by his son that he met Schubert. His next visit was for the first performance of *Euryanthe* on 25th October of the following year, 1823. Weber's was no small triumph at the Kärntnertor Theatre, the pro-Rossini stronghold of Barbaja, and his acclamation—probably exaggerated in letters to his wife—cannot but have pleased Schubert, who was present at the performance. But there was a difference between *Euryanthe* and the opera of the preceding year. *Freischütz* had its feet in the older tradition of separate arias and choruses—in spirit if not in fact. Out of the general stuff of melodramatic recitative came bewitching romantic tunes which could be hummed on the way home. Schubert expected to be carried away by another work as he had been by its predecessor. How ravished the ears and hearts of the Viennese audience had been by *Der Freischütz* we can tell from the fact that Weber's letter to his wife says little of the details in *Euryanthe* which he claims to have pleased the crowd, but dwells at length on the reception he received when he first stepped into the orchestra. The next great acclamation was, very rightly, for the brilliant overture. (What overtures quite equal Weber's in their demand for applause?) But what of the work as a whole? Neither Vienna nor Schubert was carried away into a magic world as formerly both were; the work did not hold the boards for any length of time, Rossini was not displaced from his supremacy at the Kärntnertor, and if Weber caused no rout of the Italian fashion, what hope for Schubert?

Schubert's opinions of *Euryanthe* reached Weber's ears at a time when that composer was not in the best of spirits, for he may have been convinced by the knowledgeable ones of Vienna that his music had been expended on a poor libretto, the work of Helmina von Chézy, society poetess, who was later to serve Schubert as badly with the words of *Rosamunde.* Furthermore Weber was much overworked from composing and producing *Euryanthe,* the overture having been written in the few days before performance. Then Schubert called at Weber's lodgings with the score of *Alfonso and Estrella.* Weber let him know that he had heard of his remarks concerning *Euryanthe*; Schubert is said to have acknowledged that he passed the quoted opinions and to have repeated them then and there—that the piece was to be admired for its texture, but that it lacked the melodic beauty of *Freischütz*. It is reported that Weber lost his temper, and that all he said at the time about *Alfonso and Estrella* was that 'first puppies and first operas are always drowned.' Yet no grudges were nourished on either part, and it is to Weber's credit that he did his best to procure a performance of Schubert's opera at Dresden.

In following up Schubert's affair with Weber we have moved forward to 1823, and also noticed only his operatic ambitions and dis/appointments. Two of his faithful friends set out to do him a good turn as soon as he returned to Vienna from the St. Pölten holiday; but we do not know how his father regarded the company his son now kept, with the addition of sparks like Schwind and Bauernfeld. It was probably at Spaun's and Jenger's instigation that Schubert was elected to honorary membership of the musical societies at Linz and Graz. His application for membership of the Vienna Phil/harmonic Society as a viola player was rejected on the ground that he was a professional. The unfinished Symphony had been intended for Graz, though its first performance was given at a Phil/harmonic concert in 1865, Herbeck, the conductor, having obtained the score from Anselm Hüttenbrenner. (It should be added to the credit of Grove and August Manns that a performance was given two years afterwards at the Crystal Palace as soon as the printed parts were available.) Josef Hüttenbrenner was the other friend who tried to help Schubert at this time, but his efforts, first to secure performances of *The Devil's Pleasance* in Vienna, Munich and Prague, and next to interest the Leipzig publisher, Peters, in Schubert's manuscripts, were unsuccessful. One of the opera directors got as far as to send for score and parts, and regretted that he had not made Schubert's acquaintance while in Vienna. Peters sent a charming letter of many pages, making it clear that only works by composers who had already earned considerable recognition could be accepted as a commercial speculation.

The year 1823 makes a dividing/point in Schubert's life, for the possibility of failure never seems to have shown itself to him before his disappointments with *Fierabras* and *Rosamunde*—works which had raised his hopes so much; one had been 'commissioned' and the other performed. Serious illness overtook him for the first time, and he faced in a way never before experienced the feeling of being alone which is known to less convivial and childlike natures at a much earlier age. For an artist and a romantic Schubert's was by no means a very introspective nature. However pathetic his music, no morbid subjectivity is implied therein. His letters occasionally put forth his troubles, but not at all in the quantity one might have expected. Before turning to the new chapter in his life, one may therefore quote a fanciful but serious document, among the first to reveal the darker side of his nature. It is an allegorical tale written by the composer himself and dated 3rd July 1822. It runs as follows:

MY DREAM

I was the brother of many brothers and sisters. Our father and mother were good people. I was deeply and lovingly devoted to them all.—Once my father took us to a feast. There my brothers became very merry. I, however, was sad. Then my father approached me and bade me enjoy the delicious dishes. But I could not, whereupon my father, becoming angry, banished me from his sight. I turned my footsteps and, my heart full of infinite love for those who disdained it, I wandered into far-off regions. For long years I felt torn between the greatest grief and the greatest love. And so the news of my mother's death reached me. I hastened to see her, and my father, mellowed by sorrow, did not hinder my entrance. Then I saw her corpse. Tears flowed from my eyes. I saw her lie there like the old happy past, in which according to the deceased's desire we were to live as she had done herself.

And we followed her body in sorrow, and the coffin sank to earth. From that time on I again remained at home. Then my father once more took me to his favourite garden. He asked whether I liked it. But the garden wholly repelled me, and I dared not say so. Then, reddening, he asked me a second time: did the garden please me? I denied it, trembling. At that my father struck me, and I fled. I turned away a second time, and with a heart filled with endless love for those who scorned me, I again wandered far away. For many and many a year I sang songs. Whenever I attempted to sing of love, it turned to pain. And again, when I tried to sing of pain, it turned to love.

Thus were love and pain divided in me.

Then one day I had news of a gentle maiden who had just died. And a circle formed about her grave in which many youths and old men walked as though in everlasting bliss. They spoke softly, so as not to wake the maiden.

Heavenly thoughts seemed for ever to be showered on the youths from the maiden's gravestone, like fine sparks producing a gentle rustling. I too longed sorely to walk there. Only a miracle, however, can lead you to that circle, they said. But I went to the gravestone with slow steps and lowered gaze, filled with devotion and firm belief, and before I was aware of it I found myself in the circle, which uttered a wondrously lovely sound; and I felt as though eternal bliss were gathered together into a single moment. My father, too, I saw, reconciled and loving. He took me in his arms and wept. But not so much as I.

FRANZ SCHUBERT.

How unprofitable, in such a study as this, to attempt a detailed interpretation of the document! Though couched in the literary style which he, Schwind, Mayrhofer and the rest loved, it is obviously a personal document. The interest lies in the fact that it exists at all.

CHAPTER V

MENTION has been made of Schubert's meetings with Weber, but the *Euryanthe* incident belongs to the autumn of 1823, which was altogether a crowded year for Schubert. Compositions included the piano Sonata in A minor, Op. 143, and many fine songs, quite exclusive of the Mill Cycle. This was the year of no less than three attempts to gain a foothold as a stage composer—*The Conspirators, Fierabras* and *Rosamunde*—and many of the Mill Songs[1] must have been written between Schubert's composition of the acts of *Fierabras*. When we consider that his illness was so grave that he did not expect to recover, and that he also managed to make another summer tour of Upper Austria with Vogl, we may well marvel at the Mill Cycle alone.

These songs are settings of twenty poems, from a volume containing twenty-three, with the addition of a prologue and epilogue. It was published at Dessau in 1821 and entitled *Poems found among the Papers of a Wandering Horn-player* by Wilhelm Müller, who was by no means a simple soul—though Schubert was, for which we may be truly grateful. It is a sign of the spirit of Schubert's times that within two years the volume reached his hands in Vienna; for the verses are an obvious imitation of the anonymous *Des Knaben Wunderhorn* lyrics, edited early in the century by Arnim and Brentano, and enjoying the huge popularity paralleled in the British islands by romantic collections like *Border Minstrelsy* or the Irish ballads sung by Moore. Randhartinger was indirectly responsible for the writing of the Mill Songs. Kreissle relates the story of Schubert's calling on Randhartinger when the latter, before his days of professional musical activity, was secretary to Count Széchényi:

Hardly had he come into the room when the secretary was summoned

---

[1] The use of this abbreviated title for *Die schöne Müllerin* (*The Fair Maid of the Mill*) is justified by Schubert's use of it in letters. On the Continent the songs are known as the 'Müllerlieder,' after their poet as well as their subject.

to the count. He hurried away, telling the composer that he would be back in a few minutes. Schubert came to the writing-table and found lying on it a book of poems, one or two of which he read at a glance. He then put the book in his pocket and went away without waiting for Rand-hartinger's return. The latter missed the book from the table, and the next day went to Schubert to recover it. Schubert's excuse for his conduct was that the poems had so greatly interested him that he could not resist the temptation. As a proof that the borrowing of the book had not been without results, he presented to the astonished secretary the composition of the first Mill Songs, which he had finished in the night.

Signs of Schubert's illness had shown themselves during the previous winter; by the summer of 1823 his condition was serious, necessitating his going into hospital and causing the complete loss of his hair. These circumstances, the medicines used, the constant baths, the illusory 'cure' after the first few months and the later pains in the joints have led some writers to suspect venereal disease. Schubert worshippers, like Grove, are reticent on the subject. There is no extant or accessible evidence of diagnosis, but the symptoms were giddiness, depression and debility.[1] The holiday with Vogl and old friends at Steyr and Linz did much to repair his health and spirits temporarily. A few letters from and to his friends are worth quoting:

(*a*) *From Anton von Spaun to his wife, Steyr, 20th July 1822*:

Vogl is very much embittered against Schober, for whose sake Schubert behaved most ungratefully towards Vogl and who makes the fullest use of Schubert in order to extricate himself from financial embarrassments, and to defray the expenditure which has already exhausted the greater part of his mother's fortune. I very much wish that somebody were here who would defend Schubert at least in the matter of the most glaring reproaches. Vogl also says that Schober's opera is bad and a perfect failure, and that altogether Schubert is on quite the wrong road. . . . *Memnon* and *Antigone* enraptured me in spite of my bad accompanying.

(*b*) *Schubert to Schober, Steyr, 14th August 1823*:

Whether I shall ever quite recover I am inclined to doubt. Here I live

---

[1] The contributor to the fifth edition of 'Grove' states that Schubert contracted syphilis and that he was led into careless conduct by Schober. The disease was certainly rife in Schubert's Vienna.

simply in every respect, go for walks regularly, work much at my opera and read Walter Scott.

With Vogl I get on very well. We were at Linz together, where he sang a good deal, and splendidly. Bruchmann, Sturm and Streinsberg came to see us at Steyr a few days ago, and they too were dismissed with a load of songs.

(c) Schubert to Schober, 30th November 1823:

First of all I must pour out a lament over the condition of our circle, as well as all other circumstances; for which the exception of my health, which (thank God) seems to be firmly restored at last, everything goes miserably. Our circle, as indeed I had expected, has lost its central focus without you. Bruchmann, who has returned from his journey, is no longer the same. He seems to bend to the formalities of the world, and by that alone he loses his halo, which in my opinion was due only to his determined disregard of all worldly affairs. Kupelwieser, as presumably you already know, has gone to Rome. . . . True, as a substitute for you and Kupelwieser we received four individuals. . . . What is the good of a lot of quite ordinary students and officials to us? If Bruchmann is not there, or even ill, we go on for hours under the supreme direction of Mohn, hearing nothing but eternal talk of riding, fencing, horses and hounds. If it is to go on like this I don't suppose I shall stand it for long among them.

With my operas things go very badly, too. Kupelwieser has suddenly left the theatre. Weber's *Euryanthe* turned out wretchedly, and its bad reception was quite justified, in my opinion. These circumstances, and a new split between Pálffy and Barbaja, leave me scarcely any hope for my opera. Besides, it would really not be a great stroke of fortune, as everything is done indescribably badly now.

Vogl is here, and sang once at Bruchmann's and once at Witteczek's. He is taken up with my songs almost exclusively. He writes out the voice-part himself and, so to speak, lives on it. . . . I have composed nothing since the opera, except a few *Maid of the Mill* songs. The Mill Songs will appear in four books, with vignettes by Schwind.

For the rest, I hope to resign my health, and this recovered treasure will let me forget many a sorrow; only you, dear Schober, I shall never forget, for what you meant to me, no one else can mean, alas!

(d) From various letters sent by Schwind to Schober, December 1823– January 1824:

Schubert is better, and it will not be long before he goes about with his own hair again, which had to be shorn owing to the rash. He wears a very cosy wig. He is much with Vogl and Leidesdorf. The dratted doctor is often with him, too.

. . . .

Our New Year's Eve festivity went off happily. We gathered at Mohn's. Bruchmann and Doblhoff returned on the stroke of twelve from the city where they had expected and sought Schubert. You, Senn, Kupelwieser,[1] Bruchmann and everybody's sweethearts all had their health drunk. Soon afterwards Schubert and Dr. Bernhardt announced themselves by a small target-shooting match. Schubert hit, and the shattered window-pane set everybody astir. With the doctor I have fraternized, which should suit me well. I got home at 4.30 a.m. It was all a bit crude and common, but better than we might have expected. . . .

(e) Weber to Castelli in Vienna, Dresden, 8th January 1824:

Baüerle sent a violent notice of the failure of *Rosamunde* to the *Abendzeitung* c/o my address. He probably thought this would give me pleasure, but it has only increased my embarrassment. Winkler, of course, refused to print it, which suited me very well.

. . . .

No doubt Weber's correspondent thought that a bad notice of Schubert's melodrama would soften the disappointment over *Euryanthe*, and convince Weber (if he needed convincing by this time) that the trouble lay in Helmina von Chézy's silly libretto for each of these works. Schubert's music, including the items in the lurid drama not generally known nowadays (to-day we play only the *Magic Harp* overture and the ballet music), is better than Weber's. Unfortunately newspapers then, as now, though quick enough to mention faults in a young composer, were guarded in their criticisms of a society bluestocking like the Chézy woman. Schwind, though biased in the other direction, is shrewd in his remarks to Schober:

The day before yesterday the Theater an der Wien produced a piece by the wretched Frau von Chézy, *Rosamond of Cyprus,* with music by Schubert. You may imagine that we all went to it. . . . Schubert has taken over the overture he wrote for *Estrella*, as he thinks it too 'homespun' for *Estrella*, for which he wants to write a new one. It pleased so much that, to my great joy, it had to be repeated. You may imagine how I followed the basses and the scoring. You were worried about them, I know. I noticed that

---

[1] No doubt Josef, as Leopold had gone to Rome.

the flute, to which half the theme is given, came in a bit too soon, but that may have been due to the player. . . . After the first act there was a piece which proved not sufficiently brilliant for the place it occupies, and too repetitive. A ballet made no impression, nor did the second and third act-tunes. Well, people are accustomed to begin talking immediately the curtain has dropped, and I do not see how they can be expected to notice such serious and lovely things. In the last act was a chorus of shepherds and huntsmen, so beautiful and so natural that I cannot re-member ever hearing the like before. It was applauded and repeated, and I believe it will deal the chorus in Weber's *Euryanthe* the sort of blow it deserves. An aria, too, though most atrociously sung by Mme Vogel, and a little bucolic piece were applauded. A subterranean chorus could not be heard, and even the gestures of Herr Rott, who was brewing poison, could not make it materialize.

To offset Schwind's account we have a brief entry in Rosenbaum's diary: '. . . empty, tedious, unnatural . . . paid 10 florins for my seat.' It must be amusing to modern readers to observe how both sides are concerned with the 'naturalism' of a piece; Lamb's essay on *Stage Illusion* gives an interesting commentary on the theatrical out-look of the times. It is difficult to be hard on Frau Chézy: the German romantic opera had not yet found its perfect libretto. Even *Freischütz,* with its fifty nights' initial run, was a mixture of meri-torious dramatic sequence and *ad hoc* supernatural elements included because the new romanticism loved them whether they were crude or genuinely imaginative. In Frau Chézy's inconsequential situa-tions the fancy was still more undisciplined, and when she could not fall back on super-tried fidelity, idyllic valleys where the highly born, like Rosamond, disported with fisher-folk or shepherds in unsexed attire, knightly wooing of a kind that never was, potions, faintings, sorcery and what Mrs. Malaprop called 'astronomical, mathematical, diabolical instruments,' she served up platitudinous lines no less pedestrian than those of the Italian, conventional opera of the opposing camp. It is amusing to read a Vienna correspondent's puff pre-liminary in a Stuttgart paper of 5th December 1823, announcing that Chézy is at work on a new opera libretto and has completed the drama, *Rosamunde,* but not mentioning Schubert's name.

Rosamunde was given its first performance on 20th December 1823 and had only one other, after which the parts were tied up and not disturbed until Grove and Sullivan found them in 1867. Schubert's music consisted of the overture in D major, originally the overture to *Alfonso and Estrella,* Op. 69 (see Schwind's letter above), two pieces of ballet music, three entr'actes, a shepherd's melody for wind instruments, a 'romance' for soprano solo and three choruses. It is a pity that we do not hear all this music instead of merely the ballet pieces and entr'actes.

It was in the following year, 1824, that Schubert suffered from the realization of his operatic failures. He bore Rossini no malice, as some of his friends certainly did. He was musician enough to recognize that Rossini did not depend upon a 'good libretto' in the new sense of the word. Rossini's was a different, an older art, having its roots in the operatic conventions and dramatic order of Metastasio and Mozart. (In mentioning Mozart, *The Magic Flute* must be regarded as an exception which was the precursor of all that Weber, Schubert and the young romantics stood for.) This new art, with its evocation of the past, its folk-lore and enchanted world, this German melodramatic opera, stood little chance in Vienna of post-Congress days, when Metternich himself attended the Italian productions. What Rossini gave may not have stirred the young devotees of Goethe, Schlegel, Tieck and Novalis, but it was understood by the professional musicians—the theatre orchestras and the singers recruited from Naples; the grace, the facile melody, the runs and ornaments so flattering to the voice, the scoring which made no pretensions to picturesque effect that was not brilliant, obvious, clear and adaptable to smaller and larger theatre bands—these qualities made the Swan of Pesaro *avis gratissima* with Vienna. He grew fatter than ever, treated all his cast to dinner, gave an impromptu concert on the balcony to crowds waiting for his benefit at the Kärntnertor, sang 'Largo al factotum' himself, let the benefit concert run on till two in the morning, wrote a farewell song, *Addio ai Viennesi,* collected the booty and went back to Italy. What chance had German opera before he went? Barbaja invited Weber to come with *Freischütz* only because that work had been a huge popular success elsewhere. Barbaja was a business man, guilty of no greater sin than is a modern English concert promoter who sends sandwichmen down Regent Street parading the name of a star singer, strummer or conductor without mention of the music to be played on the advertised date. The Barbajas are not to blame unless we also blame the public who want the larynx or the rapierwork primarily and the composer's mind only incidentally. Schubert's Vienna was no better than is the modern public. Hegel wrote to his wife: 'As long as I have money for the Italian opera I shall not leave Vienna,' and even Baron Schönstein, enthusiastic Schubertian as he was, lamented in a letter to Esterházy the passing of Barbaja's tenure of the lease and the departure of the Italian company.

On one point only are we certain that Barbaja played a dirty trick on Schubert, for a dirty trick is none the cleaner for being done in the name of business. He virtually commissioned *Fierabras*, no doubt to please Josef Kupelwieser, and when Kupelwieser was nicely out of the way, the score was returned to Schubert, probably unread. Poor Schubert! After the failure of *Rosamunde* he must have waited from day to day, certain that the letter would come requesting his attendance for rehearsals. It was, no doubt, in the dejection following the disappointment that he wrote to Leopold Kupelwieser, in Rome, one of the most touching and unfanciful of his letters:

For a long time I have felt the urge to write to you . . . you will be sure to forgive many things which others might take in very bad part from me. In a word, I feel myself to be the most unhappy and wretched creature in the world. Imagine a man whose health will never be right again, and who in sheer despair *over this* ever makes things worse and worse, instead of better; imagine a man, I say, whose most brilliant hopes have perished, to whom *the felicity of love and friendship* have nothing to offer but pain, whom enthusiasm (at least of the stimulating kind) for all things beautiful threatens to forsake, and I ask you, is he not a miserable, unhappy being? 'Meine Ruh ist hin, mein Herz ist schwer, ich finde sie nimmer und nimmermehr,' [1] I may well sing every day now, for each night, on retiring to bed, I hope I may not wake again, and each morning but recalls yesterday's grief. Thus, joyless and friendless, I should pass my days, did not Schwind visit me now and again and turn on me a ray of those sweet days of the past. Our readingcircle, as you probably know already, has done itself to death owing to a reinforcement of that rough chorus of beerdrinkers and

---

[1] Sung by Gretchen in Goethe's *Faust*. 'My peace is gone, my heart is sore; I shall find it never, nevermore.'

sausage-eaters, for its dissolution is due in a couple of days, though I have hardly visited it myself since your departure. Leidesdorf, with whom I have become quite well acquainted, is, in fact, a truly thoughtful and good fellow, but so hugely melancholy that I am almost afraid that I owe him more than enough in that respect; besides, my affairs and his do badly, so that we never have any money.[1] The opera by your brother (who did not do any too well in leaving the theatre) has been declared unusable, and thus no claim has been made on my music. . . .

The italics in the above letter are those of the present writer; it seems plain that the chief cause of Schubert's melancholy is the curse of his disease. Extracts from letters written during the spring of 1824 tells us that:

Schubert has given up his wig and shows a charming cygnet's down. . . . Schubert is pretty well already. He says that after a few days of the new treatment he felt how his complaint broke up and everything was different . . . he drinks tea lavishly, fasts on certain days, goes bathing a good deal and at the same time is superhumanly industrious. . . . Schubert is not very well. He has pains in his left arm and cannot play the pianoforte at all. [Various letters from Schwind to Schober.] Schubertiads are hardly mentioned any more. Schubert himself cannot sing and Vogl will sing only in agreeable and respectable society. . . . Schubert still complains of pains in his bones. [Doblhoff to Schober.]

A letter from Ferdinand Schubert to the composer says: 'Now, dear Franz, write to me to say how you are, but expressly addressed to me.' We are not to know how much evidence concerning Schubert's disease *may* have been suppressed by his family, by Grove or whomsoever. Replying to Ferdinand from Zseliz, the composer assures his brother that he is well, but adds: 'True, it is no longer that happy time during which each object seems to us to be surrounded by a youthful gloriole, but a period of fateful recognition of miserable reality.'

---

[1] If Schubert sought a melancholy companion to counteract the ebullient Schwind, he could not have sought a more suitable one than Leidesdorf, with whose name Beethoven made play, calling him 'Dorf des Leides'—village of sorrow.

The departure of friends and the failure of the operas would not be enough to make a man of Schubert's nature permanently subject to moods of depression. Besides there were musical successes of this year sufficient to please any musician—the publication of the Mill Songs and their enthusiastic reception, not with the public, but by his own friends, the performance of the Octet at Count Troyer's and, later in the year, of the A minor Quartet, Op. 29. The year 1824 may not seem very productive: there are hardly any songs, though plenty of instrumental works, and it may well be said that musically, operatically and physically he reaped what had been sown in 1823, if we exclude his months spent in Hungary. The occasional gloomy letter which we find during his last six years may have been the result of an obsession, or may have been a mere temperamental matter. We are not to know for certain, therefore, that the poem written soon after the onset of illness during the previous year is a subjective document, though it is one of the first sad ones to come from his pen:

MY PRAYER

With a holy zeal I yearn
Life in fairer worlds to learn;
    Would this gloomy life might seem
    Filled with love's almighty dream.

Sorrow's child, almighty Lord,
Grant Thy bounty for reward.
    For redemption from above
    Send a ray of endless love.

See, abased in dust and mire,
Scorched by agonizing fire,
    I in torture go my way,
    Nearing doom's destructive day.

Take my life, my flesh and blood,
Plunge it all in Lethe's flood,
    To a purer, stronger state
    Deign me, Great One, to translate.

(9th May 1823.)

It was during the winter of 1823-4 that, unable to go on living at his father's home, as he had done since his return to Vienna, he moved near to the bastion, where he lodged with Josef Huber to save rent. No doubt the need of money influenced him to go back with the Esterházys to Castle Zseliz, where he spent the six months from May to October. The deep affection between the composer and his brothers, his father and stepmother, is shown in their mutual correspondence during his stay in Hungary. The father's letters are full of pedagogical but affectionate piety and pride in the hard work entailed by his position at the Rossau school. Ferdinand's are more human and jocular missives than one would expect from a school inspector; one feels that he was made of the same bohemian stuff as Franz and would fain have kept company with the gay sparks of the Moonshine House had he not been a family man needing security in his position.

We know little about this second stay at Zseliz. The comparatively few compositions were obviously written for the company there. One says 'comparatively,' since the *Grand Duo* alone is on a scale that would have exacted a year's work from most composers. Then there are the four-handed *Divertissement à la hongroise* and the Variations in A flat major, the Sonata in B flat major and the fine vocal quartet, *Gebet*, to words of La Motte Fouqué, written between breakfast and supper one day in September, immediately the countess had produced the poem. The singers were, most probably, the count and countess, the elder daughter Marie and Baron Schönstein, whose singing must have made Schubert's stay musically gratifying, since there was a big new repertory to be drawn from his songs written since the previous stay at Zseliz. If there is any interest to be attached to Kreissle's supposition that the composer felt tender towards Caroline, the younger Esterházy girl, now aged seventeen, then his temperature must have risen during this visit, and not the previous one. But social difference alone made any declaration of his feelings impossible. It must be repeated, if only on account of an unpleasant and very popular musical play, wherein falsification of history is as great a sin as maltreatment of Schubert's music, that (a) if there was any genuine love affair in Schubert's life, any 'Egeria' or 'Ferne Geliebte,' we know nothing of it, and (b) of the probable ephemeral field-work, alley-work or alliances behind the elms, we also know nothing.

The years run alternately—1825 is a happy one. For some time Schubert had grown restless for Vienna and his friends, just as he did when previously in Hungary. Schober was still at Breslau and Kupelwieser studying in Rome; but in Vienna he was again in the convivial company of Schwind, Jenger, Mayrhofer, Bauernfeld and Vogl, with whom he planned a great summer tour of Upper Austria, beginning at Steyr in May. This was probably the happiest time of his life. Sophie Müller, whose home was open to the Schubertians and whose talents and friendship were at the composer's disposal, contributed no little to his happiness once he was back in his beloved city. A letter received from Anna Milder during the winter cannot but have pleased him, for this great artist not only wished to make his personal acquaintance, but spoke highly of his songs and hoped she could secure the performance of one of his operas at Berlin where, perhaps, there would be more German national feeling than in Vienna. At Schubertiads during March Sophie Müller sang *The Young Nun* at sight and Vogl the new Walter Scott songs. Well might Schwind write to Schober: 'Schubert is here and divinely frivolous, rejuvenated by delight and a pleasant life.' Kupelwieser's betrothed wrote to her man to say that Schubert was much in Schwind's company: 'This is good, for if they are not of much use to each other, they do each other no harm, and that alone is a good deal in Schwind's case, since he is so easily influenced by his environment. He could well do with a male friend.' Schwind was delighted and wrote to Schober:

He has recently come to live next door to us, where the beer-house is, on the second floor, in a very pretty room. We meet daily, and as far as I can I share his whole life with him. . . . There is a Schubertiad at Enderes's each week . . . that is to say, Vogl sings. Apart from him the company consists of Witteczek, Esch, Schlechta, Gross, Riepl—a mixture of nothing but similar faces. Mayrhofer and Gahy often put in an appearance also.

It is to be supposed that published music or what was earned at the Esterházys' (if anything remained) kept Schubert solvent during the early part of this year.

Schubert

Vogl had set off for his native Steyr in March; Schubert joined him in May. These were halcyon months. Grove says Schubert found his music had a 'widespread reputation' in Upper Austria, but it must be remembered that he met chiefly friends of friends, e.g. Spaun's and Vogl's friends, who had followed his muse from the beginning. Kreissle tells us that Vogl and Schubert travelled like wandering minstrels on their beautiful country expedition, 'bent on making at one time a stately monastery, at another a city or town, ring with their already famous lays. They made considerable halts at Linz, Gmunden and Salzburg, making Vogl's birthplace their starting-point. Everywhere they fell in with friends and acquaintances, who received them with open arms.' This tour with Vogl provides us with the longest letters Schubert ever wrote, and those from his relatives and friends in Vienna are all happy and often interesting. One from Schwind in July tells Schubert that Grillparzer assured him that 'in ten years he would remember every figure' in the painting from *The Marriage of Figaro*; what follows shows a difference in temperament between Schwind and Schubert:

Since, in default of a Duke of Weimar to protect and pay us, we can ask nothing better than the spiritual judgment of important people, you may imagine in what a happy frame of mind I went home . . . he hopes to secure you an opera for the Königstadt Theatre in Berlin, whose manager he knows, and who is looking for an opera. He repeated several times that he was really serious about it.

At Linz Schubert was quartered at Spaun's old home, but Spaun himself had just taken up his post at Lwów, to Schubert's great disappointment:

You may imagine how annoyed I am at having to write a letter to you from Linz to Lemberg! Devil take accursed duty, which cruelly tears friends asunder when they have scarcely sipped the goblet of friendship. . . . If Jägermeyer did not keep such good beer and they had not a passable wine on the Castle Hill, I should have to hang myself on the promenade with the legend: 'From sorrow over the departed soul of Linz.' As you see, I wax positively unjust towards the rest of Linzdom, since after all I am quite happy at your mother's house, and in the company of your sister, Ottenwalt and Max [Spaun's brother], and seem to see your spirit flash from the body of many another Linzer.

To his father and stepmother he wrote:

I am back at Steyr again, but have been at Gmunden for six weeks, the environs of which are truly heavenly. . . . I lived at Traweger's, very free and easy. Later, when Councillor von Schiller was there, who is the monarch of the whole Salzkammergut, we (Vogl and I) dined daily at his house and had music there, as we also often did at Traweger's house. My new songs from Walter Scott's *Lady of the Lake* especially had much success. They also wondered greatly at my piety, which I expressed in a hymn to the Holy Virgin and which, it appears, grips every soul and turns it to devotion. I think this is due to the fact that I have never forced devotion in myself, and never composed hymns or prayers of that kind unless it overcomes me unawares.

Modesty and lack of hypocrisy are notable elements in Schubert's character, showing themselves in the most casual letters. Nowhere does he boast his musical powers, and though the reference to a sacred composition is politically reserved for his parents, the sentiment expressed is sincere enough. Later he writes:

At Steyregg we called on Countess Weissenwolff, who is a great admirer of my littleness, possesses all my things and sings many of them quite nicely. . . . I intend to use a very different procedure with the publication of these songs from the usual one, which yields so very little, since they bear the celebrated name of Walter Scott at their head, and may in that way arouse greater curiosity, and might also make me better known in England by the addition of the English words. If only some decency might be expected of those —— of art dealers ! But the wise and benevolent dispensations of the State have well and truly seen to it that an artist shall ever remain the slave of every wretched huckster.

After telling his parents of the projected visit to Gastein, he says he will be back in Vienna early in October, asks his father to pay the rent for his old rooms next to the Karlskirche in the Wieden, which he will refund, and then adds some words concerning his brothers Ferdinand and Karl, which are, I think, significant:

I suppose he has been ill seventy-seven times again, and has thought that he was going to die, as though dying were the worst that could happen to a man. . . . If only he could for once see these heavenly mountains and lakes . . . he could not regard it otherwise than good fortune to have confided to him earth's indescribable power of creating new life. [The heretical grafting of pantheism on catholicism is present in all the great Viennese composers, whether expressed directly or not.] Karl . . . must be busy now, for a married artist's duty is to supply works of nature as well as art, and if he succeeds in both kinds he will be very praiseworthy, for that is no small matter. I renounce it myself.

The longest letter—one of the longest ever written by Schubert— includes a detailed description of the scenes of their travels, specially to please Ferdinand, who requested it. Dear old Ferdinand seemed to grow very quickly into a chip of the old block. To encourage his brother's pen he sent a longish description of the outings he had made into mountain country as part of his school-inspecting travels. The description is larded with moral reflections and aspirations . . . how, among certain peasants, one may observe that robbery and violence are not known, for virtue and industry ever keep company, how he envies the opportunity to travel, a great asset to a teacher of geography, how he visited a coal mine, how travel brings to his mind sacred music, and how pleased he is to recollect Franz's contribution to that branch of his art and to hear that his hymn to the Virgin was so moving. Franz's reply has but one aside—an apostrophe to the shade of Michael Haydn, whose tomb he visited, and of whom he wrote as though he were as great as his brother. Elsewhere the letter gives a rhapsodic account of the scenery in the Salzburg area, though it seems curious that he and Vogl have nothing to say of the adored Mozart. There is a charm about Schubert's babbling style:

We drove through the valley described above as if through Elysium, except that it has the advantage of that paradise that we sat in a delightful coach, a convenience denied to Adam and Eve. Instead of wild beasts we encountered many most charming girls . . . It is all wrong, my cracking such miserable jokes in such a beautiful neighbourhood, but I simply cannot be serious to-day. So we pushed comfortably on, lost in the delight of the fine day and still finer country, in which nothing arrested our attention except a pretty building, called Month's Castle, which an elector caused to be built within a month for his fair lady. Everybody knows this here, but no one is shocked at it. What enchanting tolerance! . . . A few hours later we reached the curious but extremely dirty and horrid little town of Hallein. The inhabitants look like ghosts, pale, hollow-eyed and lean enough to catch fire. The appalling contrast of the sight of such a rat-hole etc. in this valley made the most dismal impression on me. It was as though one had fallen from heaven on to a dung-heap or were listening after Mozart's music to a piece by the immortal A. There was no inducing Vogl to view the Salzburg salt mines. . . .

It is hard not to see in this letter a deliberate teasing of Ferdinand. Yet the affection between them was deep, and Ferdinand wistfully followed his brother's music-makings. A much earlier letter from Ferdinand relates an experience which must have given the composer as great a pleasure as another nature could have derived from a laudatory press notice or a public honour. His brother wrote:

At Hainburg I had bed and board at Herr Reinberger's, the amiable town pastor. This truly dear, good man did all he could to entertain me. The first day he took us to the local castle hill and castle garden . . . he introduced me to the local choirmaster and his son, who is a schoolmaster there. . . . The former invited me to a service that took place the following Sunday, on the fourth day of my visit; and when I asked him what Mass he had chosen, he answered: 'A very fine one, by a well-known and famous composer—only I can't think of his name at the moment.' And what do you think the Mass was? If only you had been there; I know you too would have been greatly pleased; for it was the B flat Mass by—yourself! You may well imagine how I felt, and also what kind and uncommon people these must be, who took the trouble to touch my feelings in such an agreeably surprising manner. What is more, the Mass was done with a great deal of enthusiasm, and really very well.

The flighty Bauernfeld wrote to Schubert while he was away with Vogl proposing that he shared rooms with Schwind and himself (and also shared expenses) when he returned to Vienna in October. Schubert was by no means a schemer in money matters, but he seems to have been fleeced rather too often in earlier days. His reply includes the words:

As for living together, it would suit me very well, of course, but as I know something about such bachelors' and students' plans, I should not like to find myself between two stools. . . . Should anything suitable turn up, however, I shall find means of parting from my landlord in a decent manner.

The farthest point reached during the summer tour with Vogl was Gastein; the hints of a 'Grand Symphony,' and current explanations of this mysterious work, are discussed with the other symphonies elsewhere. Little is known of Schubert's movements and musical occupations between October, when he returned to Vienna, and the end of the year. The A minor Quartet, a piano Sonata and the duet *Funeral March for Tsar Alexander* were all published at this time. The year 1826 was externally uneventful. After the New Year celebrations at Schober's there is no record of riotous parties during the early part of the year, and whatever excursions had been intended for the summer months, Schubert got no farther than Währing, just out/ side Vienna. Perhaps the most important consideration to be made in connection with this year is the discrepancy between Schubert's growing popularity and his obvious poverty. In and near this year alone the following works were published:

> Seven Songs from *The Lady of the Lake,* Op. 52 (Artaria).
> Pianoforte Sonata in D, Op. 53 (Artaria).
> *Divertissement à la hongroise,* Op. 54 (Artaria).
> Three Songs, Op. 56 (Pennauer).
> Three Songs, Op. 57 (Weigl).
> Three Songs, Op. 58 (Weigl).
> Two Songs, Op. 60 (Cappi & Czerny).
> Four Songs, Op. 59 (Leidesdorf).
> Three Partsongs for men's voices, Op. 64 (Pennauer).
> Three Songs, Op. 65 (Cappi & Czerny).
> Mass in C, Op. 48 (Diabelli) ⎫
> *Tantum ergo,* Op. 45 (Diabelli) ⎪ (1825).
> *Totus in corde,* Op. 46 (Diabelli) ⎬
> *Salve Regina,* Op. 47 (Diabelli) ⎭
> Galop and Eight Écossaises (piano), Op. 49 (Diabelli) ⎫ (1825).
> Thirty/four *Valses sentimentales,* Op. 50 (Diabelli) ⎭
> Sixteen *Ländler,* etc., Op. 67 (Diabelli) (1827).
> Three Marches (4 hands), Op. 51 (Diabelli) (1827).
> Two Russian Marches, Opp. 55 and 56 (Pennauer).
> Six Polonaises, Op. 61 (Cappi & Czerny).
> *Divertissement on French Themes,* Op. 63 (Weigl).

Early in the year the string Quartet in D minor, containing the variations on *Death and the Maiden,* had its first performance, as did the brilliant one in G major later in the year. The other chief com/ positions of 1826 are the B minor Rondo for violin and piano, the two famous Shakespeare songs and the G major piano Sonata about which Schumann was so enthusiastic. Now how can any man read that list of publications (for a single year, be it noted) and suppose that the composer was without fame in his native city? True, the parts of the chamber works were not published till after the com-poser's death, but how many copies of, say, the second violin or the viola part could the publisher have sold within the first year of issue, even in so musical a city as Schubert's Vienna? It is not as if the parts were easy. Few quartets or trios could have attempted them. As Grove puts it:

Pennauer and Leidesdorf were his personal friends, and may possibly have printed his pieces from chivalrous motives; but no one can suspect hard and experienced business men like Diabelli and Artaria of publishing any music at their own risk unless they believed that there was a demand for it. . . . And even at the incredibly [1] low prices which his publishers gave for the exclusive copyright of his works, there is enough in the above to produce an income sufficient for Schubert's wants. But the fact is that he was mixed up with a set of young fellows who regarded him as a Croesus, and who virtually lived upon his carelessness and good nature.

Grove over-champions his hero; in this and other matters Schubert was not a good business man and, unlike Beethoven, took no trouble to get a good price from his publisher, or to set two or three pub-lishers in competition for a new work. Moreover, Schubert had not the sense to be guided by a better business man than himself; obstinacy was a trait in his character, as we know from the testimony of those who saw his behaviour when tipsy, in which state men very frequently verify the adage, 'In vino veritas.' Schubert obviously intended to run his own business affairs. Music would always pour from him, and if he were ever out of pocket, he would have to write something quickly and sell it, till one day an opera would set him permanently on his feet. Schubert was a fool if he could not choose good friends, that is to say, the friends who brought the best out of him because he admired them. In this matter I do not think Schubert was quite such a fool as he has been painted; his letters to his friends show that, whatever follies he shared with them, he admired each one of them for some quality or qualities which answered the 'Kann

[1] This is Grove's word. Were the prices so incredible? Is much more paid nowadays to composers who are so anxious for ready money that they sell copyright instead of doing business on a royalty basis?

er was?' test. And if it is foolish to be unstinting, as a bachelor with no more immediate obligations, to one's closest friends, there are many of us who admire such folly. Besides, Schubert was a good deal older than Schwind and Bauernfeld, and his payment for what they ate and drank at the *Gasthaus* or elsewhere gave him as much happiness as it gave them. It cannot have done him much harm.

Hope sprang eternal in his breast. He waited like Micawber for something to turn up from the Kärntnertor, the Theater an der Wien, from Berlin or Dresden. Meanwhile his friends persuaded him to apply for a salaried post. Salieri had died in 1825, and his colleague Eybler, the other examiner of young Schubert's fitness for a choral scholarship, stepped naturally into the post of first court *Capellmeister*. In 1826 Schubert applied for Eybler's former post of second court musician, along with seven other candidates whose names include Gyrowetz, Kreutzer and Anselm Hüttenbrenner. All were passed over in favour of Weigl, composer of the popular *Swiss Family*. We cannot, of course, be sure that Schubert sought this post with all his heart; if he did, his remark to Spaun: 'I wish I could have obtained this post, but as it has been given to one so worthy as Weigl I must not complain,' is a fine testimony to his generosity and lack of professional jealousy. It is true that Schubert was the kind of man who seeks regular appointment not for its own sake, but for periodicity of salary, but we have reasons for believing his application for Eybler's post to have been by no means so half-hearted an affair as was his previous application for the teaching post at Laibach. In the first place he may have applied later in the year for the post of conductor at the Kärntnertor Theatre.

There seems to be no reason for Kreissle's doubt of the veracity of Schindler's account of the Kärntnertor incident. Vogl encouraged Schubert to apply. Appointment depended upon public trial of ability, the candidate being required to write a musical setting of words by Dupont, the theatre manager, and to direct their rehearsal. During Schubert's test, Nanette Schechner, the prima donna, requested the simplifying of an aria. Dupont and several of the musicians present supported the request. Schindler says that Schubert shouted, after a tense silence: 'I will alter nothing!' He shut the score with a loud bang and marched off. This rather doubtful account is partly confirmed by one Franz Zierer, a teacher at the Conservatory, but his suggestion that the aria was beyond the singer's powers is refutable. Mlle Schechner, according to Schober in a letter to Bauernfeld of June 1826, 'revolutionizes the town by her wonderful singing in German. Since the Milder it is said that no such voice has set the air vibrating, and she is youthful, pretty and vivacious into the bargain. Schubert has heard her and chimes into the hymn of praise.'

Any disappointment Schubert may have retained from his failure to acquire the two salaried appointments was at least banished temporarily by a pleasant surprise. At the instigation of its secretary, Josef Sonnleithner, the Philharmonic Society voted him a hundred florins 'not as a fee, but as a token of the society's sense of obligation towards you, and of the thanks with which it acknowledges the interest you have shown it.'

This once more points to the fact, which it is necessary to repeat, that Schubert was not a neglected or slighted *composer*; he was passed over as a professional musician in other respects for the very good reason that there were others who would obviously have made better teachers or musical directors. Consider merely the progress of his popularity at meetings of the Philharmonic Society, although it must be conceded that the society in those days was fairly small and exclusive. The first acquaintance which these connoisseurs made with Schubert's work in public was with *Erl King*, sung by the tenor Gymnich in 1821. By 1826 so highly valued were the many works by Schubert which were given at the society's concerts that it was decided to add Schubert's biography to the others which were kept in the society's library. Jenger was therefore requested to provide the document, and in the following summer Schubert had the pleasure of writing to the secretary: 'The Philharmonic Society in the Imperial City having done me the honour of electing me a member of their body, it gives me great pleasure to say that I feel extremely flattered, and I hope that I may fulfil my duties of membership worthily.' Apart from this public recognition, we learn from letters and diaries that Schubertiads were on a grander scale than ever, especially just after the idyllic summer stay at Währing.

Those who wish to paint Schubert as ill-used and without honour usually recognize his following among the friends who only too readily organized Schubertiads, or whose ways of life provided an almost daily opportunity for a Schubertiad if only the composer could be induced to be present. It is the publishers and musical public in general who are made the villains. But it can be shown by citation of two phenomena that Schubert's claim (the fourth point made in his application for the vice-capellmeistership) to be 'well known, not only in Vienna, but in the whole of Germany, for his composition of vocal and instrumental music,' was not an exaggeration, customary on such applications. First we have to note that in December 1825 the publishers Cappi & Co., in the Graben, put the following advertisement in the *Wiener Zeitung*:

The art-dealers Cappi & Co., in the Graben, No. 1134,[1] are showing a very successful portrait of the composer Franz Schubert, reproduced by Herr Passini, from the original painting by Rieder, price 3 florins. This talented composer, whose music, especially his vocal compositions, has so often delighted distinguished audiences, appears in this picture to the life. It is a most speaking likeness, and we are sure that the numerous friends and admirers of Schubert will find it an acceptable gift.

The portrait was on sale at other shops in the city. Secondly we have yet to record Schubert's full and final recognition by Beethoven, though the material for that account belongs to the year 1827.

I cannot see that letters such as the following from Probst, which are so often quoted as evidence of shabby treatment, contain anything which could not be written to-day by a reputable business house to a composer of enterprise:

. . . thanking you cordially for your confidence, I am very gladly prepared to contribute towards the dissemination of your artistic reputation so far as it lies in my power. Only I must frankly confess to you that our public does not yet sufficiently and generally understand the peculiar, often ingenious, but perhaps now and then somewhat curious procedures of your mind's creations. Kindly, therefore, bear this in mind on sending me your MSS. . . . Once the path has been cleared, everything will find access, but to begin with a few concessions must be made to the public. . . .

---

[1] There were not thousands of houses in the Graben: the numbering in the city ran consecutively from street to street.

Those are no insulting sentences to send a man of twenty/nine. They show recognition of genius. Schubert had less than two years to live; during those two years he had illness and periods of poverty. But he was tied to no work which he did not choose to do, he was in full command of amazing creative powers, there were no signs that his invention would ever fail him, he had a large circle of admirers and, in the words of Probst, once the path had been cleared, every/ thing would find access—even the supposedly difficult symphonies —and if he occasionally spent days with an empty pocket, there were dozens of houses at which he could call just as a cloth was being spread. Being poor meant, to Schubert, being unable to pay for an evening's conviviality at the *Gasthaus* or for a show at one of the theatres which gave opera, and it is clear that Schubert never availed himself of money which would have been given immediately by one of his better/off friends. Before he began the last two years of his life, Schubert must have known what he was. He must have recog/ nized, too, that he was an older person than his immediate friends, with a heavier responsibility, for he had travelled farther along the road of artistic experience. He sometimes took part in their revels, we feel, with the strange feeling that he was playing Peter Pan when youth was over, and that he should have been elsewhere—reading, meditating, composing; and when illness came, although the specific dogmas of his inherited religion may have troubled him not at all, he must, in Johnsonian phrase, have 'felt the impress of futurity.' We cannot think that so gifted a man, even a creature so much more emotional than intellectual, did not in his last years speculate in his own way on the deepest mysteries of being, nor can we think that he deliberately frittered away his leisure time in order to banish all speculative thought from his mind.

Ultimately the life of every great artist is a lonely one, for he travels ahead of the generation he represents, but also leads. Even Schubert, most convivial of the great musicians, had arrived by the end of 1826 at the knowledge that he must go alone. He may have known it long before; but any picturesque, Schwindian, lilac/timeish con/ ception of the composer which lurks in our minds must be tempered with the more serious figure of the last two years—a Schubert who hardly revealed himself, even in his music.

CHAPTER VI

THE END

BEETHOVEN was brought in December 1826 to the sick-bed from which he never rose. After being tapped for dropsy three times, he recovered sufficient vitality to need mental occupation. Amongst other works about sixty Schubert songs, some still in manuscript, were brought in by the attentive Schindler. This musical offering contained the Mill Songs, *The Young Nun, Iphigenia, Viola* and *Bounds of Mankind*. Beethoven was surprised and deeply moved: he gave the songs repeated study. According to Schindler, 'not once but many times, Beethoven said: "Truly this Schubert has the divine fire" and "Had I come across this poem I should have set it."' The older composer was amazed that 'Schubert was able to set a song of such length that it seemed to contain ten other songs.' The present writer has not seen a satisfactory explanation of this last remark reported by Schindler. Maybe Beethoven, whose art was the construction of huge edifices from an economy of short, pregnant materials, wondered at Schubert's lavishness, at the 'profuse strains of unpremeditated art,' the unending spate of melodic invention. It is no legend that Beethoven uttered words either actually as reported by Schindler or else to similar effect, for he asked to be shown some operatic and keyboard compositions by Schubert, and declared that 'he would make a great stir in the world.' For the information and for a corroborating account of Schubert's visits to the dying man we have the testimony of Anselm Hütten-brenner, who is regarded as reliable. Before this year Beethoven had met only some four or five of Schubert's songs, and he was astonished to learn that at least five hundred existed.

Beethoven's condition soon became so serious that it was impossible to follow up his request to see Schubert's pianoforte works or operas; but Hüttenbrenner tells how he and Schubert called to see Beethoven about eight days before his death. Schindler announced them and asked which of the two men should be brought in first; Beethoven said: 'Let Schubert come.' It is said that a further visit was made by Schubert, along with Josef Hüttenbrenner and the painter Teltscher, but Beethoven could only stare at them and make with his hand some signs which they were unable to interpret. At the funeral on 29th March Schubert had an honoured place as torchbearer with the finest and most prominent artists of Vienna either around him or sharing the same ceremonial duty—Grillparzer, Raimund, Lenau, Czerny, Lachner, Anschütz, Castelli, David, as well as lesser lights such as his friend Bauernfeld. At the graveside the actor Anschütz delivered the oration written by Grillparzer. One of Schubert's fellow-torchbearers was the great Italian bass, Lablache, for whom he wrote the *Three Italian Songs*, Op. 83, dedicated to the singer. On the way home from the funeral Schubert, Schwind and Schober met at the 'Castle of Eisenstadt' tavern to talk chiefly of Beethoven. At another inn Schubert is said to have proposed two healths, the first to the great man they had just seen buried, the second unconsciously to himself—'To him who shall be next.'

However much we reject of the reported talk at meetings between the two great musicians, it is certain that only Beethoven's death prevented his expressed recognition and close following of the younger man's musical achievements. And there is every sign that had Schubert lived a little longer he would have enjoyed honours beyond his own city. Just before the events recorded above two firms of publishers wrote independently from Leipzig for manuscripts. The tone of the letters, from H. A. Probst and from Breitkopf & Härtel, is decidedly flattering. Publishers do not frequently write such letters, even nowadays, to composers under thirty.

Critics have been unusually wise after the event in explaining the pathos of the *Winter Journey* cycle, which constitutes Schubert's supreme achievement for the year 1827. The seriousness of these songs at first surprised Schubert's friends. Schober liked only *The Linden Tree*, but its silly tale was the sort of thing that appealed to the exquisite Schober. His musical experience was of just the right depth to be captivated by the little figure evoking the flurry of the wind in the tree, so cruelly blowing a cloak away! Spaun, on the other hand, though as much subject as any Schubertian to the romantic tastes of his day, was a musician of sound judgment, and he tells us:

Franz had for some time appeared altered and depressed, and upon my inquiry as to what was the matter he only replied: 'You will soon understand.' One day he said: 'Come with me to Schober's and I will sing you a set of songs that will make you shiver; I am anxious to know what you think of them.' They touched me more deeply than any songs I had ever heard. He sang in a voice vibrant with feeling the whole *Winter Journey* cycle. The tragic and passionate tone of these songs took us aback. . . . Schubert said: 'I am more pleased with these songs than with any others, and you will get to like them too.' He was right; we were soon mad about them, with their yearning pathos, when Vogl sang them in his masterly style.

Now it is not to be denied that the Schubert of ten years before the *Winter Journey* songs could hardly have sustained the spirit of pathos all through twenty-four poems, scarcely one of which reflects the idyllic happiness of the former Müller collection. The maid of the later set, cruel baggage, never shows her face; the hapless lover is alone in a frost-bound countryside, or in spiritual sympathy with the poor old organ-grinder. But the extremes of human pathos had been sounded in many a *single* song dating from Schubert's youngest days as a songster, and we are being very wise after the event to support a theory that Schubert was himself approaching the winter of life —he was only twenty-nine—or the extremes of illness, wretchedness and poverty. His health did not deteriorate to the point of seriousness until late in the year, and Professor Deutsch's collected Schubert documents show even more than the usual number of convivial gatherings at this or that tavern both before and after Beethoven's funeral; and since the first half of the *Winter Journey* cycle was written before March 1827, Beethoven's death cannot have cast any shadow over Schubert's mind while he composed some of the most pathetic songs in the collection. Surely the consistent seriousness of *The Winter Journey* is sufficiently explained by the effect of the poems themselves on a mature and very sensitive artist; their appeal was so powerful that, once the composer had set his imagination in sympathy with their hapless central figure, he was unconsciously in his shoes and unable to get out of them just because a friend called on him while there were still more verses in the volume to be set.

We have accounts of two particularly fine music-makings in the period between March 1827 and the summer holiday which Schubert took in the Graz district. The first is described by Hiller, who at the age of sixteen visited Vienna with the veteran Hummel, arriving just in time to attend Beethoven's bedside. Hiller recalled the tremendous experience of hearing Schubert and Vogl in partnership at an evening party given by Madame von Lascny, who had great reputation as a singer under her maiden name of Buchwieser. Hiller says:

> Schubert had little technique and Vogl but little voice; but they both had such life and feeling, and went so thoroughly into the thing, that it would be impossible to render these wonderful compositions more clearly and more splendidly. Voice and piano became as nothing; the music seemed to want no material help, but the melodies appealed to the ear as a vision does to the eye.

The other gathering referred to above was arranged by Anna Fröhlich for a birthday fête at Döbling; her position as singing teacher at the Conservatory enabled her to obtain the picked voices for the performance of Schubert's specially composed Serenade for alto solo and female voices ('Zögernd leise,' Op. 135). It was sung by moonlight in the garden, and 'numbers of the dwellers at Döbling stood and listened at the garden gate.'

The manuscript sketch of Schubert's last opera (*The Count of Gleichen*) is dated 17th June 1827; although the whole work is sketched, no part is fully scored. Bauernfeld gave Schubert the libretto in 1826.

On Sunday morning, 2nd September, Schubert set out with Jenger for his last holiday in the enchanted hills of Upper Austria, the lovely Styrian capital of Graz being the place of his first fortnight's stay. For some time the Pachler family, whose house was well known as a haunt of musicians and artists, had looked forward to the visit of Schubert and Jenger, and several letters from the Schubertians assured the Pachlers that Schubert would be persuaded to come. The advocate Dr. Karl Pachler was a generous connoisseur of the arts and Frau Pachler a fine pianist, on friendly terms with

Beethoven and Anselm Hüttenbrenner. Graz was as picturesque as a medieval toy town set in the richest green. The Schubertians picnicked, walked up the Schlossberg and marvelled at the valley below them and the distant mountains, visited the terraced gardens of this or that baroque castle, with its fantastically lovely flowers, its sundials, gods and urns, drove out through forests, fields and vine-yards, danced, made music, warmed their hearts with good wine, acted the fool and flirted. The peak event of these days was a visit in two carriages, one for the Pachlers, one for Schubert, Jenger and Hüttenbrenner, to the idyllic little castle and estate of Wildbach, the property of the Pachlers' aunt, Frau Anna Massegg, and bower of her six lovely daughters. As to indoor hospitality at the Pachlers', the Styrian dances, the 'Grätzer' galop and waltzes, the concert organized by the Styrian Musical Society at which Schubert accom-panied his songs and the letters written after the holiday was over—all these testify to everybody's pleasure and perhaps the most happy time Schubert had ever known outside Vienna or in it. The Pachlers and their friends knew how to make a distinguished party both genial and homely. Schubert was appreciated for what he was and not formally lionized. Himself sensitive, he enjoyed his stay with sensitive hosts. After their return Jenger wrote:

Through Josef Hüttenbrenner, who is lucky enough to be returning to Graz, we, Friend Schwammerl [Schubert's nickname] and myself, thank you, dear and gracious lady, most heartily for all your kindness and friendship, which neither of us will forget as long as he lives. Seldom have Schubert and I enjoyed such glorious times as in Graz and its surroundings, and we shall always remember Wildbach, with its dear inhabitants, as the crowning delight.

There follows an account of the journey home, punctuated by pleasant visits to Jenger's friends.

It is remarkable that, for once, Schubert seems to have lingered mentally at Graz, to have wished to be back there rather than in Vienna. Formerly he always wanted to get back to Vienna, however beautiful the place of his exile. Perhaps the dispersal of his old circle explains this change. It was at this time that Spaun and Kupelwieser married, and even the old dandy Vogl led a charming pupil to the altar. The circle had grown up. Schubert was essential to festivals of farewell, but he must have felt lonely at the thought that a man whose natural life has its time of gregarious pleasure and flirtation should not prolong that time artificially after his first affections have turned to home-making and family life, unless he is burdened with the vocation of genius, the devotion to a cause, the obsession of a crank or the folly of a libertine. The gentle Schubert, like the wistful and bewildered Mozart or the defiant Beethoven, had to face the knowledge that he was not as other men are. Not even a strong religious faith or a fine physical constitution has spared genius its moods when the recognition of loneliness has been strong; and Schubert was neither a fine physical specimen nor the child of a religious age.

Yet this parting of the Schubertians cannot have had anything to do with the seriousness of the second volume of the *Winter Journey* songs, which are on the whole the more pathetic of the collection. He began work on them immediately after the great refreshment of his holiday in Styria, and the farewells to his close friends took place during the winter, when Schwind, the closest, moved to Munich. Other compositions of 1827 include the German Mass and the fine Trio in E flat major (Op. 100) for piano and strings. On his return to Vienna Schubert lived in rooms taken by Schober at the 'Blue Hedgehog' in the Tuchlauben.[1]

That his friends by no means forsook him is proved by their persuading him to give a concert on 26th March 1828, in the Musical Society's hall; that they were numerous and his local fame was by no means so small as some would have us think is proved by the fact that the concert attracted 'more people than the hall had ever before been known to hold,' and that the takings for Schubert were 800 gulden, about £32, which were spent in paying off old debts, celebrating the event and paying five gulden three days later to hear Paganini. The one visit was not enough: Schubert had to go again to take Bauernfeld, who 'had not five farthings while with Schubert money was as plentiful as blackberries.' It is a tribute to Schubert's

[1] We do not know precisely when he settled in the house near the country which had been taken by his brother Ferdinand, the school inspector.

generosity that he seems to have joined in the general admiration of Paganini's virtuosity, despite the fact that the more grudging news-papers saw fit to compare Schubert's reputation with Paganini's, depicting the composer as one of the many 'who are content to be put in the shade' of the star fiddler. As one account says:

> Vienna was plunged into the throes of a great agitation, more remarkable even than that which Rossini's visit had previously induced. Paganini appeared, and all classes of society came under his spell, including the dandy and the small shopkeeper. Hats, gloves, boots were all worn *à la Paganini*. Walking-sticks and snuff-boxes bore the virtuoso's likeness. Even *restaurateurs'* dishes were named after him.

It may have been well that Schubert's concert came before the first of Paganini's, though Schubert's audience must have consisted chiefly of those whose hearts he had already won in the intimate circles of private gatherings. The programme included some of the latest and best songs, the Serenade written in the previous year for Anna Fröhlich's garden party and the fine E flat major Trio. It is plain that, had Schubert lived a few years longer, he would have seen his already considerable following swollen to as great a size as any artist has enjoyed in middle life. A few weeks before the concert Probst and Schott had written to him from North Germany re-questing manuscripts, of which Schott accepted some of importance.

A further exaggeration to be avoided in a just account of Schu-bert's later years, and especially his last, is a misplaced sympathy with his financial poverty, most of which was due to himself—one is careful not to say 'to his own fault.' Haydn or Brahms could have lived on the takings from publishers which we are so often told were beggarly. Schubert lived on rolls and coffee at Bogner's for a day or two and then had a convivial day or night with friends in which he either threw away some temporary alleviation of his poverty or else ran up a fresh debt. One account remarks:

> For giving lessons, as Mozart had done, Schubert had neither the gift nor patience. His bitter experience in youth as a schoolmaster put him off trying this method of bringing grist to the mill. Rather starve and be free to dream, to sing and compose as an independent artist!

Indeed, what artist, or even artistic person, however much smaller in stature than Schubert, would not like to be 'free to dream'? Who is not sorry that the world has not yet found a society which ensures us musicians the freedom to work out our artistic salvation? But let there be no false sentiment towards one who 'had not the patience' to do something that he knew would bring the money in; he wanted something else more than the money. He made the deliberate choice. Why shed a tear over a man who knew quite well what he was doing? All his life Schubert did more or less as he pleased: he neither stayed in a post nor attended a musical evening nor accepted an invitation unless he wanted to. There is no comparison between his suffering and that of Mozart, saddled with wife and family, with the ailments of others as well as his own physical frailty, yet keeping up brave appearances to the end.

Yet we may be grateful that Schubert made the choice of freedom, knowing himself and the price he would pay for that freedom. He hated the thought of others being in straitened circumstances, and a letter written to Anselm Hüttenbrenner early in 1828 is yet one more testimony to the generosity of his nature:

MY DEAR OLD HÜTTENBRENNER,

You will wonder at my writing now? So do I. But if I write it is because I am going to get something by it. Now just listen: a drawing-master's place near you at Graz is vacant, and competition is invited. My brother Karl, whom you probably know, is anxious to get the post. He is very clever, both as a landscape painter and as a draughtsman. If you could do anything for him in the matter I should be greatly obliged to you. You are a great man in Graz, and probably know someone in authority, or somebody who has a vote. My brother is married and has a family, and would therefore be very glad to have a permanent appointment . . . what you do for my brother, you do for me. . . .

It seems that he hoped to go again to Styria in the summer and had invitations both from the Pachlers at Graz and from Traweger at Gmunden. His friend Jenger had to write explaining frankly that 'pecuniary difficulties have prevented him from carrying out his project. He is at present working at a new Mass.' And Schubert wrote to Jenger as late as September (for his friend hoped for a last-minute acceptance to begin the journey with him): 'It's all over with my visit to Graz for this year, for my pecuniary prospects, like those of the weather, are downright gloomy and unfavourable.' So the composer got only as far as Baden and Eisenstadt in his last year.

The compositions of Schubert's last year are astounding in number and magnificent in quality. In March after his first and only concert he first wrote the curiously Handelian *Song of Miriam*, and followed it with the great C major Symphony which all succeeding generations have regarded as one of the great examples, if not the greatest, of its kind. It was presented to the Vienna Philharmonic Society, but found too long and difficult in rehearsal. At the composer's sug- gestion the earlier C major Symphony (No. 6) was submitted for the greater work at the concert. Shortly afterwards came the composition of the C major string Quintet and later, it is usually supposed (for the Quintet bears only the date '1828'), some pieces for piano solo and piano duet. In the summer months he produced the E flat major Mass and the 92nd Psalm in Hebrew, the latter for the Vienna synagogue, of which Salomon Sulzer was cantor. Before autumn he had written thirteen songs, seven from Rellstab and six from Heine, which, with the addition of Seidl's *Die Taubenpost*, form the collection posthumously called *Schwanengesang,* though there is no particular reason why they should be treated as a song cycle. Neither for emotional piquancy nor for technical economy and virtuosity can any Schubert songs claim to be finer than these fourteen, though their composer must have already been a sick man before they were completed. In the October he turned his interest specially to church music. A new *Benedictus* for the early Mass in C major, substituted for a reason which is not known, cannot help showing its disparity with the rest of the Mass, so magnificent is its conception; there are also few church compositions by Schubert of greater dignity than the offertory *Intende voci*, with its almost Mozartian contrapuntal felicity, or of greater beauty than the *Tantum ergo* which followed during the same month. Once more we are unable to know why Schubert took his *Hymn to the Holy Ghost*, written for a concert earlier in the year, and scored for eight male voices with piano accom- paniment, and added parts for thirteen wind instruments. It seems clear that such work was done for a special performance. A lovely work (rarely heard, alas! though the concert-going public would soon make it a favourite) composed during this autumn is the lengthy cantilena *The Shepherd on the Fells*, for soprano voice with pianoforte accompaniment and clarinet obbligato; the work was probably intended for Anna Milder.

Towards the end of the summer Schubert had left his rooms at the 'Blue Hedgehog' for a new house in the Wieden, taken by his brother Ferdinand. Grove describes these quarters, now No. 6 Kettenbrückengasse, as

a long house with three rows of nine windows in front, a brown sloping roof, and an entry in the middle to a quadrangle behind; a quiet, clean, inoffensive place. . . . He made the move with the concurrence of his doctor, von Rinna, in the hope that, as it was nearer the country—it was just over the river in the direction of the Belvedere—Schubert would be able to reach fresh air and exercise more easily than he could from the heart of the city. The old attacks of giddiness and blood to the head had of late been frequent, and soon after taking up his new quarters he became seriously unwell.

Though he never regained health, Schubert made sufficient temporary recovery by the end of October to take a walking excursion towards Eisenstadt, twenty-five miles from Vienna, with his brother and two other friends. A visit was made to Haydn's grave. The whole expedition took five days, during which Schubert showed no bad symptoms; but on his return to the city his illness was aggravated in so marked a degree that his friends were alarmed. Two incidents testify to his physical and nervous condition. On the evening of 31st October, during supper at a favourite tavern, the 'Red Cross,' he suddenly dropped his knife and fork, declaring that the fish tasted like poison. On some other day during this period he was taken by a musician who belonged to Schuppanzigh's quartet party to hear Beethoven's great Quartet in C sharp minor. To see Schubert deeply moved or excited at a work of such quality was no unusual experience for his companions, but the extreme agitation which he displayed on this occasion 'made us all afraid for him.' On 3rd November he walked out to what is now the suburb of Hernals to hear his brother Ferdinand's Requiem Mass, which was being sung within the octave of All Souls' Day. He considered his brother's work well written. He returned, after three hours' walking, in an exhausted condition.

His brother's Requiem was the last public musical performance that Schubert seems to have heard; there must surely have been an instrument in Ferdinand's house, however, and it cannot have re/ mained silent, even during Franz's last illness. Before taking finally to his bed, the composer was much impressed by Handel's scores, possibly those included in some of the Arnold volumes which had belonged to Beethoven and had been put up for sale after that master's death. Schubert told members of the Fröhlich family that these Handel works showed him that he had much to learn. Like other masters, including Beethoven himself, Schubert desired contrapuntal virtuosity beyond that which he already possessed, although no new skill in counterpoint could have made us wish that one of his great songs should be rewritten or the structure of his two finest symphonies altered. Had Schubert lived to make a new study of texture, to which Handel's magnificent part/writing inclined him, we should have perhaps been given a new series of works—choral works, masses, or perhaps string quartets of a new kind. Passages in com/ positions like the motet *Intende voci* leave us with no doubt that his natural perception of style would alone have ensured that such works would have been technically excellent and not cribbed, cabin'd and confined by the new study; and would the spate of inspired songs have been slowed? We cannot tell; few composers have prolonged their song/writing days beyond early middle age, and Schubert was not destined to become even fully middle/aged. He showed the sincerity of his resolve to make a special study of counterpoint by arranging, poor as he was, to pay fees and take lessons from Sechter. Marpurg's treatise was commended as the aspirant's *vade mecum*, but it must be pointed out that Sechter, of whom Bruckner became a devoted pupil, was a far more intelligent teacher than Albrechtsberger to whom Beethoven submitted.

Within a week Schubert had written his last letter:

Dear Schober,
I am ill. I have eaten and drunk nothing for eleven days, and am so tired and shaky that I can only get from the bed to the chair and back. Rinna is attending me. If I taste anything, I bring it up again directly.

New Development Arrested by Death

In this distressing condition, be so kind as to help me to some reading. Of Cooper's I have read *The Last of the Mohicans, The Spy, The Pilot* and *The Pioneers.* If you have anything else of his, I beg you to leave it with Frau Bogner at the coffee-house. My brother, who is conscientiousness itself, will duly bring it to me, or anything else.

Your friend,

SCHUBERT.

Schubert took to his bed on 14th November. His chief musical preoccupation in the previous weeks seems to have been the projected completion of his opera *The Count of Gleichen,* and he had held a specially enthusiastic conversation about it with Lachner, who had come to Vienna after the notable success of his own opera *Bürgschaft* at Pest. Even on his deathbed, Schubert spoke to Bauernfeld and Lachner about his operas. He spent a considerable time sitting up and correcting the proofs of the *Winter Journey* songs, wherein he must have been struck with the recurrence of such themes as desertion, solitude, poverty, forebodings. We have only the untrustworthy Bauernfeld's assertion that most of the old companions—Spaun, Randhartinger and the Hüttenbrenners—visited his sick-bed, though it is certain that he was visited by Randhartinger and by Bauernfeld himself.

Schubert died on Wednesday, 19th November. Bauernfeld saw him for the last time on the Monday, towards the evening of which day the composer became delirious, to remain so till the end. The doctor diagnosed typhoid fever as the cause of death, which was untouched by any beauty except the devoted nursing of his stepsister, Josefa, and the loving care of his brother Ferdinand, whose behaviour at the end was consistent with his attitude to Franz throughout the thirty-one years of the composer's life. Sentences muttered during the last three days of that life are variously reported ('What are they doing with me?' 'I implore you to put me in my own room, and not to leave me in this corner under the earth'), but are of no significant value, though Beethoven's name was mentioned.

Schubert's father issued the following obituary notice:

Yesterday afternoon, at three o'clock on Wednesday, my beloved son Franz Schubert, artist and composer, died after a short illness, having received the Holy Sacraments of the Church. He died in his thirty-second year. We beg to announce to our dear friends and neighbours that the body of the deceased will be taken on the 21st of this month, at half past two in the afternoon, from the house No. 694 standing in the new street on the New Wieden, to be interred near the bishop's stall in the parish church of St. Joseph in the Margarethen, where the holy rites will be administered.

FRANZ SCHUBERT,
Schoolmaster in the Rossau.

VIENNA, *20th November 1828.*

The place of interment was changed to the Währing cemetery, on the strong recommendation of Ferdinand Schubert, who declared that his brother had wished to be buried there and expressed this desire while on his deathbed. Schubert's remains were therefore buried only three graves distant from the place of Beethoven's burial. An inventory of the composer's effects includes only clothes and bedding for himself and a quantity of music, mostly printed; the value of his whole possessions (he left no will) was estimated at sixty-three florins. The doctor's bills, debts and funeral expenses amounted to nearly two hundred and seventy florins.

On 27th November Mozart's Requiem was sung, and on 23rd December a Requiem composed by Anselm Hüttenbrenner was given in St. Augustine's, the church in which the second performance of Schubert's first Mass had taken place. Concerts sponsored by Schubert's friends within a year or so afterwards drew crowded audiences, and had to be repeated. Grillparzer wrote for the memorial stone set up from the proceeds of some of these concerts: 'Music has here entombed a rich treasure, but still fairer hopes.' It is the testimony of subsequent generations that few such inscriptions are as truthful and terse as this tribute to Schubert.

CHAPTER VII

THE SYMPHONIES AND OVERTURES

SCHUBERT'S symphonies are so nearly the contemporaries of Beethoven's as to invite comparison; and were magnificence or magnilo-
quence the sole attribute of greatness, then Schubert, judged by what
he wrote before his death at thirty-one, could be considered a greater
potential symphonist than was Beethoven at the age of forty- or
fifty-one. Since no generation has held such an opinion, there must
be a shifting of symphonic ideals between the two composers; moreover, since in Beethoven the symphonic forms reached that perfection
in which form and utterance are one, no advance of technique in
their kind can be regarded as vital or necessary. Schubert's quartets
and symphonies are therefore luxuries whose decadence is historical
or biological—'decadent' is applied in no pejorative sense. The
forms and formulas, the zodiac of tonalities which underlie the
architecture of classical symphony—these were easily at his service,
so that if our greatest artistic experience is to feel the mind at work
with its materials, Schubert cannot interest us architecturally as
Beethoven does.

This does not mean that Schubert's structures are weak in the few
master-works that his few years allowed; it means that we do not go
to Schubert primarily for architecture. His delight and ours lies
in his expanding and gloriously enriching the details of symphonic
technique, but with that expansion and enrichment a slenderness in
the main building was not only inevitable: it was desirable. Those
who cannot distinguish slenderness from weakness should be careful
in judging any major work by Schubert.

If Schubert's songs did not exist, their place in musical history
would have to be postulated; his instrumental works form no such
entity. One may liken their place in the Viennese school to that
'perpendicular' phase of church building which marks the decline
of medieval Gothic in England; asked to name our most magnificent
Gothic buildings, we think of Gloucester choir, King's, Cambridge,

or the great Fenland churches, with their minimum of stone and maximum of coloured glass and rich tracery. Yet this 'biologically unnecessary' development of the fifteenth century in England had already been superseded by the 'biologically vigorous' classical renaissance, and on the Continent there is no trace of it except at Calais. The point to be emphasized is that many consider this final stage of Gothic to be aesthetically as well as historically decadent, and there are not wanting many who feel similarly towards Schubert's stuff. That stuff reveals as little of the structural problems which had concerned a former generation as does the stuff of the Perpendicular architects. Roof, pillar and buttress, once vigorously functional, the impressive witness of human mastery over material, had become themselves decorative and slender; invention and imagination were directed towards the enrichment and ornamentation of vast structures which others before had made possible. So with Schubert: he belongs to the succession, he is content with inherited sonata and symphonic forms, but he thinks in them without thinking of them. In the big works, where a bar's purple patch may be the sole transition from paragraph to paragraph, only the *Wanderer Fantasy* shows a conscious attempt to reach beyond accepted forms. The design of his predecessors was never questioned; it could be stretched to any length according to the length of inspiration.

But that length was not always 'heavenly'; each part of an inspired whole was not always inspired. There are patches of inferior work made all the more apparent by contiguous magnificence; there are mere repetitions of whole passages, put down in haste to complete a design of which the composer had tired; there are dull rhythms and instances of harmonic complaisance which sacrifice vigour to melliflousness—but rarely in the works of his last three years. On the other hand the very nature of Schubert's writing, its place in history, made it easy for his weak places to be called flabby, whereas Haydn's weak places are only called pedestrian, Mozart's arid and Beethoven's crude, and flabbiness seems less pleasant than crudity. It is therefore well to observe that, had Schubert lived only for the extra five years granted to Mozart (let alone to Haydn's ripe old age), it is not likely that he would have left a proportion of inferior music any greater than theirs. The sheer conception of his one complete mature

Symphony was impressive enough to keep him at full glow through every moment of it, and the musician who sees structural weakness in the unfinished B minor is like a pedant who cannot admire a lyric drama because it does not happen to be a classical tragedy. His finest extended works have earned him the title 'The last of the giants.'

Schubert's temperament was exactly suited for his place in the classical line; a different nature would have been forced either to develop a technical renaissance or else to leave a pile of enervated formalities, well-written essays in the forms and idiom that had previously enshrined genuine prophetic utterance. But Schubert was not even tempted to write symphonies with a literary programme. The instrumental music on which he was nurtured delighted him as the heroic couplets delighted Pope, who 'lisped in numbers, for the numbers came'; often he is at his best when most derivative. If the music in him did not well up in his mind, he did not write, and no doubt he had the most sincere artistic reasons for leaving the B minor unfinished. The spontaneity of his musical thinking and the individual nature of his colouring make it impossible to judge a whole movement from an incomplete outline; they also make it of little interest to examine the few cases of alteration made to a manu-script; recensions give no glimpse of his mental workings, for the music is entirely pre-natal. When Beethoven recasts a theme, he recasts a good deal more; indeed he cannot work till the recasting is done, since his theme is a key-pin, not a facet. But Schubert's few alterations are made to material which is already filling an adequate space in a general scheme. The alteration improves or enriches the space, as in the *allegro* of the C major Symphony (see page 104); if we are inclined to call this a pillar rather than a space, then a pillar is being carved, and it can bear it, so light is the weight it has to support and so evenly is that weight distributed throughout the work. Schubert's alterations have been well called 'inspired afterthoughts.'

Of the four great masters in the classical line Schubert is the only one whose lispings include full-blown symphonies—not the semi-chamber works in three movements from which Haydn and Mozart evolved their greater symphonies. Thin stuff, but well honeyed, may be poured into the youthful Schubert's symphonic mould; but the mould is of full size. Our architectural parallel helps to explain why the tendency of the earlier Schubert symphonies is towards a rambling slenderness. The first Symphony is prolix for the same causes which make his last Symphony tremendous. It was written at the age of sixteen while he was still a pupil at the Seminary and is supposed to have been played for the name-day of Dr. Lang, to whom No. 2 was dedicated. Its four movements, not counting the enormously extended slow introduction, make a length which the most indulgent cannot find heavenly. This D major Symphony is scored for full Beethovenian band, including trumpets and clarinets; but the orchestra, even without the old pupils and friends who probably sat with it on such occasions, did not seem to muster two good flautists as well as oboists—at least not when clarinets were present—for there is no flute part. There is nothing very distinctly Schubertian in this very competent work, though being wise after the sequel we may suppose that no other made the slow movement:

The D major Symphony dates from Schubert's sixteenth year. Each following year brings its symphony artistically better, though not always more attractive or personal, than its predecessor.

Symphony No.	1 in D major	October 1813.
„	No. 2 in B flat major	December 1814.
„	No. 3 in D major	May 1815.
„	No. 4 in C minor	April 1816.
„	No. 5 in B flat major	September 1816.
„	No. 6 in C major	October 1817.

A whole decade passes between these and the two works which might have been the first of eight or nine supremely magnificent symphonies. It should be pointed out that the above chronology of the youthful symphonies gives the month and year which head the score-paper, the time when each work was begun.

The second Symphony is well worth playing occasionally to-day, and not just at an afternoon studio concert. It is more athletic in proportions that the D major, its opening having slimmed from fifty-odd bars to a good purposeful ten, and its *allegro*, while by no means aping Beethoven, pays tribute to young Schubert's acute perception of style in the work of his musical forbears:

The scoring, throughout the work, for the same orchestra as in the first Symphony, would not have been likely from a youngster who had not admired Mozart. Particularly Mozartian are the held wind chords against staccato strings in the opening *allegro*, and the general lay-out of the minuet—a fine, bold specimen in C minor:

Cadences and rhythms such as the following are now identifiable as Schubertian fingerprints:

The third Symphony is again technically excellent, but disappointing to those who search among these early orchestral works for an advance in personal utterance comparable with Schubert's expressive development as a song-writer, for in 1815, the year of this merry Symphony, Schubert happened to give us, amongst other gems, *The Nun, The Hedgerose* and *Erl King*. The opening *allegro* theme at first arrests us as we transpose it into C major and fit it into a great context, but then it makes us wish there were more context and less theme; young Schubert can be rather too persistent sometimes:

The fourth Symphony is by no means the great matter that Schubert's own description, 'Tragic,' would lead us to expect. It is, however, his first symphony in a minor key and approaches in places to the kind of pathos found in the 'daemonic' works which Mozart prefaced with a C minor or G minor key signature.

The C minor is not, however, the workaday writing of a busy composer, and it is a pity that one so rarely hears a performance which shows signs of careful rehearsal; for even when the rhythms seem lacking in freshness the scoring is that of a man who writes from inside the orchestra as easily as from inside a handful of chamber instruments. The C minor uses four horns as well as trumpets.

The other Symphony of 1816 is a perfect little gem—the diminutive being forced from one's pen both by the endearment which the work wins and by the unwonted reduction of orchestral forces to flute, oboes, bassoons, two horns and strings (no clarinets, trumpets or drums). The texture and rhythms are Mozartian, with a vernal tenderness which belies the fact that it is technical details of *late* Mozart that have received Schubert's careful observation; the very places which most recall Mozart are the most inspired and the most Schubertian—the tune of the slow movement, for instance. Its ripeness is utterly unlike the feline, aristocratic sweetness of Mozart; its romance is without the Mozartian sadness; but where is the Mozart *andante,* so different in feeling, which lurks somewhere in the memory?

Had Schubert heard the G minor Quintet? Is the figure (see page 94) of the opening *allegro* (there is no slow introduction) a half-conscious or unconscious allusion? It will be noticed that, wherever Schubert recalls Mozart, or for that matter Haydn and Beethoven, the similarity is rhythmic. This is not remarkable when we bear in mind that, apart from one or two favourite measures which Schubert brought from the Vienna streets into orchestral music, there are few rhythmic novelties in his work to show any technical advance comparable with his wonderful adventures in harmonic modulation. One cannot resist the surmise that his easy-going nature found out many of the harmonic treasures at the keyboard; the rhythms were just what the mind brought up. To be rhythmically inventive requires a little detached thought—and why bother to take thought when such a stream of music wells forth without it? The truth of the above remarks may be examined by reviewing the minuets of Haydn and Mozart and comparing them with those of the composer who had the benefit of knowing them. The minuet in this B flat Symphony is indeed worthy of its place. It shows various links with Mozart—the scoring, the chromatics at the usual spot, but not the stiffening cross-rhythm. But it is a Schubertian trick to give us a minuet in the relative minor:

while only Schubert, the one 'Viennese' composer to be born and bred in Vienna, could have written the trio (third example above).

The dominant cadence at the end of the quotation is one of those little honey-drops which, so far, have not been used too generously. The Symphony abounds in quotable passages, and a casual dip at any point would impress the dipper: the opening is as apt and masterly as anything to follow:

We learn from Kreissle that the B flat Symphony, like its C minor and C major companions, was specially designed for the 'amateur' orchestra whose open rehearsals must by this year (1816–17) have been more important for knowledgeable young musicians than many a public concert with a charge for admission. Amateur the society was, only in the best sense of the term, for the enterprise of its pro-grammes attracted the participation of professionals, as well as of first-rate singers. The nucleus had been the home quartet at the elder Schubert's, but as the society expanded it sought more and more elbow-room. By the time of the 'specially designed' symphonies it met at Otto Hatwig's home in the Gundelhof. Now though the sixth Symphony shares the technical mastery of the fifth, with the added bravery of clarinets, trumpets and drums, it is surely stretching a theory too far to suppose, as some do, that the superiority of these three symphonies over the first three is attributable to Schubert's 'specially designing' them for the society. One could say that the first three were 'specially designed,' as the first two certainly were, for the Seminary band; secondly the great symphonies unborn owed their greatness to no demand other than that made by an ideal orchestra, for Schubert never heard them played. After all, an artist matures sooner or later, and there is usually a work or collection of works which marks the end of his pubescence. With Schubert they came later in symphony than in song, and nineteen is a creditable age for their achievement. Moreover the line of demarcation is by no means sharp. The sixth Symphony, wherein there is no sign of adolescence in the handling of materials or mastery of form, has less to say of importance than had its two immediate predecessors. Its summer atmosphere soon belies the dignified gestures of its opening, and the *allegro* puts us in mind of Weber, or perhaps of the Boïeldieu and Méhul overtures which Schubert's orchestral society liked to play.

This C major Symphony is no music for the man who does not think the title justified unless the work contains speech at a prophetic level. The earnest student may well ask: 'Why do the endless cadential figures, the German sixth modulations, the chromatic salacities, seem so significant in a Mozart symphony on this scale, yet become the small change of music in this Schubert work?' Apart from the main reason that Mozart's symphonies with trumpets, drums and clarinets, or with a slow introduction, are nearly all crea‑ tions of his maturity, and that young Schubert was not impelled by size of score‑paper to do more than *desipere in loco,* there are technical reasons which partly account for the impression of superficiality. In the first place there is none of the Mozartian subtlety of detail, especially with regard to rhythms; the ♩ | ♩ ♩ ♩ | ♩ of Schubert's scherzo (first called by that name in this sixth of the symphonies) does not invite the kind of cross‑rhythm which produces an odd number of measures: all is ease and balance. If ever the balance can be made by plain repetition of an eight‑ or sixteen‑bar paragraph, a plain repetition there is. Audiences accept Schubert's ease of conscience if the repeated material is as attractive as in the fifth Symphony, where at the reprise of the first movement Schubert actually begins his first subject in the subdominant key (E flat) so that he is spared the trouble of rearranging the material of his exposition; he has nothing to do but transpose. But the material of the sixth Sym‑ phony is not quite so attractive as that of its predecessor. One feels that, in such full movements, there should be fewer simple cadences, be they plain closes or German sixths. How different are Mozart's magical protractions of expected cadences, or his witty denial of the cadence that a whole passage has led one to expect. (The slow move‑ ment of the 'Prague' D major symphony is an example of this.) In his last works Schubert supplied a felt need not so much by subtlety of detail as by a fullness of it; a presage of that fullness is found in the wind polyphony of the slow movement in the Symphony now being discussed—a work which, on the whole, would make pleasant inci‑ dental music to a picnic scene.

Of the symphonies written after an interval of four years, only one remains in its entirety, though evidence indicates that all four—if four there were—had the same ample dimensions and rich texture that are found in this surviving specimen and in the two first movements of the B minor. It used to be customary to call this great C major the seventh Symphony, and to give the B minor no titular number. Nowadays the numbering in favour calls the E major No. 7, the 'unfinished' No. 8 and the great C major No. 9, allotting no number to the supposed 'Gastein' Symphony. Thus the list of symphonies following the sixth, after the four-year interval, is as follows:

(*a*) Symphony in E minor and major (No. 7). August 1821. (MS. incomplete.)

(*b*) Symphony in (?) C major. *Circa* August 1825. ('Gastein,' lost.)

(*c*) Symphony in B minor (No. 8). Early 1822. (Unfinished.)

(*d*) Symphony in C major (No. 9). March 1828.

(*a*) *The Symphony in E minor and major.* The manuscript of this passed from Ferdinand Schubert to Mendelssohn's brother Paul, and from him to Grove, who left it to the Royal College of Music in London, and who is quoted here:

It occupies 167 pages . . . *adagio* in E minor and *allegro* in E major; *andante* in A; scherzo in C and trio in A; *allegro giusto* in E major. The introduction and a portion of the *allegro* are fully scored . . . from that point to the end of the work Schubert has made merely memoranda. But every bar is drawn in; the tempi and names of the instruments are fully written at the beginning of each movement; the nuances are all marked; the very double bars and flourishes are gravely added at the end of the sections, and 'Fine' at the conclusion of the whole . . . there is not a bar that does not contain the part of one or more instruments; at all crucial places the scoring is much fuller; and it would no doubt be possible to complete it as Schubert himself intended.

J. F. Barnett in 1883 at the Crystal Palace and Felix Weingartner in our own time performed the work with the empty parts reverently scored, but the results do not seem to have been sufficiently impressive to put the Symphony permanently in the repertory. The quotation is taken from the opening bars:

(b) The 'Gastein' Symphony. Gastein, which lies some forty miles south of Salzburg, was the farthest point from their base at Steyr in the summer tour of 1825 made by Schubert and Vogl. Grove adduces letters from Schubert's friends as evidence that the greatest creation penned and actually completed among the mountains was a 'Grand Symphony' in C, a 'special favourite with the composer.' No trace of this Symphony exists. In his analysis of Joachim's 'Symphony in C, orchestrated from Schubert's Grand Duo for pianoforte duet,' the late Sir Donald Tovey expressed his belief that the Grand Duo could have been a keyboard arrangement of the lost Gastein Symphony, but admitted that 'the special authorities on Schubert' were unwilling to entertain the suggestion. Today it is widely believed that the only 'Gastein' symphony was the one now called the Great C major, and that nobody would have sought any other unless Sir George Grove had supposed another to exist.

(c) The Unfinished Symphony, B minor. Incontrovertible seems Professor Gerald Abraham's evidence that the B minor entr'acte, stylistically incongruous within *Rosamunde*, was intended as the finale of this symphony, of which it is worthy. Even more difficult to deny is the musical evidence of one's ears when this piece concludes the work.

Abraham scored Schubert's scherzo and used his music, including the melody of a song, *Der Leidende*, to provide a trio which does convincingly what one imagines Schubert might have done. The scherzo is of the right dimensions for its context, but its persistent expansion of the opening idea does not make it quite the equal of the corresponding movement in the C major symphony with its counter-melody and abrupt modulations. Yet it is a very fine movement, somewhat Beethovenian and saturnine, to be played more briskly than the C major scherzo and with strong (unmarked) accents, and never suggesting, as the other work does, affinity with the waltz.

Normally, then, we should no longer present this work as a torso, even if we treat it, as we often do Mozart's K.334 symphony, 'without minuet,' since it is difficult not to feel a certain decline after such tremendous opening movements. This, not Tchaikovsky's, is the greatest pathetic symphony, for pathos embraces much more than aspects of life which bring pity.

The first theme which one thinks of in connection with the first movement is the long singing one in G major:

Its A—B—B—A shape, probably an unconscious inspiration, is interrupted only by the figure of rising notes before the second A, which causes its development within the exposition itself. But this theme is but the leaven, the relief, to the material which characterizes the movement, and many performances vulgarize it by 'bringing out' the G major tune—it is marked *pianissimo*—playing it too fast and, most disgusting of all, playing tricks with the tempo of the few preparatory bars which lead to it from the previous B minor material. Grove comments on the simple sublimity of those bars in which Schubert gives us the syncopated accompaniment alone before the lyrical section; this is by no means the single instance of the practice which is found in the following movement, in the slow movement of the C major Symphony and several other places. The technique of the song-writer has fertilized that of the symphonist.

The opening bass theme of this B minor movement sets its character, and as in a great poetic tragedy there seem to be two parallel emotional struggles, one a struggle of events, producing the action, the other a conflict within the hero's soul, finding expression in the glowing poetry. The action is a matter of rhythms, volumes, tonalities and all the elements of musical form; the hero is the receptive listener, and it has been the witness of all generations since Schubert's that in no work does he make the listener, albeit an unsophisticated listener, so active a participant in his emotional conflict. This is but a long way of saying that he never wrote a work so deeply pathetic in the classical sense of that misused word. Let one example be quoted, and let us ask where is its fellow elsewhere in Schubert, or in music? [1]

One type of listener may be more excited by Beethoven's modulations, such as the swerve into F major at the reprise of the 'Eroica' first movement; but he is not excited in the same, pathetic way. The Beethoven modulation is architecturally functional and therefore thrilling beyond the wonder of its passing colour; the thrill comes from the mind's ear, aided perhaps by the mind's eye, going back to a corresponding place in the expository material which happened to take a different turning. But with Schubert modulation is used for its own appeal; it is the purple patch of a given point. There are some points (plenty in a work like the unfinished C major Sonata) where even modern admirers are a little dazzled, where ears cannot quite accept, though it is obvious that Schubert knew what *he* was about: the purple is put on firmly enough. Had the riches of the unfinished Symphony been lavished on Schubert's contemporaries, it is likely that some bewilderment would have been caused among the schoolmen.

[1] The two chords of this modulation are almost stock-in-trade—German sixth and minor triad 6-4.

99

The *andante con moto*, often played so slowly that its movements is lost, and with so little obedience to the many *pianissimo* directions that its remoteness is lost, seems to take the hero into a secluded, transfigured world of consolation, where remain only shadows of the external conflict of the first act:

Once more, among Schubert's many modulations is the odd one belonging uniquely to this Symphony and movement:

The variation of this passage in the major—a procedure common enough in Schubert—makes in this particular place an effect of incomparable loveliness:

(*d*) *The Great C major Symphony.* Among the claimants for the honour of being the composer of the greatest symphony is there any but Schubert who offers a specimen in which the purpose is so homogeneous yet the manner so diffuse? Even the introductory slow tune, having been presented with lovely orchestral variations, sets off on a burgeoning development which every student knows does not belong there—except in this work; and as it is meant for this work, what fool will call it misplaced? Of course the C major sprawls, but its sprawling moves us as profoundly as the most close-knit and apposite orthodox symphonizing; so we glory in what Gounod did not quite call, in a different connection, 'the affirmation of incompetence raised to an art.' No one has yet dared to call its fullness adipose, and no generation has contradicted Schumann's dictum, originally applied to the *andante,* concerning its 'heavenly length.' Are we to regard everything previous as an early work? Or did the mature series begin with the E minor or the unfinished B minor Symphony? All we know is that the one and only complete symphony of Schubert's last years makes it impossible for the mind to conceive the glories that were silenced by his death. There must be technical reasons for the excellence of the C major, for there has been no inspiration in the art so far whose expression cannot be examined technically. Our first question must therefore be: 'Since this work digresses like others from the same pen, why does it hold our attention at the *n*th hearing?' The very opening gives one clue. The horn theme measures eight bars, not a balanced four-plus-four, but two sets of three, with an augmented echo of two bars:

Here, then, is that rhythmic vigour which is characteristic of every great instrumental composer as soon as his personality becomes distinctive. To notice this we have but to compare the Weber-like phrasing of *Rienzi* or *The Flying Dutchman* with the sinuous periods of *Tristan* or *Parsifal,* or the subtleties of Brahms's Intermezzi with his early Schumannisms. Even of two contemporaries like Brahms and Wagner one can say: 'By their rhythms ye shall know them.'

The new rhythmic muscularity invigorates thematic material throughout the C major; the stealthy metre of the *andante* pulsates beneath constant variation; the bass of its 'accompanimental' opening shows seven bars of irregular accentuation:

and the first phrase of the march-tune three bars:

the last spondee and that in the previous example correspond—for reasons which are made significant later in the movement. Finally, in spinning the trio to this heavenly long march, Schubert did *not* write:

a form which might have satisfied him in former times. The Beethovenian energy of the scherzo theme:

wrestles with a flowing *Deutscher Tanz*:

which again is not built on the four-measures-plus-another-four which one finds in the piano waltzes of Schubert's teens. Rhythmic squareness is again eschewed even in the *Ländler* of the trio, which has received hard words from one quarter on account of its hurdy-gurdy sixths and thirds. Tovey, on the other hand, calls it 'one of the greatest and most exhilarating melodies in the world.' Most Schubertians, while hardly rising to Tovey's extreme of enthusiasm, will feel that the fair-ground spirit is in just the right place, the trio being the traditional *locus* for rusticity,[1] and that the effect is admirably brought off if the conductor is careful with Schubert's very full use of wind instruments.

The scherzo may well illustrate the second reason for the formal satisfaction of this long and diffuse work—for a long work by Schubert is by nature diffuse: the scherzo goes at a speed that will bear the persistent reiteration of its opening figure, and that figure is almost ubiquitous; with its repetitions, however, there is an organic design of smaller and larger climaxes, the repeating figure hurrying most closely towards the major climaxes. At the point of climax we have those contrasts of which Schubert had been master for many years—not always dramatic modulations. This, for example:

is quite as effective at a smaller climax as this modulation at a greater, double-bar, climax:

---

[1] See the article, 'The Minuet-Trio,' in vol. xxii, No. 2, April 1941 issue of *Music & Letters*.

The same is true of the other movements, especially in the whirling finale, and in the magnificent codas to first movement and finale. (So often in previous works on the 'magnificent' scale, it is the coda which fails to realize the ideals of its conception.)

And that brings us to the third technical reason for our delight in the C major: instead of choosing the most immediately character-istic figure of a theme for imitative development, so that we have an exhilarating rhythm repeated till it ceases to exhilarate, Schubert delights us by making real 'points'—not formal developments—from the Cinderella pieces of his tunes. (Both here and elsewhere Schubert prefers to make his transitions by a mere short gesture; it is a pity that later symphonists did not learn a lesson from him in this respect.) Thus, in the first movement, instead of stuffing the middle of his *allegro* with imitative derivations from its first motif:

as he did in his D major Symphony, No. 3, the trombone makes thrilling reference to the introductory theme (see 'x' on page 101) which is apotheosized in the coda. What grand play he makes, too, with the opening rhythm of his second theme; and was ever the despised dominant seventh so strongly used?

¹ The notes crossed out show Schubert's first version of this theme.

The *andante* shows similar dramatic reference: here the spondees are included in the two transition themes of the march and put to wonderful effect at the close:

It is in the finale, however, that this process of exalting the humble is most astoundingly used. After the grotesque opening:

a texture follows of whirling energy landing with a bang and jump full stop in orthodox G major; a tense silence, like that of an acrobat leaving his spectators guessing as to the direction of his next caper, is ended not by a sudden spring of more energy, but by four minims on the horns which seem merely to paw the ground. To our great delight these quiet repeated minims are not merely preparatory, but are combined with the grotesque triplet of the example just quoted into the giant theme which alone could maintain the giant proportions of the movement:

There are two amazing facts to record about this passage and theme: first, they constitute one of Schubert's 'inspired afterthoughts'—his original move after the G major close was the announcement of a little fugato, which was very fortunately crossed out, since it certainly would not have maintained the giant proportions; secondly, this was the very passage which was marked by derisive laughter when Mendelssohn first tried to rehearse the work in London with the Philharmonic Society's orchestra.

Even nowadays one is rarely satisfied by performances of this finale. It is often taken too fast. A firm rhythm and the right conductor can secure the atmosphere of impetuosity at a speed which allows the exquisite detail to be heard clearly. Rarely do we hear the bows bouncing their triplets throughout the treatment following the last example; rarely does the *decrescendo* at the end of exposition and just before coda achieve the effect both of distance and perfect clarity. But the C major is such an ideal work that one can hear it at intervals throughout a lifetime and still wait for the perfect performance.

None of Schubert's overtures belongs to his last years, and none is on any grand scale, even among the one or two discursive pieces for four hands, which may or may not have been abortive orchestral essays. The early overtures are efficient and brilliant, and it is difficult to find anything particularly Italianate in the two 'Italian style' overtures of 1817, said to have been dashed off at speed to prove to his friends, who were full of admiration for *Tancredi,* that there were no trade secrets held by the purveyors of the glittering materials which had captured the opera houses of Vienna. No doubt these very comely fruits of Schubert's bravado were acceptable at the meetings of his orchestral society, together with the other overtures listed in the appendix catalogue.

Of greater interest are those overtures, some of which are regularly played, intended for Schubert's operettas and melodramas; the picturesqueness of a stage theme did not fail to vitalize the purely musical parts of the score. For instance the diabolical pleasance in the early opera *Des Teufels Lustschloss,* though situate in a neighbouring parish to Don Giovanni's, adjoins the less precisely charted wildernesses and woods surrounding the Wolf's Glen, for the libretto is by Kotzebue and the work is entitled 'eine natürliche Zauber-

Oper.' On the very first page we have a roll on the timpani from *p* to *ff*, syncopated string chords—uncommon chords too—plenty of *sforzandi*, and the general direction *con fuoco*. The course of the overture is pathetically interrupted by a section marked *largo* in triple time, wherein the three trombones are left to their portentous selves and a minor key.

Three Schubert overtures are still popular—*Alfonso and Estrella*, *Rosamunde* and *Fierabras*. The first is excellently scored and makes happy enough prelude to the stuff its play is made on. Musically it is no greater matter than the 'Overtures in the Italian style.' It was originally used in 1823 for the play *Rosamond, Queen of Cyprus*, but was again called after the opera to which it is attached, *Alfonso and Estrella* at its first publication (in a four-handed piano arrangement) in 1827. What is now called the *Rosamunde* Overture was originally the overture to *Die Zauberharfe*, a melodrama of 1820. This overture is always with us, and it seems a pity it cannot bear its original title, so much do we respond to a name, and the name of *The Magic Harp* invokes the phase of popular romantic drama between Mozart and Weber which has now taken on sufficient period flavour for us to hold in affection. How deliciously does the simple string writing sound:

what a fine judgment of effect Schubert displays in sounding the F sharps of the basses and cellos against the violin and viola G's:

and how delicate is the mixture of string *spiccato* and wind *staccato* in the passages which follow! The overture to *Fierabras*, the opera rejected by the Kärntnertor Theatre in 1824 after its composition late in 1823, has a calibre such as befits a full-scale opera. It abounds in romantic tremolo bowing, pathetic alternations of passages in minor and major tonality and contrasts of dynamics. The whole piece may be regarded as Schubert's best overture in a serious vein; if there is no strikingly memorable or quotable section, the work either smoulders or flares throughout its length.[1] It appears that some of the overtures which are not often played nowadays were great successes when they first got a hearing, for we read that the overture to the musical play *Die Zwillingsbrüder* (*The Twin Brothers*) was encored at the Kärntnertor at its first performance in 1820.

---

[1] The magnificent B minor entr'acte in *Rosamunde*, now recognized as intended for the B minor symphony, is even finer.

CHAPTER VIII

THE LARGER CHAMBER WORKS

SCHUBERT'S judgment of the sounds he wanted from various chamber groups seems an innate gift, but it must be remembered that in boyhood he played the viola in quartets at home and in symphonies at school. Even when the shape of an early movement owes more to a favourite symphony than to a quartet by Haydn or Mozart, Schubert strains neither a part nor the whole effect. He composed for immediate rehearsal and knew his players well; but the brilliant sureness of his effects in the ambitious and difficult chamber movements of his maturity suggest that he knew no less well the first-rate professional performers who first gave them. Why, then, is it true that he composed many supremely great movements in his chamber works but few works that are supremely great in all movements?

It is more easy to recognize the reason than to mention it in words that do not imply, even if they do not state, the mistake that great art should be solemn. If we judge an age or society by the quality of its entertainments, we rejoice that the classical giants of music often used a light style without vulgar condescension. If in their unbuttoned movements they can compel an admiration equal to that which is drawn to their prophetic utterance, they show themselves greater than modern composers who cannot, and whose humour is either vapid or sardonic. We should not object to an effervescent scherzo or entertaining rondo in a work which began with an imposing first movement, but we may be justly disappointed if the composer changes his level of workmanship with his change of mood. Westrup writes: 'There is always a danger that a piano trio will remind us of restaurant music. The trouble with Schubert's trios is that too often his material confirms the associations of the medium. It is not a question of gaiety . . . but of the accents in which the gaiety is expressed.'

If a concert includes quartets by Mozart or Beethoven and Schubert, it is well that the composers be represented in the reverse of historical order. Otherwise we are deeply impressed with one set of standards, and those the master-set for quartets: we need different criteria for Schubert's changes from elevated to popular styles, from concentrated to merely colourful music.

Of Beethoven it may be said, as Wordsworth said of Shakespeare and the sonnet: 'With this key he unlocked his heart.' This is not true of Schubert, by whose time the daily music of Vienna, apart from simple dances and songs, was written in the sonata-symphony, overture, quartet, quintet forms. 'Music,' to young Schubert, meant any writing in these forms; if he wrote for string quartet, despite his splendid feeling for the particular combination, he did not feel impelled to voice therein any particular type of thought or emotion different from that which finds utterance in sonata, symphony, overture or keyboard piece. There is no mistake about his feeling for the medium. If any one points to a place in any Schubert chamber work and says 'That is a tea-shop effect,' then Schubert intended the effect. How can one question the technical ability of one who writes, without a single miscalculation, first a piano quintet with one fiddle and a double bass, and then a string quintet with two cellos?

The difficulty lies entirely with the heavy responsibility handed on by his predecessors, especially Beethoven. Haydn's quartets, composed for the cream of his performers, show in their most vivacious movements the cream of his technical skill in composition. Mozart's quartets, among the most aristocratic conceptions of an aristocratic mind, not only pay open or implied tribute to Haydn's, but were intended for players like his Sunday quartet—all connoisseurs and composers. With Beethoven the quartet reached a mystical world, at once the farthest and the innermost region attained by any musician. Schubert gives us nothing but beauty. He needs fine professional players as much as did his forbears, but he takes them into a domestic *milieu*, though not the music-room of a grandee, unless it be also the meeting-place of the Viennese middle-class music-lovers who delighted in the new poetry and songs. It might well be argued that Schubert's most acceptable contributions to chamber music are the B flat Trio, the Octet, the marches for piano duet—those works which reflect the picturesqueness, even the rhythms, of popular verse.

No edition has been made to show us Schubert's twenty quartets in chronological order. The most up-to-date account of their chronology, publishers, first performers, etc., is that by Otto Erich Deutsch in *Music & Letters* for January 1943. While, as Deutsch remarks, not even the earliest works are childish, the fact that they include a quartet-overture and a set of minuets, trios and waltzes, shows that Schubert by no means regarded the medium with awe. Indeed a quartet of 1814 was fabricated from a guitar trio composed by one Matiegka, Schubert adding the cello part. There is little opportunity nowadays to hear the first dozen or so quartets, written chiefly for Schubert's family circle; yet at least three of those included in the Peters edition of nine quartets belong to the period before Schubert began to be noticed by the quartet leader Ignaz Schuppanzigh, who had done so much for Beethoven; every one of them may be commended to performers, since they are written on a scale which precludes the comparisons invoked by more ambitious works, and we can enjoy their delicious competence for sheer love of workmanship. Particularly fine is the quartet style of Op. 125 No. 2, in E major.

The only Schubert quartets which can be considered as in the permanent professional repertory to-day are those of 1820 and onwards, designed by the composer for some of the finest players of his time. They are as follows:

(a) *Quartettsatz* (Quartet movement) in C minor, written in December 1820.

(b) Quartet in A minor, Op. 29 No. 1, written in February or March 1824.

(c) Quartet in D minor, 'Death and the Maiden,' written in March 1824.

(d) Quartet in G major, Op. 161, written in June 1826.

(a) The manuscript of the *C minor Quartettsatz* came into Brahms's possession. Forty-one bars of an *andante* in A flat major follow the fine *allegro* movement, of which a critic has said: 'It is to the quartets what another unfinished work is to the symphonies.' The opening immediately suggests the B minor Symphony:

as does the singing second tune; but the course of the movement is by no means stereotyped; it has all the ambulatory ease of a typical

Schubertian first movement, together with a departure from the traditional order of themes and keys, yet maintains a magnificent homogeneity. It is difficult to imagine that Schubert, writing at his usual speed, would ever have composed three other movements worthy to be its fellows.

(*b*) The *Quartet in A minor* was first performed in the spring of 1824 by a team led by Schuppanzigh, probably including Weiss and Linke, two other members of the famous Rasumovsky quartet, since all three players are known to have taken part in Schubert's Octet of this year. No work from his pen is more Schubertian than the A minor Quartet: a piece of its opening melody shows how different the details of Mozart's vocabulary become in Schubert's sentences:

The very intervals are Mozartian, but the range of Schubert's melody implies modulations which the older master would not have allowed in an expository statement. The texture accompanying this melody has often been quoted, and it illustrates one of the most enchanting features of Schubert's instrumental technique, the perfect tonal background for a melodic theme. How much more than accompanimental is the setting provided by this figure:

How simple yet subtle is the similar passage from the D minor Quartet! (see page 115). Hadow, writing of Schubert's ability to enchant us by sheer sensuous beauty, likens him to Keats, whose poetry immediately takes us into a region of magic, a kind of dream country. But, since the visionary is greater than the dreamer—even when he fails to maintain his vision, or is less competent as a technician than the dreamer—we must be careful to have Schubert before Beethoven on our programmes.

The *andante* is a strophic movement using the familiar theme from the *Rosamond* music which occurs later in the Op. 142 piano Impromptu. The workmanship here is of a far more complicated order than the ingenuous tune would lead one to expect—a remark which might be applied with equal justice to the minuet and finale. In the finale especially we find an easy blending of capricious rhythmic components one could call Mozartian in its organization if one could suppose that Schubert ever organized anything; one simply declares such movements to be inspired as much in their whole as in their delicious parts. It is interesting to glance over the score and see how much is marked *pianissimo*; how perfectly placed are the little *sforzandi*, rests, *ritardandi* and other quirks of tempo. The A minor Qua nowhere inhabits the pathetic world of the *Quartettsatz* or the D minor Quartet, but as a work it is not a whit inferior to them. Indeed, there may be musicians who think it Schubert's most perfect chamber work.

(c) For the *Quartet in D minor* is not a perfect work, though it contains some of the finest passages in Schubert's whole output. There is no reason to suppose that the use of the song, *Death and the Maiden,* in the slow movement shows that Schubert intended to write a 'Pathetic' or 'Tragic' quartet, in the sense that certain sonatas and symphonies are given these epithets. In a letter of 31st March 1824, to Kupelwieser, Schubert writes:

I have written very few new songs, but against that I have tried my hand at several kinds of instrumental music, and composed two new quartets, and I want to write yet another quartet and so prepare the way for a big symphony.

The two Quartets are the A minor and D minor; probably the third was never written. The D minor is not proved to be specially programmatic: we are not even to know whether the *Death and the*

Maiden movement was planned before he wrote the first movement. It is noteworthy, however, that all four movements are in a minor key—three in D minor and the slow in G minor. This is unique; so, among the chamber works, is the mood of dramatic pathos which runs through all first three movements as it does through the two movements of the B minor Symphony. On the other hand, too much has been made of what is surely an unconscious reference in the finale to the tune of 'Meine Töchter sollen dich warten schön' in the *Erl King*; some folk would suppose that Schubert's self-quotation (a mere two bars of typical Schubert) testified to his thinking of Death as engaged in dreaded pursuit of a young life, as was the Erl King, and that the preceding six-eight stuff represented Death in full gallop. But the finale, however fine a conception in itself, is the very movement which is hardly in keeping with the pathos of its fellows.

If we are not foolish enough to listen with Mozartian ears to the proportions of the first movement, we shall find that in few movements by Schubert has the texture so Mozartian an organization of its parts. Here are a sample two bars from the middle section, showing three of the leading themes played simultaneously almost in the style of the G major Quartet or 'Jupiter' finales:

The cello triplets derive from the opening, preparatory bars of the movement; the second fiddle double-stops emphasize the first subject (first in order—it is well in this work not to talk about two principal themes), while the first fiddle recalls the enchanting second subject:

What are the features in this movement which prevent our regarding it as a masterpiece in all respects? The defects, which are almost entirely architectural, arise from Schubert's giving rein to his rich fancy at any given point, yet feeling the impress of a traditional mould on either side of that point. Thus the middle section, which is so full of good things that it would almost seem to belong to a later age, has neither a great central climax nor a climactic goal. There is no reason at all why there should be a definite 'point of reprise,' cunningly approached in the manner of Mozart or dramatically timed as with Beethoven, and if Schubert wanted to organize his materials after their exposition in an original manner, provided that his result were musically convincing, only a fool would have deplored his departure from 'sonata form.' But Schubert is not quite convincing: in deference to tradition he repeats a considerable amount of his exposition, with the necessary transposition of keys, and his middle section overworks rhythmic figurations previously heard. Even more contributory to the Schubertian impression of diffuseness is a sort of double coda, the second element of which goes back to *Tempo I* after the usual *Più mosso*. Was this one of Schubert's 'inspired afterthoughts' produced after deciding to use the 'Death' theme in his slow movement? That it is inspired no one would deny; and so is any particular part of the whole movement, especially the very places in which we are aware of the composer's inability to use the classical scheme without the classical symmetry.

The only satisfactory way in which to demonstrate the beauties of the *Death and the Maiden* movement is to quote the whole, or play it. As that is impracticable, one may perhaps quote Mr. Brent Smith's words:

If I had to award the title of genius to any composer for two bars of music, I would be inclined to award it to Schubert for the first two bars of the second section [of the theme in discussion] . . . no wrenching, aching harmonies! just a faultily written chord of the sixth. Would not a thousand other composers have written a common chord of B flat major, thereby missing the poignancy of that G in the second violin part?

Schubert's melody and texture seem to commend Death as a benignant, if mournful figure whose arms reach to enfold one who would sleep 'after life's fitful fever.' In these simple chords we sense at a glimpse Schubert's poetic contribution to chamber music, just as in the Lydian chords of the 'Heiliger Dankgesang' we experience the most rarefied flight of Beethoven's mysticism.

The opening of the scherzo sends us forward in time to Mime's motif in the *Ring*:

but the symmetrical barring of this opening is not maintained: the glory of the movement lies in its rhythmic caprice, of which the two cadences before the double bars may serve as samples:

The trio plays the same tricks, making a stimulating contrast in the major key out of materials whose harmonic and melodic slightness is surely deliberate.

It is difficult not to believe that the finale of Beethoven's 'Kreutzer'

Sonata was unconsciously fermenting in Schubert's memory when he wrote the opening theme of the finale to this Quartet. Those who are ardent Schubertians like the persistent rhythms and repetitions, and at the same time commend the interspersed rhythmic asymmetries and harmonic abnormalities—some of them worthy of Berlioz—but no pontiff has yet decided whether the listener or Schubert is on trial. One does not expect, in Schubert of all people, to find a subject obviously introduced at a certain point for a structural purpose. If Schubert's *subject-matter* (the italics are important) is brought into being for any other purpose than delight in itself as music, it has an uncanny way of hiding the purpose; but the second main theme of this finale, so grandly bursting in after the tense silence which has preceded it:

continues with the contrapuntal 'business' of a student following a model; to some ears this is amusing in so unorthodox a movement.

(d) The most remarkable consideration evoked by a perusal of the *G major* Quartet of 1826 is its neglect by musicians in favour of its predecessor. The mere fact that it is Schubert's last quartet should give it at least priority of examination. It is possible that the reader, like the present writer, was until recently unfamiliar with the work. As we look at any sample bars, it is difficult to recognize Schubert, so very Beethovenian are the short pregnant themes and the interplays of parts:

Can it be that this Quartet is something of an essay? Of all the quartets it is the least typical of its composer—that is to say of the Schubert we know, who died so young; but does it not, perhaps, give us some indication of the next technical advances he would have made? Would the Schubert we do not know have proved, in his middle or third period, a deeper artist than the enchanting poet? If so, it is likely that the medium for his new utterances would have been instrumental, for composers write most of their songs during the springtime of life. Kreissle states that Schubert, when offering the C major Symphony to the Philharmonic Society, declared that he intended to write no more songs.

The extracts quoted immediately above show two of the contributory elements to the magnificent texture of the first movement. Daring as are the demands of compass and agility made on the instrumentalists, Schubert is always sure of his effects, of his organization of sonorities. Throughout the Quartet it seems that to this ability he had added a study of the techniques used in Beethoven's most advanced quartets, and then sought to add another to the middle-period set which Beethoven dedicated to Rasumovsky—for there can be no question of Schubert's entering at the age of twenty-nine into the *spiritual* adventures of Beethoven's final quartets. Furthermore, it is almost certain that some ears which had heard the Rasumovsky quartets heard either the first, private performance of Schubert's G major or else the public one of the first movement on 26th March 1828. The players may have included two or three of the original Rasumovsky quartet team.

The dynamic range and harmonic daring of the slow movement may be judged by this purple patch:

The scherzo, in B minor, but of playful temperament, sharing nothing of the pathos of the Symphony in that key, derives its chief interest from contrasts, from juxtaposed *pianissimo* and *fortissimo*, emphasized by the opposition of few parts toying with the little *spiccato* theme and the whole quartet sawing away with tremolo bowing. The virtuosity of the part-writing in the trio can be inspected in this sample:

It is useless to quote any part of the finale to illustrate a new and quite un-Schubertian kind of audacity. Superficially there are resemblances to the finale of the D minor Quartet—the six-eight tempo and the broad theme which breaks the onrush, as in the first example on page 117. But the novelties of the D minor finale become in this work almost a new technique. We are used to new and moving modulations in all Schubert's mature work: their object is sensuous and their impression richly dramatic; but in this Quartet we meet a new, cerebral type of harmonic audacity in the main materials, not just at transition points or dramatic climaxes: it produces a stimulation found only in the last of Beethoven's sonatas and quartets. Just as novels which try to depict civilized life in the distant future are not really prophecies but projections of current hopes and ideas for the future, so this new technique, or attempt at a new technique, was never actually pursued by Weber, Wagner, Chopin and other later composers who advanced harmony into the lush pastures of romanticism. Thus the G major Quartet must be given an honoured place even by those who like Schubert to be the Schubert they know. It is in some respects his most masterly quartet, and the one farthest removed from those works by the same composer which, in Johnsonian phrase, engage our affection without incurring our respect.

Schubert wrote one complete Trio for violin, viola and cello. The date, 1817, makes it probable that it was intended for home performance, and it has the same Mozartian flavour as the delicious B flat Symphony composed a few months before this E flat Trio. Despite the slenderness of the medium, the Trio is neither thin nor pedestrian, and it may be heartily commended to three players who cannot find a second violin. The two famous works for 'piano trio' are preceded in the catalogue by a so-called Sonata written in Schubert's fifteenth year, a work which need not detain us. No chamber work by Schubert is more popular than the B flat major Trio, Op. 99, written in 1827, though the composer favoured its successor in E flat major written the same year, Op. 100. In a letter to Hüttenbrenner he speaks of a performance at Schuppanzigh's, in which Bocklet, Schuppanzigh and Linke played the E flat Trio 'exquisitely,' and then demonstrated their enthusiasm in serious pantomime. Schumann, writing ten years afterwards, was roused to similar emotional heights: he refers to this Trio as 'an angry meteor' which 'blazed forth and outshone everything in the musical atmosphere of the time.'

Certain crisp rhythms and other features of the E flat Trio are decidedly Schumannesque. The opening of the slow movement:

or the canon between strings and piano in the scherzo might very well have come from the whimsical mind of the later master. It is difficult, however, to explain why Op. 100 should have brought forth so much more expressed enthusiasm than its B flat predecessor, for the B flat Trio has its own Schumannisms:

It is for the expert musical psychologist to answer the question: How is it that the *particular* unprepared dominant seventh quoted at example (*b*) above could never have occurred in the scores of Mozart and Beethoven, who were both as adventurous as Schubert in harmonic technique, even though they were less lavish with their harmonic riches? Either Schubert or Schumann could have written so familiar an inversion of the same chord as the following:

There is no reason, it seems, why former composers did not use it; no doubt they did, but not quite in the same way. The example comes from the first movement of the B flat Trio.

Two movements of the B flat Trio are highly Schubertian. The singing slow movement belongs exclusively to the composer of the unfinished Symphony, and the finale has a fascinating texture and structure.

To ears which have known the beauties of nineteenth-century pianism Schubert's writing for the pianoforte is wholly acceptable only in the Trios (and the Quintet). This does not mean that Schubert, either in these chamber works or elsewhere, wrote 'good' pianoforte music of the kind developed by Schumann and Brahms: his keyboard style quarries from Beethoven and is without any trace of keyboard invention. (It is plain that young Schubert had no training in the older keyboard style upon which young Mozart had been nurtured.) What Schubert had, most strongly too, was a feeling for the sound produced by any instrument, keyboard or otherwise, and for the sound produced in any part of its compass. An inspection of the pianoforte part of these Trios shows little but change and change about upon some five applications of technique —repeated chords, broken chords such as are used in song accompaniment, octave triplets, chromatic scales bubbling up in octaves like the flute and piccolo in imperial Elgar, pulsating octave-figures in the bass, or 'glass chandelier' octaves in the top register, usually to repeat a pretty tune while the strings take over the repeated chords.

SCHUBERT
From a Lithograph by Josef Teltscher, 1826

VIENNA, VIEW FROM THE UPPER BELVEDERE

From a Coloured Engraving by F. C. Zoller, c. 1800

JOHANN BAPTIST JENGER, ANSELM HÜTTENBRENNER AND SCHUBERT
From a Coloured Drawing by Josef Teltscher, c. 1827

SCHUBERT EVENING AT JOSEF VON SPAUN'S HOUSE

From an Oil Sketch by Moritz von Schwind c. 1870

SCHUBERT

From a Water-colour by Wilhelm August Rieder, 1825

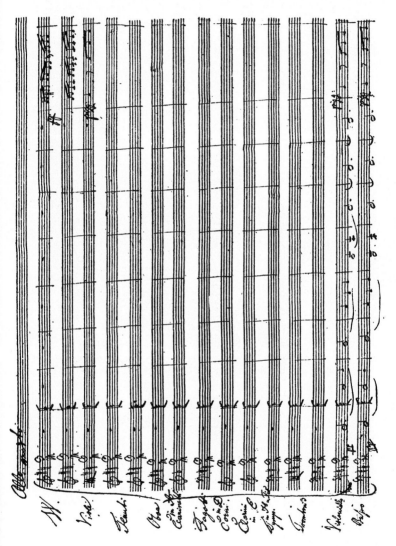

THE UNFINISHED SYMPHONY.   THE OPENING OF THE FIRST MOVEMENT

COURT AND GARDEN OF SCHUBERT'S BIRTHPLACE WITH THE 'TROUT' WELL ON THE RIGHT

'TO MUSIC'. AS WRITTEN IN THE ALBUM OF ALBERT SOWINSKI

But Schubert judges perfectly the right part of the keyboard on which to play his octaves and the exact number of doublings to allow in relation to the string registers in use at a given place, so that a bar which looks nothing sounds enchanting.

Some of the foregoing remarks might be applied to the *Nocturne* for piano trio, a straggling but pleasant work in E flat major with a middle section in E major. It is rarely heard and makes no rhythmic adventures of any importance, though there seems to be no reason why it should not be given as respected a place as are some of the little pianoforte pieces.

Scarcely more ambitious is the A major 'Trout' Quintet, written for Steyr after the summer tour with Vogl in 1819. The unusual combination—violin, viola, cello, double bass and piano—probably represents the professional ability of the gatherings at friend Paum, gartner's. Disappointment in the work need come only when it is played after a more serious or elevated chamber work by Mozart, Beethoven or Brahms. It is not a very great work, but it thoroughly deserves its popularity. Schoolboys love the variations in which the tune can be heard with slight but delicious alteration, and old boys who do not love them are advancing in sin as well as in years. The work is a perfect choice for a homely summer party. Were there a little less bump in the scherzo it might pass for Mendelssohn in his Puckish moods, or perhaps Schumann in his usual mood:

The great string Quintet, Op. 163, for the beautiful combination of two fiddles, viola and two cellos, is held to have been composed in the summer of 1828, though no reference to the fact survives in letters by Schubert or his friends. There was no performance, so far as is known, during Schubert's life; Josef Hellmesberger led what seems to have been the first performance in 1850. While nobody disputes Grove's opinion that the C major Quintet is

Schubert's finest piece of chamber music, there are few who would not imagine that, if he had lived a few years longer, he would have revised it, especially the last two movements. 'Scale' and 'size' are not exactly synonyms in music and, as in the B minor Symphony, we can enjoy movements following the unique and magnificent first two without considering them to be on quite the scale. It is mistaken, however, to be disappointed in the serenade-like happiness of the finale—its almost Hungarian opening rhythms and the lilt of its distinctive second subject. What, for want of precise terms, one must call 'depth' of expression in those first two great movements is surely not tragic, and Moser's belief that Schubert had premonitions of death while composing them is utterly without evidence. His letters during the spring and summer of 1828 suggest good spirits.

The probability is that, on his return to Vienna, he wanted to revive the chamber music he had enjoyed in his father's and brother's houses. His father was a cellist and his favourite brothers, Ferdinand and Ignaz, violinists; Schubert himself usually played viola. Linke, the cellist in the Rasumovsky quartet, was a friend of the family. For all its marvellous effects, the quintet does not make extremely difficult demands on the players. Even the first cello which, when not doubling the second, must keep largely to the alto register, does not take risky leaps high on the A string.

Though all five instruments are almost continuously in play, all movements show a rich textural variety. The first page contains a fine contrast in tones, the tune being first presented in the soprano, with the second cello silent, followed by a second lay-out in the tenor register with the first violin silent. From this point nearly every bar in the work shows every instrument in use. This passage, just after the opening:

is no formal counterpoint, but it makes the homophonic beauty of
the two next themes seem all the finer by contrast:

Disappointment comes with the middle section: two pages of the
miniature score (pages 13–15, Eulenburg edition) repeat the former
two pages a tone lower.   The two themes quoted immediately above,
so finely conceived for quintet that they are ineffective on a pianoforte,
pass through various keys in a leisurely, unclimactic but never
enervating way.   Yet a quotation from any one part of this middle
section would show its worth.   The approach to the reprise is
excellently done and the reprise itself shows another beautiful variant
of the opening texture; it is followed by a recapitulatory section which
transposes the exposition note for note before it reaches a coda wherein
extra effort marks a return of inspiration.

The slow movement is very beautiful.   Schubert was probably
unconscious that he was using a Dorian idom when he changed the
harmony of his opening theme at its first repetition and gave it a
flavour found in Brahms or Dvořák:

The scherzo, with its robust horn effects, is a unique conception, despite some melodic enervation soon after the double bar. The trio is also unusual, being neither waltz nor rustic dance, but a soulful measure in slow quadruple time. If all the repeats are played, as is customary, this trio drags, and we ask whether this is novelty or originality and, in any case, what is its relationship to the scherzo? Why was this form of contrast selected, which seems to belong to a dramatic *andante*?

That the finale might have been revised or replaced by Schubert seems likely when we listen to a recording of it immediately after hearing one of the two first movements. Its materials seem to belong to a work with the emotional effect of the Octet. The great paragraphs and the play of sun and shade in the first movement seem to have promised a finale which even Schubert could not finish in a month or so. The delightful one he did write is almost too easy going for its context.

The Octet in F major for clarinet, bassoon, horn, string quartet and double bass is a splendid example of Schubert's facility in blending and contrasting instrumental tones, a facility which is evident even in the earliest symphonies or in the Funeral Music of 1812. The musical content of the Octet is by no means profound: the work inherits the characteristics of Mozart's serenades and divertimenti and gives us a bourgeois equivalent to summer-party music in the gardens at Schönbrunn. The workmanship is exquisite in each of the six movements, which have a counterpart in the Beethoven Septet. It seems fairly evident that Schubert took the Septet for his model. The Octet, Op. 166, 'was written for Count F. von Troyer, chief officer of the household to the Archduke Rudolph, Beethoven's patron.' Troyer was a clarinettist, and the Rasumovsky players, Schuppanzigh, Weiss and Linke, are known to have taken part in the first performance of the Octet, soon after its composition in March 1824.

The very Schubertian *allegro* is preceded by a short *adagio* whose figuration, as in the C major Symphony, turns up in the middle section and at the coda, giving the whole movement a brilliant consistency. The quality of the writing, with its easy combination of themes, is shown by the fact that it is difficult to make quotations of any aptitude without using up the space needed for the eight staves

of score. Parts of the development having failed to compress themselves neatly into three staves, I refrain from quoting at all.

The slow movement pays compliment to the noble clarinettist by
giving the Big Tune to Troyer's instrument, and it is to be hoped that
the noble clarinettist returned the compliment cash down. Tune
and accompaniment remind us of the *Ave Maria* song composed
a year subsequently, though the Octet movement is rather drawn
out, being in binary form from which the interest retires a little
after the half-way mark, only to be stimulated first by the inspired
rhythmic variants of the accompaniment and then by an original
stroke of modulation at the coda, just when one expects a full close
into B flat.

The scherzo and the *andante* for the variation movement are delight-
fully ingenuous:

Ingenuousness can be as disgusting as the lisps and dimples of a
child actor verging on the desperation of its ninth birthday, but a
quality which fails to convince in Mozart, who was never a child,
can be engaging in Schubert, who to the end preserved a child-like
delight in the materials he played with, even in the consecutive
dominant sevenths on a rising-fourth bass which were mere reach-
me-downs to later composers:

The variations are brilliantly done in the same unpretentious vein
as those in the 'Trout' Quintet. The minuet which follows is a
sweet placid thing, and deserves to be one of the most popular movements in the work. The clarinet tune of its trio grows almost

over-sweet but serves well to put into relief the dramatic introduction to the final movement:

Here are the final bars of the minuet followed by the opening of the sixth movement:

This sombre introduction is but a foil to the *allegro* proper, which is on a mock-symphonic scale, wondering whether to be impressive or informal. Its lengthy subject runs thus:

Informality wins, of course, and the cadence recalls a popular song of a few years back with a refrain 'round the cock-eyed world'; and that is the spirit in which the happy Octet leaves us.

CHAPTER IX

CHURCH, CHORAL AND DRAMATIC MUSIC

OUR prevailing English taste in church music is to that of Schubert and his contemporaries as the lily to the hollyhock, but it is grossly erroneous to assert that Vienna of the classical epoch had no taste, or that there was no difference between its music for church and its music for the stage. Church authorities to-day, who pay lip-service to plainsong and Palestrina, but find little room for them on service lists, inveigh against the 'tyranny of the bar line' and find continued harmony secular. They are captivated by the tonal idioms, as by the visual symbols, of a former age of faith; nowadays Dorian and Phrygian cadences grace the sacramental atmosphere, whereas composers from Haydn to Schubert became somewhat 'baroque.' Formal dress is never modern. To whatever school the critic belongs, he should not doubt the sincerity with which a former age curbed its artistic expression in deference to taste.

Schubert's church music also defers to taste, but he does not seem to have been punctilious in religious observance. Not only his brother Ignaz, but many of his musical circle were either unorthodox or anti-clerical.

We have every right to declare that Schubert's age was humanitarian rather than catholic in its most exalted moments. Beethoven's *Missa solemnis* paid tribute to a real enough Presence, but that Presence is not focused specifically upon the *res* of the altar; priests themselves had not long before belonged to masonic lodges and found a truer agapemone in the brotherhood of Sarastro than in their Communion of Saints. This seeming discrepancy can exist in any age and did not prevent Viennese church musicians from having a definite taste in their art, though tasters of to-day measure it only in paltry concessions to ecclesiastical conservatism. A musician whose private aspirations reach to an inarticulate 'O altitudo!', whose spiritual quest is as nebulous as the Orphic mysteries, whose mouth utters the small change of pantheism, Buddhism or Nietzscheism, may be a protagonist of 'good taste' in the religion he has inherited, and may bring to

his liturgy a heart solaced as much by eclectic deism as by the orthodox formulae of the rite. So Beethoven's masses did not find their
way to the imperial chapel, where the prevailing taste required that
masses should have a *pianissimo* written between 'altissimus' and
'Jesu Christe,' and should present abortive fugues at 'cum Sancto
Spiritu' and 'et vitam venturi saeculi.' We may ridicule this taste,
but taste it is; we may dislike the dancing hockets in Purcell's
Magnificats, but no part of a Purcellian dramatic extravaganza is
labelled 'Canon 4 in 2,' and no secular writing by Schubert is quite
so unlike Schubert as some passages in the 1814 Mass, composed
for the Liechtental parish church.

That work was sufficiently tasteful by the canons of the time to win
Salieri's enthusiasm. It was an attempt by the young composer to
clothe the sacred rite soberly—far more soberly than Haydn and
Mozart had done. Yet two Masses of the following year, in B flat
and G respectively, show him hoping, as did Haydn, that God
would not reject the offering of a cheerful heart. It is curious that
these two Masses, the very ones which in their own day paid least
deference to ecclesiastical sobriety, are the only two frequently heard in
Anglican churches. The B flat major recaptures the smiling curves
of Mozart's little C major Mass. Its 'taste' may be judged from the
vernal lilt of the final clause. Did Schubert recognize the liturgical
meaning of *pax*? Not he. *Pax* was the gift of happiness—Viennese
happiness—and Schubert was as sure of benediction as the wisest
preacher with his list of theological connotations:

Do - na no - bis pa cem, Do - na no - bis pa - cem

The G major, banished from Westminster Cathedral, but
nourished at St. Paul's, is a grand little service, which could be said
to correspond to the sturdy B flat major Symphony were not the Symphony, like the Mass in that key, highly Mozartian, whereas the G
major Mass is more Schubertian than the Schubert masses to follow.
In the *Kyrie* and in the ritornello to the *Agnus,* Schubert's unique vein
of pathos suffuses traditionally lyrical portions of the Mass. An
achievement especially remarkable in Schubert is the compactness of

lengthy portions like the *Credo* and *Gloria*, whose prose forms defy symmetry. Schubert's four-square chords over a bass of marching crotchets make his *Credo* a worthy affirmation, while the subject of the *Osanna* fugato is typical of a work with no weak places:

The C major Mass of 1816, dedicated to Michael Holzer of the Liechtental church, pays more tribute to taste than to inspiration; yet Schubert was fond of it, for he gave it a new *Benedictus* in 1828, shortly before his death. The Mass in A flat major, begun in 1819, but not finished till September 1822, tends to sprawl and fails to fulfil its original conception. (Its title was *Missa solemnis*.) The examples seen on page 132 serve to show the composer at pains to temper exuberance to dignity.

In some places tenor and bass parts divide and make contrast with a similar burgeoning of the upper parts. A trio of soloists is imposed above the chorus in the *Benedictus*, and there is no doubt that, had the words been secular and picturesque, Schubert, fresh from his holiday tour with Vogl, would have let his fancy roam and left us a choral work as wholly gorgeous as this Mass is in parts:

The A flat Mass shows that Schubert particularly desired to master the grand style. Despite the inscription 'completed September 1822' on a manuscript unusually marked with corrections, he took up the work again in his last months and made more alterations.

In 1826–27 he wrote a work which plainly indicates the direction in which his style would have gone had he lived to become an honoured *Capellmeister*. This work is the *Deutsche Messe,* a type of devotion that had some popularity in certain parts of southern Germany and is not to be confused with the Lutheran communion service of the north. In country districts of Austria and south Germany it was no novelty, by Schubert's time, to hold a kind of instructional devotion which included the mass sung in vernacular; the attitude of the instructed seems to have been similar to that of northern congregations of Bach's time to the Sunday cantata. In 1782 Michael Haydn, *Capellmeister* to the notorious Hieronymus Colloredo at Salzburg, wrote one of the first of these 'German Masses' which can be examined to-day. The text was provided by one Kohlbrenner; Schubert's was by Johann Philipp Neumann, professor of physics at the Vienna Polytechnic, members of which institute may have provided the male voices. The text of a German mass is thus neither stereotyped nor that used in Protestant communion services. Schubert's score appeared subsequently in different arrangements, including one for men's voices, but it was designed originally for mixed choir, organ and wind instruments.

Its musical style is interesting. Once the text becomes unliturgical, human emotions take the place of those spiritual exercises which are assumed at a particular moment in the ritual sacrifice. The *Kyries*, for instance, which are the ritual parallel of the ceremonial censing and preparation of the altar, acknowledging the unworthiness of the celebrants and the inadequacy of all human offerings, retain their ternary form when translated, but lose their objectivity—the feeling that humanity as a whole is humbly approaching deity; in place of this comes subjective human piety, taking comfort in the contemplation of anthropomorphic love. Divine mercy is expressed by music which could quite as suitably reflect human pity, and the mass music of the humanitarian nineteenth century shows that the *mensa* of the altar, civilized successor of the sacrificial block, was a symbol less venerated than the crucifix above it. *Credo*, once a categorical statement of faith, with music avoiding the picturesque and linking the doctrines in business-like order, began to develop certain sections, even in short settings, as surely as did the intentionally sectional *Credo* of Lutheran Bach; human sympathy was expressed with the sufferings of Jesus.

Schubert's music for this unliturgical text is in places curiously similar to late Victorian church music of the type composed by Sir Joseph Barnby and Sir Arthur Sullivan. Dogma and ritual, by nature, remain intact; remove the setting which honours them and we see Liberal humanitarianism invading Catholic piety as surely as it invades Protestant piety. This music of the *Deutsche Messe,* in what Professor Dent calls the 'harmonium style,' is the expression of Schubert's piety, not of his racial faith. Protestantism, with its love of the vernacular scriptures, has always emphasized the subjective emotions; its hymns and sermons dilate on human sin and human love, and the 'saving' of the sinner by love shown in vicarious suffering on the cross. Protestant teaching consists chiefly in telling the sinner how to claim the benefits of the divine sacrifice. But is Catholic teaching so very different? What is the mass but the same teaching dramatized? This stress on the personal relationships of the individual soul with its Saviour is characteristic of democratic Protestant communities in which the individual matters; the 'German Mass' was used for instructional purposes in an age that developed individualism—the age of self-made men—and the expression of subjective, personal devotion invaded not just the 'German Mass' but the Latin; the sublime functional music of Palestrina, the operatic elegance of Mozart—these are succeeded by music recognizable as the kind we associate with those hymns we were taught in our youth, and employed the first personal pronoun: 'I could not do without Thee,' etc. This particular period of church music has as straight a development from Hummel to Bruckner as it has from S. S. Wesley to Sullivan and Barnby. Schubert came under the general influences; but where did the actual musical style come from—the pathetic suspensions and chromatics? Since moral uplift was formerly marked by crabbed dryness and fugato entries, whence the change to lush homophony? Certainly not from Beethoven, whose Rousseauist humanitarianism is as universal as the old mass music. Probably from France—post-revolutionary France that was fast becoming bourgeois, with a spiritual horizon neither that of Pascal nor of Voltaire, but of Chateaubriand. Schubert's operas show strong French influence for the plain reason that Italian and French opera had invaded and gripped the German theatres well before Beethoven's death. Schubert was not the man to set a fashion. He wrote in the styles he heard and absorbed them into his own; we may suppose that his church music came under the same influences as his theatre music.

Schubert's last Mass, that in E flat major of 1828, is both a fine work, to prove which one must know it as a whole, and an interesting historical study, to demonstrate which shall be our concern now. There are three types of writings: (1) Recognizable Schubert, in occasional lyrical passages, such as 'Et incarnatus'; it is noteworthy that these passages are not found in parts of the mass usually conceded to lyricism, and also that there are very few of them. (2) Large portions of writing in 'harmonium style.' Schubert is the child of his time, and such items as the *Kyrie* show taste 'progressing' towards the 'sacred' style of the Chevalier Neukomm. Here is all the unctuous sweetness of Gounod's *Messes solennelles*:

(3) The element of conservatism which has always been a feature of church music. Schubert's reverence takes him almost to the imitation of Bach or the C minor Mass of Mozart.

Schubert so obviously wanted to be respectable that he began seven fugues in this normal-length Mass, though he seems to have gauged his contrapuntal style by intuition. Had he been granted Mozart's ability to study older contrapuntists, his perception and general musical facility should have made him a master of the formal polyphonic forms. At the age of thirty-one he certainly had no definite criteria to guide him even in the choice of a fugal subject. All that is needed to complete his conception of joyful futurity is this:

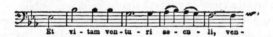

There is not space in a small book to examine every *Salve Regina*, *Tantum ergo* or elaboration of the liturgical *proprium*—antiphons, graduals, etc. Schubert's increasingly serious settings of the *ordinarium* are proof of his interest in church music and possibly of his hope for church appointment. He thus makes strong contrast with Mozart, whose masses are sufficiently few in number and secular in style (with one great exception, the C minor, and that only in parts) to show that he had no burning desire for the chief duties of a *Capellmeister*, whatever his father thought about the subject. The Salzburg masses are operatic and rococo; the best portions of the C minor and the Requiem are not highly liturgical. Yet Mozart was punctilious in sacramental practice, and it is not evident that Schubert's religious observances were even habitual.

That Schubert's writing for the liturgy was always of a standard comparable with that for the mass itself is shown in so excellent a work as the offertory *Intende voci orationis meae* of 1828, which opens with the same kind of long-phrased sweetness and is dignified by the same contrapuntal stiffenings as the E flat Mass:

Another magnificently dignified work of 1828 immediately puts us in mind of Mozart's masonic music: this work is the setting of Psalm 92, in German,[1] for baritone solo, quartet and chorus. It was written for the Vienna synagogue, and it is a pity that both this psalm and the motet do not get a regular hearing in public.

Several of the short choral works for various types of voices—male chorus, mixed or female voices—some unaccompanied, have religious words. But it is noteworthy that, as in certain solo songs, such as *Die Allmacht,* these non-liturgical texts are treated without churchiness of either the old contrapuntal-dignified or the new fluid-sentimental type observed in the masses. The general flavour is pantheistic, and it is not surprising that works like *Gott der Weltschöpfer* or *Gott im Ungewitter* (for mixed chorus with piano accompaniment) recall similar essays by Beethoven, at least in their more vigorous passages; elsewhere we find a Mendelssohnian tenderness, particularly in the partsongs for female voices, of which the well-known *Twenty-third Psalm* is a fair specimen.

One or two of these semi-religious vocal works have a square-cut

[1] The original setting was to Hebrew words.

classicality which makes one suppose that Schubert had acquired, like Mozart, a love of the old cantata writers of Mattheson's and Handel's time. This is not just a feature of late Schubert; it is as noticeable even in 1816, in the setting of Klopstock's *Das grosse Halleluja* (for female voices), as in the *Song of Miriam,* a more lengthy product of 1828 which used to be a favourite in this country, probably because of its very Handelian idiom:

This cantata, to words by Grillparzer, is laid out for solo, chorus and pianoforte accompaniment, the orchestral scoring being the work of Franz Lachner. Schubert seems to have been a most practical creature in matters purely musical. The offertory *Intende voci,* discussed above, is scored for oboe, clarinets, bassoons, horns, trombones and strings, whereas the 'Miriam' cantata, like many another largeish choral work, has only the keyboard accompaniment. One cannot but suppose, as one sees the ambitious works written for pianoforte duet, that wherever the composer wrote for big forces, he at least *hoped* for a performance and probably had one in view.

It would therefore be interesting to know for what performers or place of performance Schubert wrote his one oratorio, *Lazarus,* or why the work was not completed. The text, by Niemeyer, professor of theology at Halle, is entitled *Lazarus, or the Feast of the Resurrection,* and as Schubert made his setting in the February of 1820, he obviously intended it to be sung in connection with the Easter festival of that year. No music at all was written for Part III, which would have been the section dealing with the resurrection of Lazarus. But the world does not seem to have lost a profound musical commentary on the mysteries of life and death. Schubert was incapable, at least in 1820, of experiencing the spiritual adventure of a mystic in contemplation of the great truths, and *Lazarus* is simply a melodrama upon a scriptural subject. Though no part of the text is taken directly from the gospels, the solo portions are assigned to half a dozen characters, as in the Lutheran Passions of which Bach's St. Matthew is the chief glory. A chorus makes comment at the end of each of the two

existing parts, and scenery and action are described in outline, thus:
'The garden of a rural dwelling,' 'Lazarus dies,' 'Simon, a Sadducee,
trembling with dismay' (at the sight of an open grave). Oratorio
as a form got its title from the religious plays given with music in an
oratory, such as that of St. Philip Neri; so it would be wrong to say
that Schubert's work is not an oratorio. But just as his operas are
best described as musical melodramas, so *Lazarus* is best described
as a religious melodrama. Human emotions are portrayed therein at
a picturesque and tearful level, though in no place so convincingly
as in some of the simplest songs. The accompanied recitative is
carefully done from sentence to sentence, but lacks climax and depth
simply because those qualities can be present in music only when
they are part of a musical conception, and for a musical conception
to be expressive and convincing the composer must feel so much at
home that he can see in whole lengths. Schubert was not at home
with the type of recitative and aria used in this religious melodrama.
Though the music is neither crabbed nor glutinous, despite occasional reflections of the sentimental religiosity of its day, Schubert
does not seem free to let himself go; nowhere within these pages is
the obvious exuberance of his first-rate works.

The melodrama of his secular pieces is of so unbridled a fancy that
it ought to enjoy the same popularity as the ballet music, overtures
and *entr'actes*. Never, however, were his libretti worthy of his
music. Since he mastered the *durchkomponierte Lied,* and in such songs
as *Gretchen, Erl King, Postilion Chronos, The Young Nun* or the later
Warrior's Foreboding made glorious unity of melodramatic balladry,
why should we doubt his success where he had faith in himself?
The sources of Schubertian operatic melodrama are those Weber
knew, and it must be remembered that Schubert had made at least
six essays in dramatic music before Weber's important operas appeared. Schubert's chief influences were probably Gluck, *The Magic
Flute, Fidelio* and the pieces of smaller men like Weigl, Winter and
Süssmayr.

Just as the orchestral scoring of those operatic pieces which have
survived shows subtlety beyond Weber's brilliance, so we cannot
conceive of harmony like the following from a Chorus of Spirits in
Rosamunde being found anywhere in *Freischütz*:

It would be misleading to discuss Schubert's theatre music under the categories of its title pages—opera, Singspiel, melodrama—for in *Biedermeier* Vienna the genres were no longer clearly differentiated. The popularity of such pieces as Weigl's *Schweizerfamilie* (Swiss Family Robinson) in a city that also loved *The Magic Flute* and *Fidelio* proves that many people enjoyed in the greater works only what they found in the ephemeral ones. Schubert, from youth a theatre-goer, no doubt knew fine expression from trivial, but had no Mozartian judgment of dramatic technique, the means of characterization and the timing of situations in broader construction. He enjoyed scenes, expressions and effects of an order called 'poetic' by critics who meant that they 'aspired to the condition of music' (Pater's phrase applied to more than lyric poetry).

In other words, opera and romantic drama feasted Schubert's fancy and gave him what Richard Capell calls 'the rapture and poignancy of first sensations.' This experience and imagination made the greatest of song composers but was not enough to make a successful opera composer. The seven fattest volumes of the collected works record Schubert's persistent attempts to capture the stage—five *Singspiele,* three operas, one melodrama and half a dozen incomplete works. Here is no lack of splendid music for at least three grand operas. Many a student who supposes that Schubert's 'heavenly lengths' are found only in the superb instrumental movements of his last years can find himself corrected by perusing only *Alfonso and Estrella* and *Fierabras,* the two operas deemed worth producing in

1854 and 1897 respectively. The first is full of brilliant arias, the second of lengthy scenas in which leitmotive technique is wonderfully used.

The composer of *Fierabras* would have left his mark on opera if he had found the right play for his own kind of expression or a counsellor with a shrewd judgment of dramatic vitality. His masterpiece would probably have been a 'grand' opera with oracular trombones or a concealed wind band (as in *Rosamunde*) for rich supernatural effects; it would have differed from the 'grand' operas of Paris not only because of its German romanticism, but because scenas, choruses and melodrama, in the sense used in *Fidelio,* would have made the work a treasury of large-scale forms rather than of songs and arias. Huge unified 'complexes,' made possible by Schubert's command of modulation and colour, would have been the dramatic equivalents of his great symphonic movements. His master opera would thus have differed not only from Meyerbeer's or Rossini's, but also from Weber's; the theatre as well as the concert hall would have claimed Beethoven's successor, whom we can recognize even now when enterprise lets us hear some of the best pieces in the seven volumes.

In Schubert's lifetime only *Zwillingsbrüder* (The Twins) and *Rosamunde* were staged, and their short run was partly attributed to Schubert's noisy scoring. The opinion need not be considered, for *Biedermeier* Vienna was almost incapable of discovering the true reasons for its disappointment and ready enough to pass around an excuse. The Schubertian circle were of their period although, in the theatre, they failed to oust the conqueror, Rossini.

If proof is wanted that Schubert could have written magnificently for operatic solists and choruses, finding shades of vocal colour as varied as his orchestral colours, it will be found in the number of fragments for chorus, either male-voice, female-voice, accompanied or *a capella,* so unaccountably neglected by our choral bodies, and in the choral texture of his best sacred music. Given the libretti which poor Schubert never found, how well would the male-voice *Song of the Spirits over the Waters,* or the vocal dance *Welcome Spring,* or the solo scena with clarinet and piano, *The Shepherd on the Fells,* embody the atmosphere of a passing operatic movement.

CHAPTER X

WORKS FOR AND WITH PIANOFORTE

(a) Piano Sonatas

A few years ago the only Schubert pianoforte sonatas to find an occasional place in recital programmes were the A minor, Op. 42, and the so-called Fantasy-Sonata in G major, Op. 78, edited by Liszt. At the present moment, however, academies and public performers are favouring the Sonata in B flat major, written in Schubert's last year, and opening with the phrase:

There are admirable parts and features in the work, but it is by no means a favourite with the present writer, and it is difficult to say why, especially since one knows that the very parts one man dislikes in certain works by Schubert (or another composer) are those held in affection by other people. Consider, for instance, the theme just quoted. To one man it seems weak; to another it is endearingly Schubertian, and a distaste for the type of Schubertian expression which it exemplifies does not come from any memory of a similar cadence in one of the more pinchbeck tunes of *Madame Butterfly*, nor from the anticipation of its appearance with the following harmonization:

One is unable to find the words with which to describe this particular vein, though one could quote a good many examples from the piano pieces of Schubert, rather than from songs or works for orchestra. They represent a type of sentiment, which cannot be dubbed sentimental. When a composer is sentimental, he just 'lets himself go'; he is not fully self-critical, is not, in the case of an artist Schubert's size, fully himself, whereas the sentiment of the B flat theme quoted above is decidedly Schubertian. When Schubert becomes merely sentimental, we can see how and why, can explain the lapse in technical terms—easy stock suspensions, loosely used chromatics, as in another part of the sonata:

It is not proposed here to discuss the merits of each sonata, but to seek some reason for the comparative unpopularity of the sonatas as a whole. Schumann, Liszt and other pianists, including some distinguished modern performers, have shaken the dust from this or that specimen, found enough superior-quality Schubert therein to make neglect seem unjustified, and have tried to get the musical public to accept the sonata as a whole. Schumann declared the G major Sonata to be 'the most perfect work, both in form and conception' that Schubert left; Schumann's enthusiasm was useful and courageous at the time, but many of his remarks on the keyboard works, together with some later opinions of Grove and Parry, reflect only a passing taste. The public has judged for itself, and many a homely amateur plays the first two movements of that A minor Sonata without any august recommendation. Indeed these two movements appear in popular albums and cheap editions, along with the *Moments musicaux,* waltzes and *Impromptus.* Since there are seventeen piano sonatas (counting the G major, which is as much a real sonata as any), why is the first movement of the A minor so marked a favourite? In the first place, despite the Schubertian flavour, its texture is Beethovenian; it is grateful to the fingers and it is written in the grand manner, with plenty of dramatic contrast; it grants a time to make the piano sing and a time to rap out the chords. Yet it is difficult to understand why professional favour is bestowed on the B flat and amateur on the earlier A minor when there exists a fine work like the Sonata in A major, dating, like the B flat, from 1828, and being not only very attractive musically, but also far better laid out for the keyboard than are most of its fellows. Surely it is the best of the seventeen, with the exception of the unfinished C major, which is to be admired rather for its conception than its pianism. No quotation is made from the A major, since one of its merits lies in the size of its paragraphs. To quote a snippet from the first page of any movement, especially the opening *allegro*, would be to give a false impression of the movement as a whole. That the work abnormally 'pleases the hands' and, also abnormally, maintains its excellence in the last two as well as the first two movements, is partly due to the strong influence of Beethoven: this is very noticeable in the final rondo and in the 'jumps' of the scherzo which provides keyboard, not orchestral, playfulness.

One of the first reasons for the neglect of the sonatas is that they seem crude to ears familiar with the fine texture of nineteenth-century pianist-composers. The crudity would be acceptable if there were ideas to interpret in the grand Beethovenian manner. This style Schubert could not quite catch, although, lacking keyboard inventiveness, he used Beethoven as a huge quarry from which to chip basic figurations. Beethoven placed a heavy responsibility upon any composer who wished to write 'Sonata' at the top of his paper, incurring a test no less comprehensive than that made by a symphony. In sonata after sonata Schubert sets off with a heroic gesture in the grand style, but soon has to fall back on stock triplet figures:

There may follow a pleasant idyll sung to an Alberti accompaniment, until the heroic gesture makes a long-overdue recurrence.

More will be said later of Schubert's pianistic deficiency, but that alone is not responsible for what we miss in his sonatas. One or two of the least impressive of them are quite grateful to the fingers, as is also the Sonata in B major, Op. 147, whose first movement none can call unimpressive. The opening gesture of the D major Sonata quoted above may remind the reader of the opening of Brahms's first piano Sonata, the early work in C major. Now Brahms is one of the last composers to be thought pianistically

deficient: his rhapsodies, ballads, and still more his exquisite intermezzi, are the delight of every one who enjoys the subtleties of pedal-
ling, of carefully placed suspensions within arpeggiated chords, of
juxtaposed delicacy and sonority; but do his sonatas appear at recitals
much more frequently than Schubert's? No: probably not even as
frequently. On the other hand Schubert's short piano pieces are
scarcely recital material as Brahms's are.

It is worth noting that the first and the last music by Schubert that
is extant was for piano. For no previous composer except Beethoven
was the piano so much the confidant of his solitary hours, notably the
hours when Mayrhofer or others with whom he shared lodgings went
out to business and left him in the house with the piano. We may
even underestimate his ability as a player. The people whom he
enchanted included many who engaged the most esteemed teachers
and could play well themselves, and almost all of them were regular
concert-goers in the city which, above any, attracted the finest recitalists. In a limited sense Schubert was therefore a public performer
whom writers may underestimate as a pianist because his career was
not public in the same sense as Mozart's and Beethoven's, or because
his smaller piano pieces are not essential in tracing the ancestry of the
rich crop of short piano lyrics that came during Schumann's lifetime.
Yet how much were those later piano composers inspired by Schubert's
songs, including their piano parts?

Brahms's smaller pieces, like the lyrics of Schumann, Chopin or
Grieg, owe their loveliness to the composer's use of the powers of
suggestion possessed by the pianoforte. The instrument's limitations,
such as the lingering evaporation of held or pedalled notes, are
exploited as felicitously as are its direct capabilities; the composers
cited may not consciously have recognized keyboard limitations.
Nor did Schubert; one quotation from the Grand Duo is enough to
prove that:

But Schubert had no need to be a good player in order to utilize his
instrument's powers of suggestion; all musical Vienna of his time,

every owner of a new pianoforte, was aware of them; hence the joy of the friends in Schubert's song accompaniments. No doubt they listened to his piano pieces, including the sonatas, supplying for themselves what we seem to miss. We have but to read letters by persons present at Schubertiads to find that not only songs but pianoforte pieces, and even extemporizations, conjured up romantic landscapes from China to Peru and took their sensitive hearts through a whole Alexander's Feast of emotions. To his contemporaries, Schubert's pianism was obviously as evocative as Debussy's still remains for us. We can complete the atmosphere suggested by Debussy, but when there is no voice or violin, those Schubertian movements which do not satisfy modern ears may be likened to a painting with definite background and foreground but no middle distance.

But there is a more potent suggestion than that of romantic scenery: Schubert consistently and obviously evokes in his piano sonatas the sounds of concerted orchestral instruments. Too often do we declare a man's keyboard writing to be orchestral when our fingers rather than our ears find it awkward. To say that Beethoven wrote orchestrally just because he recognized the sonority and percussive range of the pianoforte, or because there is a horn effect in 'Les Adieux,' is to talk nonsense; one might as well say that he wrote vocally because of the recitative-like soliloquies in the D minor Sonata. Beethoven was trained at the keyboard; he was a fine player who knew the older keyboard technique together with the adventures of the Bachs and of Mozart. Like Brahms, he exploited the instrument's limitations, as we can see from the almost Schumannesque texture in the *adagio* of Op. 2 in C major. Schubert, deprived of pictorial inspiration, could use only the more obvious powers of the keyboard—its chords, arpeggios, scale passages, octaves, triplets and traditional variation-formulae. He used them particularly well in trios, songs or piano duets; that is to say, he could write an excellent piano *part*, treating it as an orchestral instrument which he was able to play musically but not virtuosically.

Now if we exclude pictorial and literary evocations, such as delighted the French impressionists, we still have an instrument which can suggest other sounds than its own. Long before the Elizabethan spinets took to imitating cuckoos, bells, trumpets or the carman's whistle, keyboard composers had written music as they knew it— the music for concerted voices on which they had been nourished; and the limited compass of vocal texture was easy to find on the regals and virginals. When Schubert wrote the music on which he was nourished, he derived it from quartet and symphony, sonata and serenade; because he also happened to write it for the keyboard we must not suppose that he did not *intend* to write pianoforte music, but once he let his fancy go he thought musically rather than pianist- ically. As a result, the most magnificent of the solo sonatas is the least adequately served by the keyboard.

The two movements of this unfinished Sonata in C major,[1] written in 1825, are the only two pieces for pianoforte solo comparable in conception with the same composer's symphonic achievements, and comparable (as music only, not as pianism) with Beethoven's key- board masterpieces. How obvious is the call for horns and bassoons in the thrilling modulation which makes the first big transition! How difficult it is to believe we are not playing from a transcription as our hands jump from bass *pizzicato* to 'wind' octaves:

How Schubertian is the modulation to B minor, how Schubertian to use that key for his second subject, and what a perfect example of specifically orchestral accompaniment he gives his new subject! In other places we have the sensation of score-reading a string quintet,

[1] Usually referred to as the 'Reliquie' sonata.

only to find ourselves soon among the trombones and flying wind
triplets of the great C major Symphony:

How magnificently effective in every movement of that Symphony
is the repeating of chords with varied placings of the bass; therefore,
knowing the Symphony, how much are we forced to read into
Schubert's use of the same device at the feeble keyboard!

The task of orchestrating this first movement would be a ticklish
one, whereas the glorious *andante* which follows it gives us the instrumental outlay almost precisely, even telling us where to use
tremolo bowing:

The incomplete minuet alternates between keyboard idiom (the repeated chords of which Schubert was so fond—cf. minuet in the G major Sonata or B flat Trio) and the suggestion of horns, bassoons and other instruments. The even more fragmentary finale is totally inept and disappointing as far as it goes. The first few pages are 'complete,' but how hopelessly incomplete! In general, the minuets and finales of the sonatas are their most disappointing movements. The novelties brought off in corresponding movements of symphonies have no parallels, despite the examples of whimsical invention set by Beethoven. (An exception is the scherzo of the A major Sonata of 1828, so obviously derived from Beethoven.)

(b) Miscellaneous Pianoforte Pieces

The smaller pianoforte works are of considerable documentary significance. The *Écossaises*, galops, waltzes, *Ländler* and German dances (including the *Grätzer* and *Atzenbrugger*) may mean little to us, though we sometimes amuse ourselves with the *Valses nobles* and *Valses sentimentales*. Yet these trifles are the chief extant representatives of the popular dance music of *Biedermeier* Vienna. They come from street, suburb, private party and public festival and have more direct jollity in them than the more languishing waltzes of Strauss's Vienna which had moved further towards decadence; here is the true Viennese *Gemütlichkeit* with the flavour of beer, rather than the more heady wine of the later waltz, so alluring, so suggestive of private romance and personal languishment. Allurement of a kind there is in Schubert's dances, but subjective romantic emotions take subsidiary place in a general come-all-ye; these waltzes, whatever Lanner and the older Strauss may owe to them, belong to the Vienna of Beethoven's youth, not to the post-*Biedermeier* period. Their purely musical value is, of course, slight.

Not so the little treasures entitled *Moments musicals*—the plural of the adjective is Schubertian French, so let it stand for once. These pieces, together with other short piano pieces entitled *Klavierstücke* or *Impromptus* or *Allegretto*, make Schubert the first composer to feel himself one of the great new class of unprofessional home-pianists. (Beethoven's *Bagatelles* are chips from a great workshop, and we are aware of the proximity of highly professional works in the grand style.) The *Moments musicaux*, etc., are thus the first of a great line of 'genre pieces'—Schumann's *Scenes of Childhood*, Mendelssohn's *Songs without Words*, Grieg's *Lyric Pieces*—which have endeared the pianoforte to humble folk and opened enchanting vistas to learners of the instrument, young and old. There is no need to quote them here.

None of Schubert's sets of variations is particularly noteworthy, though sets like that in the B flat major *Impromptu*, using the *Rosamunde* entr'acte tune, are pleasantly and delicately laid out, as are others among the favourite *Impromptus*. Schumann thought so highly of these works that he regarded them as the movements of a sonata not assembled—a strange theory!

Increasingly heard in recitals by great players is the pianoforte Fantasy, known to us as *The Wanderer*, though not so called by Schubert; yet the faults one would expect in such a daring experiment—poor transition from section to section, scrappiness or formal imperfections—are hard to find even by those who like neither Schubert nor Liszt. We usually hear the work with Liszt's orchestral framework and support, and we can understand how very attractive the task must have been to Liszt. The 'transformation of themes,' a technique supposedly adumbrated and developed by the later master, is here a *fait accompli*, though the work which most ideally follows Schubert's example on a big scale is Franck's *Symphonic Variations*. The sections of the Fantasy follow the basic tempos of a four-movement symphonic piece, the finale being a

strepitous fugue and the slow movement an *adagio* containing the
short quotation from the song *The Wanderer* followed by meditative
and variation-like developments. The rhythm of Schubert's self-
quotation is the basis of his themes in the opening movement and in
the fugue, and this rhythm holds the work together far more obviously
than the theme-transformations. The latter occur chiefly in the
fourth, scherzo movement, which forms a kind of parody of the
grandiose matter stated in the opening *allegro*:

(c) Piano Duets

When we turn to Schubert's four-handed essays we again find
the grandest conceptions, such as the *Grand Duo*, to be highly orchestral, but without the feeling imparted by the two-handed sonatas
that inner parts are missing. We have instead the illusion that we
are playing duet arrangements of symphonic scores:

The *Grand Duo*, fired by a complete Schubertian orchestral conception, includes not only a scherzo worthy of its first two movements, but a finale whose first held note shows us that Schubert had forgotten that he was writing for the keyboard:

It is therefore a splendid final movement to a splendid work. Its first tune reminds us of the finale to the B flat Trio. (Was it at the back of Brahms's mind when he wrote the corresponding movement of his F minor Quintet?) The tune, like the triplets in the C major Symphony or the saucy march tune in the Octet, prepares the ground excellently for a heavy chordal second subject, but only Schubert, and he in his more inspired moments, could have worked these materials into so magnificent a coda. The *Grand Duo* has been fully discussed in Tovey's *Essays in Musical Analysis* (vol. i) as a symphony orchestrated by Joachim, whose scoring is somewhat Lisztian and therefore too much of its age to be wholly acceptable to some ears. Elsewhere I have quoted the theory mentioned by Tovey that the work may be the lost Gastein Symphony; a rival candidate for that honour is the C major 'Reliquie' Sonata written in the same year, whose two movements would have quite as good a claim but for the story that the lost symphony had all four movements complete in detail.

Almost contemporary with the *Grand Duo* is the *Divertissement à la hongroise*, Op. 54, once the most popular of Schubert duets, probably on account of its local colour—the alternation of melancholy *cantabile*, quick vigorous march themes and Hungarian syncopated dance rhythms. Schubert is said to have been induced to write it after hearing a girl singing local folk music while on his walks near Castle Zseliz in the company of Baron von Schönstein. Two other four-handed pieces on a magnificent scale and written in the last year of his life are the *allegro* in A minor, Op. 144, entitled *Lebensstürme*, and the *Fantasia* in F minor associated with Countess Caroline

Esterházy to whom it was dedicated, some say with hidden love, though concealment, worm i' the bud or no, never seems to have done much damage to Schubert's complexion.

No composer has left such a wealth of music for piano duet, but I think too much is made of the theory that a great deal of the pile represents Schubert's failure to secure performances of major orchestral works. No doubt he suffered keen disappointment from his operatic misadventures, but few composers of thirty can have had a very much better orchestral innings, and had he lived another ten years he might well have heard both the B minor and C major Symphonies—the former finished, perhaps. Moreover, very little of the duet music emulates the pathos and symphonic dimension of the *Grand Duo*. Four-handed writing is essentially a sociable branch of music, and what musician does not recall the four-handed orgies of his bachelor Schubertiads? If he is lucky enough to be married to the right wife, how he must still enjoy the encroachments over the half-way line of a stool made for one, the side-kicks for control of the pedal when phrasing is at variance and the vicious straying of the female little finger-nail! Schubert was a most sociable creature; his best work was done for his circle of friends and for the good ladies and gentlemen on the edge of that circle who gave invitations and held Schubertiads, so that the friends could forgather in larger rooms than those of their lodgings. These more prosperous citizens, the Paumgartners at Steyr, the Pachlers at Graz, the Spauns at Linz, Sophie Müller, the Fröhlich sisters, the Witteczeks, Bruchmanns, Sonnleithners and Hönigs in Vienna—these people were to him what the van Swietens, Lobkowitzes, Rasumovskys, Lichnowskys and other aristocrats of a type fast disappearing had been to the former generation of musicians with their old-time 'academies' and *salons*.

For these middle classes and for the more intimate circle—Schwind, Kupelwieser, Bauernfeld and Co.—the piano duets were written, rather than for awe-struck posterity. Thus, beneath the title of the Rondo in D major, Op. 138, Schubert writes 'Notre amitié est invariable,' while on a sheet of the Children's March in G, for little Faust Pachler to present on his father's birthday, he writes an affectionate letter to Frau Marie Pachler while Jenger adds a longer one to Faust from 'Schwammerl and me.' There is not space to review all the duets in detail, but they contain some of his best light music, and good light music for the piano is not plentiful in substantial lengths. How enjoyable at gatherings of musical folk are works like the *Grand Rondo* in A major, Op. 107, the D major Rondo mentioned above or some of the four-handed overtures! One recalls with pleasure the choice of the first-named of these pieces by two members of a summer school held at Oxford; what Falstaff would have called a 'yarked up' concert was proposed one evening in a dining-hall. The college music library was examined, and one felt that the chosen Rondo was to us and to Schubert's bourgeois friends what serenades and divertimenti had been to a more formal age. This is the same pleasing kind of music as the Octet.

There can be no need to recommend Schubert's duets to under-graduates and music students whose leisure hours offer just the atmo-sphere for a Schubertiad; yet one wishes that some of the duets, important or light, could be included in such concerts as those held during lunch hours in some of our big cities. If great virtuosi cannot unbend to 'glass chandelier' music, let us exalt more humble players, one of whom, however, draws a line at the more clangy sets of variations. Schubert is *not* interesting as a writer of variations, though the duet volumes show sets which, by their dates, represent all stages of his musical growth, and a very slender growth it would appear if judged by variations alone. The polonaises, too, are pretty pedestrian, but nearly all the marches are attractive, especially the *Characteristic Marches*, Op. 121. Why do we hear only the one in D major of the three *Military Marches*? These pieces in general make us wonder whether the friends had a special liking for marches or whether Schubert thought there was an opportunity to score them for military band. Do we not hear the whiff and dub of a parade occasion in the second of the six-eight *Characteristic Marches*?

(d) Works for two instruments

Since he could use good violinists and cellists among both relatives and friends, it is strange that Schubert wrote so little for piano and single stringed instrument. There are but four such works dating from the time after Schubert had drifted from regular practice with his father and brothers, and only two of those are in his advanced, mature style—the Fantasy and the *Rondo brillant* for piano and violin.

The Fantasy, Op. 159, brought forth a good deal of adverse comment at its first performance from critics who, finding sonata form abandoned even in its broadest elements, could not tell what the composer was about. We should hear the work more often, for it is a highly successful and homogeneous attempt on Schubert's part to find a more direct means for his particular expression than sonata movements provided—surely more convincing than the more celebrated *Wanderer* Fantasy for piano. In the violin work the composer does not meander; the opening *adagio*, wherein the piano emulates the tremolo of a whole string body, shows that its purpose is colour, and the movements that follow without any break throughout the work employ a wide compass and range of techniques for both instruments. The lengthy *allegretto* in C major which follows the opening *adagio* makes it clear that, by discarding the formal title 'Sonata' (later composers would feel themselves under no such obligation), Schubert felt free to develop or repeat his themes when and as he liked, as he does only in the middle sections of acknowledged first movements. The middle movement is a most interesting and beautiful *andantino*, consisting of variations on a lengthy lyric in A flat, the finale is a quick march movement in C, broken just before the end by a short *allegretto* reference to the A flat variation theme, but returning *presto* for a vigorous coda.

No less interesting is the fine *Rondo brillant* in B minor, Op. 70, written in 1826, which treats the form with the utmost freedom and contains the composer's characteristic modulations and harmonic purple patches more abundantly than does the Fantasy; both Fantasy and Rondo should appear in programmes with a frequency they deserve. After an introduction with a rhythm like that which opens the *Wanderer* Fantasy, the variations on the song *Trockne Blumen* (No. 18 of the *Maid of the Mill* cycle) are well done, but of no great emotional interest. They were originally intended for flute. The *Duo* in A major, Op. 162, is a sonata, an early work (it dates from 1817) but a very good one, particularly in the quality of its pianoforte accompaniment. The scherzo comes second in order of movements, probably because the finale is an extended movement in scherzo tempo; the third movement consists of the usual *andantino* theme with picturesque variations.

Excellent examples of Schubert's youthful orthodoxy are the three Sonatinas in D major, A minor and G minor, Op. 137, composed in 1816, and no whit inferior as specimens of their kind than are the early symphonies. It is plain that when there are two instruments Schubert takes more trouble to make his piano part pianistic than he does in the solo sonatas. Pieces of the classical epoch more enjoyable for home players it would be difficult to find, and it seems a pity that we do not hear the sonatinas more often in these days when it is fashionable to play even those of the Mozart violin sonatas which are only arrangements from clavier works. The Schubert sonatinas have four movements, except the work in D, which omits a minuet.

One thing remains to be mentioned. This is a melodious but not striking work written in 1824, a Sonata for arpeggione—a bowed instrument played like a cello but with the six strings and fretted keyboard of a guitar. This instrument was invented by one Stauffer of Vienna in 1823, but evidently did not prove a popular success, for Schubert's sonata is the only work that seems to have been written for it. In 1930 Cassadó converted it into a cello Concerto.

CHAPTER XI

THE SONGS [1]

HAD Schubert written for nothing but the human voice and its accompanying pianoforte, both musicians and musical historians would have still regarded him as a major composer. No songs written before his could fit comfortably into a chance-selected Schubert collection, and the songs of later composers which pay Schubert the sincerest flattery—Mahler's beautiful *Rhine Legend*, for instance—cannot be mistaken for Schubert's own. Vocal solos which have been mentioned as immediate 'ancestors' to Schubertian song, such as the *arioso* portions of Zumsteeg's Schiller settings, have no more affinity with Schubert than has folksong, though Zumsteeg, a friend of his poet, was sincerely fired by Schiller's odes. The unique song which anticipates Schubert's art is Mozart's *Violet*.

Schubert, too modest personally and too youthful temperamentally to be thought the father of anything, must yet be regarded as father of the form we know by the inept title 'Art Song.' The proper temple of art songs is a concert hall, but the man who gave us the first, the most and the finest moves us chiefly at a Schubertian gathering of friends, or at home, self-accompanied. Neither operatic air, nor folksong, nor street ballad, a specimen from Schubert may reveal the professional skill, the freshness and the fascination of all three, and one may well ask: 'Why did no such song exist before Schubert?' The Elizabethans had the lyric poets and the musicians, but their idioms are of courtly derivation, and it is possible for songs to be domestic though not homely; the eighteenth century developed the *salon*, which could be intimate, even bohemian, yet far removed from the romantic-bourgeois Schubertiad.

Our legacy of Schubertian song is largely attributable to the synchronized confluence of three phenomena: first the new German lyric verse, homely even when fancifully peopled with the personages of pastoral convention; secondly the improved pianoforte, which

[1] It is foolish to call Schubert's songs *Lieder* unless we call Fauré's *Mélodies*, etc. *Lied* denotes no distinctive genre of German song between the *Lieder* of Luther's friends and those of today.

found its way into drawing-room, farmstead and aesthetic bachelor apartment in time to wed its suggestive tones to the lyric poetry; thirdly the birth of young Schubert in the city whose *Biedermeier* period probably saw a more musical and romantically minded population than has ever been known in a European capital. Schubert loved the verse, the instrument, the city. He recognized in Beethoven one who had sounded a range of poetic expression from the instrument without specific reference to the verse, and had there been no Beethoven, it is highly probable that Schubertian song would not have been of the same quality; for Schubert, inheriting a great keyboard technique and naturally responding to lyric poetry, was but an amateurish versifier and made no remarkable advances of technique in his solo writing for the pianoforte. As for Schubertian melody, that would have been poured out had there been neither verse nor keyboard.

Schubertian song is so complete an alchemy that we can rejoice in the melody while being unaware that it is rarely an entity like the melody of folksong; we recall it with at least some evocation of its pacing accompaniment. The perfect union of poetry, instrument and personality is immediately recognized, however profitless the attempt to define. In his great study of Schubert's songs Richard Capell opens with a chapter entitled 'Schubert's Sentiment,' pointing therein to its primary quality in the words:

All his songs are the songs of youth. Poets have told of times when youth had the world to itself . . . but Theocritus and Boccaccio were wise compared with Schubert, who knew nothing but the rapture and poignancy of first sensations, the loss of which is the beginning of wisdom. The poets have had to invent worlds unworldly enough to allow youth to wonder, love, and suffer purely youthfully; but such a world was naturally Schubert's.

Let the truth of this be shown by recalling merely the songs dealing with love, happy or unhappy, and asking: Which one enables us to meet the expression of full sexual love? Where is the erotic warmth of Schumann's *Ich grolle nicht* or *Im wunderschönen Monat Mai*, of Brahms's *Sapphic Ode* or Wolf's *Lebe wohl*? It is no explanation that romantic harmony had not developed to its luxurious stage; the erotic emotions of Elvira, expressed by Mozart in the last bars of her recitative 'In quali eccessi,' are as adult, as sexual, as those of Isolde, and some of the phrases might well be taken from their context and passed as coming from Wagner's drama; moreover the composer whose command of colour and modulation made the pathos of *The Winter Journey* or of the unfinished Symphony could have turned it to the expression of adult eroticism had such an emotion existed in his lyrical world. It is not suggested that Schubert's real sexual life (about which we know so little that suggestion is either malicious or exculpatory) was a simple, pastoral affair; however long a particular attachment lasted, we cannot regard the Schubert of the songs as its participant or protagonist if he knew 'more than the rapture and poignancy of first sensations.' Is it possible to think of a married Schubert? Or a paterfamilias Schubert? Or even a Don Juan Schubert? If it were, we should have to write of him as an enigmatic dual personality, and submit a biography at variance with the picture communicated by the personality of the songs. Adult only as a faun is adult, the songster has made some of us seek in *The Winter Journey* and *Schwanengesang* a deeper, more speculative Schubert than the composer of the Mill Cycle. The quest is a mistaken one. Schubert responded directly, as would a child, to a pathos more poignant and prevalent than in former verses from the same pen, but nothing was elicited from him 'too deep for tears,' however pitiful the lover or the organ-grinder, however bleak their prospects.

Few statements are more misleading than those which accuse Schubert of setting a vast quantity of greeting-card verse, or of having no literary taste whatever. Schubert had a very definite taste in verse; but it was the taste of a songster, not of a philosopher or literary aesthete. In other words he knew just the kind of verse which suggests musical expression, and for seventy-one songs he found it in Goethe. Could he have done better? The chief reason for his getting verses from a score of little verse-spinners, who compare with Goethe only through Schubert, was that only seventy-one Goethe lyrics, instead of six hundred and six, fulfilled the demands made in the composer's quick scrutiny. Let us compare that scrutiny, albeit unconscious, hasty, instinctive, with the excellent *literary* scrutiny of our highly educated modern song writers. These ambitious men are not content to let music express 'nothing but the rapture and poignancy of first sensations'; not one but many young English and American composers have tried to set poems by Donne or Hardy, or sonnets by Shakespeare or Milton, and in doing so fail either because single lines are far too sententious to be prolonged by the process of singing or because the poetic form (especially with sonnets) has been sacrificed without the creation of a new musical form, or because in straining to illuminate each recalcitrant image and meaning of the words, the musical texture is usually congested, inconsistent and formless. Delius had the sense, in his great choral setting of *Sea Drift,* to miss out the disquisition or reflection on death which a poet might consider to be the most important part of Whitman's piece. Schubert chose to make a setting of Cibber's *Blind Boy* ('O say what is that thing called Light'), the sentiment of which is simple and sufficiently wide-spread to evoke just one strain of musical pathos; but the several modern composers who have attempted Milton's sonnet *On his Blindness* remind one of Aldous Huxley's sentence-meet-for-translation: 'Eupompus added splendour to art by numbers.' Again, Shelley's *Music when soft voices die* may be a lyric, and a very musical lyric, turning on a single thought presented by three or four different images. But is that thought a musical one? Has not a composer to think several times when tempted to set the poem? Had he not better leave it alone?

Schubert never thought several times, nor did he leave a verse alone if he was ever inclined to set it; that is why he lit on the superficial image of certain of Goethe's lyrics and did not notice (at least musically) the deeper significance they contained. It was his good fortune to be born in an age which served him with over ninety poets whose verses are innocent of any significance beyond the expression of a mood or the mention of a picturesque situation. For some reason he missed Eichendorff; he was just in time to catch Heine. If some of his best songs were inspired by Goethe, so were at least as many by his friend Mayrhofer, who supplies forty-seven poems, hardly a single one bringing an inferior song from Schubert. This shows that, though the picturesque verses of Mayrhofer, Müller, Schober, even Hölty, have a smaller literary content than Goethe's, Schubert was not concerned with the more in Goethe. He could set Mayrhofer to the full; he could set Goethe only to the Mayrhofer content. Schubert, called by Liszt 'the most poetic musician ever,' should rather be called 'the most musician-like musician ever' in his attitude towards poetry. Perhaps that is why we find so few songs of the finest Schubertian quality to Schiller's words. Of the forty-two Schiller settings the mind immediately recalls only the *Group from Tartarus* and *Dithyramb*. It is doubtful whether he would have set so many Schiller poems but for the fact that, since German schoolboys are brought up on Schiller, Schubert must have become familiar with this poet before others; but to wring limpid music from Schiller's lofty abstractions is like trying to write Cicero in limericks.

Schubert was not without criteria of verse, any more than he was without love for it; but the criteria were expressed only implicitly. We deduce them from the kind of poem which inspired the greatest songs. The right rhythm, the right sequence of images, the right situation, mood or atmosphere generated the musical conception, which could only be in terms of the music he knew, and all Vienna knew—the kind of music found in Beethoven's piano sonatas. Could not the first or second themes of the 'Waldstein,' 'Moonlight' or 'Appassionata,' or of a dozen other sonatas, form the opening piano music to a Schubert song? Are not the running water suggestions which accompany the Mill Songs derived from the stock figurations of Viennese keyboard technique? But with what poetic suggestion, what subtle diversity from song to song! And as Schubert was not an inventive piano composer, it can be only the impress of poetry that makes him so in his songs. There was no certainty that he would respond consistently and magically to every poem or to every part of a poem. Felicitous enough is the strophic setting and accompaniment to the famous *Trout*, but is there not manoeuvring in the final section? Perfect indeed are *Erl King* and *Gretchen* of his eighteenth year, but many an inferior song followed. We are astounded when we ask: Where are the ancestors of *Erl King* and *Gretchen*? They are without ancestry, for no previous composer responded to that kind of poetry in the same way.

It does not seem generally acknowledged that Beethoven, had his mind been of a different, less architectonic order, might have written

more songs of a Schubertian type. Beethoven's more ambitious
vocal essays are well aired, but there are one or two little songs that
sound strangely like Schubert, and which Schubert may have heard,
though it is not likely that he did.[1] The song quoted below
comes from *Egmont*; it shows not only the Schubertian 'echo' of
vocal cadences by the accompaniment, but Schubert's favourite
device of repeating a major musical phrase in a minor key:

Freud-voll und leid-voll, ge-dank-en-voll sein

Yet it is hard to find ancestry even for the simple strophic songs.
Occasional pieces like the first song of the Mill cycle, *Wandering,*
may show the strophic symmetry of German folksong, plus the echo
mentioned above; but the marvel of most Schubert songs is that they
keep the spontaneity of a four-square folk or street song while using
various means for variety which one cannot bring oneself to call
'devices.' The opening phrase of *Who is Silvia?* is treated sequentially,
but in how many variants? Here are two transformations; the
cadences of the following phrases are similarly varied:

and what magic produced these octave leaps:

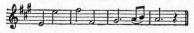

which might otherwise have been these dull ascending notes?

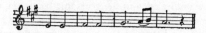

[1] Though he must certainly have known some of the songs by Zelter
and Reichardt, who had written several Goethe settings, including *The
King of Thule, Shepherd's Lament* and *Little Hedgerose.* They are often very
well turned, in the Schubertian manner, with every quality but the personal
Schubertian magic.

This may be art, but its spontaneity feels strangely like nature. We look for its parallel, not in German, but in English or Irish folksongs like *The Flight of the Earls* or the 'Londonderry Air.' But there is a vast difference between Schubert and folksong. *Du bist die Ruh* (there are some Schubert songs to which one cannot easily refer except by their German titles) may be simplicity itself, but it depends on its accompanying chords, on Schubert's particular inversions of those chords and on his keyboard disposal of the notes in those chords. So does *Silvia*. Successive notes of 'That all our swains commend her' form the component intervals of chords; the accompaniment, though it suggest the thrumming of a lute, is pianistic, especially in the crossing hands of its 'echoes'; and the keyboard is so essential that a singer would foreshorten the very first note of the song but for the measuring quavers beneath. Moreover, like most Schubert songs, *Silvia* is constructed on sequences or semi/sequences of short phrases, as are the lyrical movements of Viennese instrumental classics.

A word concerning performance may not be untimely. The collaboration of singer and player is more than usually important in Schubert. Neither is soloist; neither must be effaced. In strophic songs both must use the same kind of intelligence that prevents the reading of blank verse like a sing/song of alternate strong and weak syllables. For Schubert, unlike Hugo Wolf, never hesitates to bend metrical exactitude to his primary musical conception, though his treatment of verse is less cavalier than that of Brahms.

His first song, *Hagar's Lament*, written in 1811, is representative of the whole series of ballad/cantatas which followed and transcended the Schiller cantatas of Zumsteeg. It sprawls through many movements and many keys. There followed the *Maiden's Lament* and *A Corpse Fantasy,* in which Schiller anticipates the sensory grisliness of Edgar Allan Poe. Another essay in the gruesome belonging to this period is *The Parricide,* to words by one Pfeffel. Not till we come to the first strophic song, a setting of Rochlitz's *Lament,* written in 1812, do we taste the mature Schubert. The opening words:

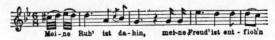
Mei-ne Ruh' ist da-hin, mei-ne Freud' ist ent - floh'n

force a comparison with *Gretchen,* which is the first supremely great song. That it took a supremely great poet to fire the composer to an achievement which he never excelled may be a coincidence, but *Margaret at the Spinning-wheel* was not written till 1814. Between it and the *Lament* quoted above Schubert wrote one or two good songs, including a setting of Pope's *Vital spark of heavenly flame* in a translation by Herder, and a whole spate of short and sweet little pieces to poems by Matthisson.

Margaret at the Spinning-wheel comes like a bolt from the blue: we cannot explain the sources of its marvellous elements, not one of which is an entity to be examined alone—the astounding accompaniment, the boy's understanding of Margaret's suffering and passion, the stopping of the treadle at the most intense moment of her false vision, the masterly recurrence of the opening lines at the end of the song. Nor can we explain why, after this perfect thing, inferior songs are found among others of the same year, some being of the old ballad-cantata kind. The only other good songs of 1814 are Goethe's *Shepherd's Lament* and the first Mayrhofer setting, *By the Lake.*

The first great vintage year is 1815. Schubert has left school in more senses than one, though he is employed as a schoolmaster. After yet more churchyard scenes and ballad-cantatas, he turns to Schiller and sets *Hector's Farewell* in dialogue form between the hero and Andromache, following it first with the *Ode to Joy,* used by Beethoven in the choral finale, then with a second setting of *The Maiden's Lament*—the favourite of his three dealings with this particular Schiller text. Of the one hundred and forty songs poured forth during the year 1815, fifteen are to Schiller's texts and thirty to Goethe's. Before we come to the second supreme Goethe song, *Erl King,* written at the end of the year, we have to pause over smaller gems. Beautiful though some of Schubert's settings of poems by Hölty may be, Brahms's songs *May Night* and *To the Nightingale* are of a loveliness that makes us approach Schubert's treatments of the same poems as museum pieces. His meeting with sagas from Ossian, such as *The Death of Oscar,* prompted him to lengthy essays which are so far an advance upon his earlier ballad-cantatas as to resemble narrative portions from Wagner's *Ring* dramas.

The Goethe songs of 1815 merit an essay to themselves—but a profitless one. What a galaxy they are!—*To Mignon, Calm Sea, Wayfarer's Night-song, Restless Love, Little Hedgerose, Knowst thou the Land, To the Moon, First Bereavement, Erl King*. What similarity is there between them and previous songs? Three or four years earlier many of these Goethe lyrics had been made into passable songs by composers whose names occasionally appear in albums of German song, but who are now interesting chiefly because they were first in the field with poems afterwards used by Schubert, such as *The King of Thule, Little Hedgerose* or *The Shepherd's Lament*. Schubert's settings of these have made us regard the earlier settings as we might have regarded his own songs if he had composed only the settings of verses by Hölty which brought forth the best of Brahms. Obviously the metres, figures and other ingredients of these songs had sources inherited by Schubert, but the tracing of the sources is difficult; one might as well ask from which of the old dance movements— sicilienne, sarabande, etc.—Mozart derived this or that andante or rondo. Let us consider just the most famous of these Goethe songs.

Erl King was written without aid from the pianoforte. Mayrhofer found Schubert in a state of extreme excitement after reading the poem. He read it again aloud, and after writing his sketch hurried off with Mayrhofer and Spaun to the piano in his old school music-room. The point to notice is that the conception was complete, the sketch written down for the whole ballad, including the surprising minor ninths at the cry 'My Father!' Temperament, age, artistic criteria may cause any one of us to call some of the *Winter Journey* songs, or even *Gretchen*, greater than *Erl King*, since the appeal of Goethe's ballad is direct and melodramatic. But the ballad was irresistible to Schubert, and the word 'irresistible' is that which we apply to Schubert's setting. There are said to be about seventy *Erl King* songs; aesthetes, who may have less liking for Schubert's familiar version just because it is the best-known, are wont to tell us that other settings, especially Loewe's, makes points which Schubert missed. Sir George Henschel, whose opinion is surely to be respected, favoured Loewe rather than Schubert, and Tovey was moved to write a masterly page for the defence of Schubert. One cannot help siding with Tovey in his opinion that Schubert missed nothing, but that in this song, as in others, instinct told him what to sacrifice that the whole might be irresistible. No other setting of *Erl King* is irresistible; none is such a masterpiece of form. Berlioz took a risk in scoring it for orchestra, but even as it is, it makes a perfect symphonic entity, a perfect example of the fact that form is more than the filling of a formal mould; for in his lavishness Schubert uses different music in the two episodes wherein the Erl King entices the lad, the second being faster and more cogent. No one element in the song is to be detached and admired; the accompaniment is marvellous, but there are pages in *Fidelio*, in the Beethoven piano sonatas, even in the Mozart 'fantasy' sonata, that show its ancestry; the voice part is a series of short cumu-lative phrases, always urging to a keystone phrase which the theorist could name as one of a chain of full closes. Not one phrase is a great tune. Why then is the whole such a purposeful, irresistible masterpiece? Because the poem is such—a point rarely recognized. Among a number of eldritch, pseudo-Gothic compilations in the name of balladry, Goethe's *Erl King* rings as true as does Coleridge's *Ancient Mariner*. It impressed young Schubert as a whole piece, and he responded with a complete musical inspiration.

In the following year another song to words by one Schmidt began in a manner which indicates the composer of *Erl King*, but which, despite its compactness, shows how unconsciously Schubert produced the greater, more truly *durchkomponiert* song to the greater poem. *The Wanderer* would not receive special mention, although singers and players both love its range of moods and tempos, did it not happen to be the song most popular in Schubert's lifetime, with the exception of *Erl King* itself. At its printing in 1821 the Patriarch Pyrker enclosed twenty ducats in a very complimentary letter to the composer, who had dedicated *The Wanderer* to the kindly prelate. Other songs of 1816 show a great increase in the range of poets sought by Schubert, probably through the influence of Mayrhofer, whom he had known since 1814. Even so, the best song of the year is to a Goethe poem; again it is the last song of its year. With Zara-thustrian love of life the poet asks Time, the Postilion, to rush on and spare not the horses: let life be devoured, not munched; experience be crowded, not tediously spun. *Postilion Chronos* is a song of ardent and defiant youth. Schubert's galloping six-eight rhythm does not relax its masculinity below the strength *forte,* for the song has weight as well as impetuosity. Youth's visions pass between modulations which are arresting even in Schubert:

Space does not allow a review of the many short songs and few long ones made to texts by various minor poets during this fruitful period. Mayrhofer's own verses were as well served by the com-poser as any, whether they recall mythology with more modern and subjective poignancy, as in *Memnon,* or dwell on the pastoral situations of youthful verse, as in *The Fisher,* or of Austrian picture-postcards, as in *The Alpine Hunter,* of folk legend, as in *Erlaf Lake,* or of subjective emotions, as in the lengthy *Loneliness.* Between these songs and the famous song-cycles Schubert wrote the pieces that have most need of exploration: recitalists, for some strange reason, tend to give us songs written by the marvellous youth in 1815, 1816 or 1817, and then to jump from these to the cycles. The in-quiring musician may find facets of Schubert's character which will give surprise, and very pleasant surprise, among the songs written just after the composer had finally turned his back on schoolmastering. There is, for instance, his solemn and proud setting of Goethe's *Prometheus,* which suffers no whit from comparison with Wolf's great song to the same text. Schubert's is a dignified and power-ful defiance of a tyrant; Wolf's a tortured utterance of despair. Where are more wonderful Schubertian modulations than in the adoring pantheism of *The Bounds of Mankind (Grenzen der Menschheit)*?

Where is a more subtle suggestion of cajoling dalliance than in *Secrets*, the only well-known song of a number of settings of Goethe's *Divan* poems?[1] How rarely we hear the Suleika songs, or the Hymns to verses of Novalis, the lovely setting of Mayrhofer's *Sunset* or the tumultuous nature-piece *In the Forest* to Schlegel's poem of a thunderstorm at night!

The first of the cycles, *The Fair Maid of the Mill,* hardly needs exploration. Here, if anywhere, is the picturesque Schubert transcending himself; for the pretty songs of his early days, which we should have enjoyed for themselves but for the Mill cycle, look now only like preparatory essays for *Wandering, Whither?* and *Mine.* These songs, with their water-music and immediately attractive tunes, are eagerly embraced by players and singers, and taken, quite unjustifiably, out of their context to be put into collections of songs—either Schubert collections or miscellaneous anthologies. But the greater demands upon good singing and true musicianship are made by those numbers wherein the brook hardly murmurs and wherein

[1] The word 'Divan' is from the Persian, and means 'anthology' or 'cycle' of verses.

that side of Schubert's nature which is more obviously manifest in later songs deals with the emotional misgivings of his journeyman-lover. Such are the songs *Pause,* in which Schubert makes wonderful play with a recurrent piano motive (representing a short recollection of lute music, for the miller's lute hangs on the wall during his uncertainty) and *Withered Flowers* (unfortunately treated later as a theme for flute and piano variations), a miniature dead march which is so sincere that nobody could parody it or smile at the fanciful conception. The same remark could be made of the songs with the fantastic titles *Favourite Colour* and *Detested Colour.*

Queasy though may seem one's harping on the neglected songs, since the popular ones are rightly those which are easiest to perform and which have the most immediate attraction, it can safely be said that between the Mill cycle in 1823 and *The Winter Journey* in 1827 Schubert wrote a number of songs which are among his greatest, and which refute the statement sometimes heard that with Schubert there is no progress, only a Peter Pan prolongation of childhood. This was the period of his finest chamber works, sonatas and four-handed compositions. The Winter songs begin really in the year of the Mill cycle, for the last settings of 1823 are four of great loveliness from Rückert, the orientalist. It speaks much of Schubert's avidity for new verse that Ruckert's poems were set very soon after their publication. They are anticipated in spirit, though not in quality, by the *Divan* settings from Goethe. Their range may be judged by comparing the introduction to the first, *Here is fragrance Dass sie hier gewesen*), and that to the last, *Veteran's Song (Griesengesang)*; the first breathes the incense of youthful infatuation:

The other declares that the memory of romantic days is warm to the heart of one whose youth is well past:

The gem of the Rückert songs (and when sung and played well it seems the loveliest of all songs) is *Thou art repose* (*Du bist die Ruh*). Of this song Capell writes:

Singers frequently attempt *Du bist die Ruh* having only the lightest notion of its requirements. The music is, of course, limpidness itself: the scope obvious. It remains one of the most difficult songs in existence, taxing the technical control as severely as the singer's taste. An exquisitely refined *mezza voce* is called for in the greater part of it, and then a power of expansion on the two scales. There is no cover for a fault; and the more accomplished the artist, the more seriously will he consider the undertaking.

Unfortunately certain she-artists have rushed into recording studios where better singers have feared to tread.

In 1824 Schubert wrote his last settings of Mayrhofer poems, and they are among the finest. The composer seemed to understand the strange assertiveness of his poet friend—assertive only in writing— and to recognize the tragedy of a soul who found peace only in escape. Thus *Victory* (*Der Sieg*), in which Mayrhofer declares that the poet has broken the bonds of human trouble and found the key to unearthly happiness, is a deep, solemn song, rather than a jubilant one; *Evening Star*, with harmony as thin as it is full in the former song, expresses the sadness of a lone-ganger, rather than the sweet pangs of love; and *The Gondolier*, a nocturne which introduces the striking of the midnight chimes from St. Mark's, has a somewhat ghostly liquidity. Only one of these Mayrhofer songs, and that the grandest, makes its phrases soar entirely exultantly. This is *Auflösung*, a title one is loth to translate except by the word 'Assumption' as used in Catholic hagiology. A song not to be passed by without comment, for it is one of Schubert's most wonderful, is *The Young Nun*, though by it alone is the poet Craigher remembered. The spirit of *Erl King* and *Chronos* is revived in the furious opening lines, depicting a night of fearful wind, thunder and lightning; half-way through, the music moves to the major key; the young nun has looked fearlessly upon the storm, which, like the storms of passion, is but the superficial raging of a beneficent nature—for the young nun is a pantheist! The marvel of Schubert's piece lies in the fact that, even at the end, when we hear the serene call of the chapel bell, the raging of the elements is still present in the background. We have here something like a musical counterpart to the 'Madonna of the Rocks'; only genius could have expressed spiritual serenity and natural turbulence simultaneously. Even during the final 'Hallelujah' we are aware of the power of natural forces. Indeed the young nun seems very fond of the storm she despises!

The most important songs of 1825 are those from Walter Scott's *Lady of the Lake*; they are seen often enough in English albums to need little comment. The present writer may be deceived in thinking that the chivalric numbers, such as *Huntsman, rest*, with its horn-calls, or *My hawk is tired* (*Lay of the Imprisoned Huntsman*), with its martial rhythm, so reflect Schubert's reaction to the spirit of his poet that they are noticeably without Schubert's essential Teutonism. It seems that only the well-known *Ave Maria*, wherein the accompaniment recalls Ellen's harp-playing, shows the spirit of German romanticism.

In the following year Schubert wrote his last Goethe songs, and these certainly need more frequent attention from our singers. The lyrics are from *Wilhelm Meister*, to which Schubert had gone before for the songs of Mignon and the Harper; indeed the duet called *Mignon and the Harper* written at this time is no other than *Who has ever known the pangs* (*Nur wer die Sehnsucht kennt*), which Schubert set no less than six times, the present duet being fine enough, though less expressive of the spirit of the poem as a whole than is the previous, best-known setting. This fact may show how music does best when guided by musical sensitivity; by writing a duet setting Schubert let himself be guided by Goethe's own 'stage directions.' The two Op. 62 songs simply known as *Mignon's Song* are each a resetting of words which formerly had brought childlike music from Schubert, but which now, in a greater conception, are made deeply tragic, reflecting the visions of a Mignon whom suffering has aged prematurely, and who in thoughts of her pathetic death prays that she may be born again to a youth that shall not fade or be broken. These last Goethe settings of 1826 bring us near to the spirit of the *Winter Journey* cycle which was to follow in the next year; it is there/ fore to be expected that, as we examine other songs which precede that cycle, our interest will be roused rather by the more pathetic compositions than by the well/known Shakespeare songs—*Hark, hark, the lark, Silvia, Come, thou monarch of the vine*—or the equally attractive *Cradle Song* (Seidl) and *Fisherman's Ditty*. Yet only snob/ bery can fail to marvel at the perfection of these favourites. The spirit of Schubert's later songs is to be observed in several of this year's settings of poems by the schoolmaster Johann Seidl, whom the com/ poser honoured in his very last song, *Pigeon Post,* and in the dedication of his four *Refrain Songs*. The 1826 *Longing* is the most serious song with that common title (*Sehnsucht*) from Schubert's pen; *The Way/ farer to the Moon* is comparable with the marching song *The Signpost* in *The Winter Journey,* using the technique of a persistent tramping rhythm. But the finest of the Seidl songs is *The Passing/bell,* suffused with a rich melancholy. Like Death, in *Death and the Maiden,* the passing/bell which tolls in almost every bar of the song is the benign symbol of reunion to true hearts that have been parted. Although the song is strophic, each of its five verses differs, not in melody but in cadences and rich modulations—perhaps to a minor key where before there has been a major. Enjoyable as are the ingenuous *Refrain Songs,* written later in the year, they are trifling beside *The Passing/bell* and other Seidl songs in the first group.

An account has been given elsewhere of the composer's circum/ stances during the writing of the *Winter Journey* cycle in two parts of the year 1827; stress was also given to the point that we have no evidence that anything but the pathos of Müller's second set of poems brought out the strong musical contrast between this cycle and the Mill Songs. That Schubert intended *The Winter Journey* to be sung in series is shown by the fact that he set all twenty/four of Müller's poems, making no omissions as he had done from the *Fair Maid of the Mill* volume. Yet *The Winter Journey* is in some ways less compact than the Mill Cycle: there is nothing comparable with the recurrent music of running water, and any one song can be put in a recital as a self-sufficient masterpiece, representative of others among its fellows. The hapless lover goes alone; every artist goes alone; but Schubert's youth seems to have taken some time to know it and is still in the pitiful state wherein, without faith, there is no permanent courage. Here, as before, is only 'the poignancy of first sensations' with the smallest extra of reflection. But the prevailing theme of loneliness is what makes the *Winter Journey* songs into a cycle, and the musician's delight is in the recognition of the many kinds of rhythm, harmony and musical techniques by which Schubert expresses the same dominant motive. It seems profitless to search out contrasts and parallels between single songs of Müller's two volumes. Can we imagine Schubert himself, during the creation of any single *Winter Journey* song, thinking about anything else, about any previous song? People have found a keyboard figuration, a turn of cadence in the one cycle to resemble one in another. Is that remarkable? What was personal in Schubert, and what was derived from Beethoven's piano sonatas, did not disappear just because new verses called for a new seriousness.

The quality of the *Winter Journey* songs forbids us to speak of any as better than another; we can only speak of those which are more popular or make a more immediate appeal. They will include those with the characteristic Schubertian march rhythm—the stealthy *andante con moto* found in the C major Symphony—which begins the journey with the song *Good Night* and returns in *Frozen Tears* and *The Signpost*. The methods by which a note of pathos is brought into songs in this cycle, even when their rhythms and melodies show similarities with other Schubert songs, are so varied and subtle as to defy classification. The pathetic note may lie in modulation or tonal shift, as in *The Signpost*:

in a masterly use of our old friend the Neapolitan sixth:

as in *Solitude* (*Einsamkeit*), or in the sudden use of plain octaves after full chords, as in *Frozen Tears*:

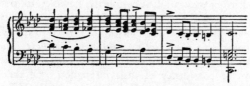

And is it fanciful to declare that the April tearfulness of *A Dream of Spring* (*Frühlingstraum*), a song which finishes on a minor chord, could not possibly belong to the Mill Cycle?

As *The Winter Journey* proceeds, the poems move from the defiance and exhilaration of wild winter storms to the rambling fancies of a distraught and weary creature: how tired are the churchy harmonies of *The Wayside Inn,* the graveyard into which the poor traveller peers, without hint of any grisly thought; with what languid acceptance he sings of *The Mock Suns*; and in what song are bleakness, pathos and resignation combined as in *The Organ Grinder*? Capell writes of this song:

Given a thousand guesses, no one could have said that the last song would be at all like this. The madman meets a beggar, links with him his fortune. . . . Almost any one else [but Schubert] would have overdone it. The lamentations of seventy pages have died away. We may read anything or nothing much into the cleared scene. All that happens is the drone and tinkle of the hurdy-gurdy, whose two-bar tune enters inter-mittently between the wanderer's half-numb sentences. . . . Only near the end is there a glimmer of warmth.

Between *The Winter Journey* and his death in the following year Schubert wrote several songs worthy of the other great music of his last year, and worthy to follow the great cycle of 1827. Such are the rapturous spring song *Das Lied im Grünen,* the Wallenstein drinking-song, or the well-known barcarolle *To be sung on the Water,* with its cascading accompaniment and charming alternation of minor and major modes. It is customary, however, to speak of his last songs, to seven Rellstab and six Heine poems, as if they were a cycle, though the name *Schwanengesang* was given to the collection, after the composer's death, by its publisher, Haslinger, who added Seidl's *Pigeon Post* as a fourteenth. They certainly make a col-lection by the consistency of their inspiration. Of the Rellstab settings the first is a happy brookside love-song of the Mill type; the accompanimental 'echoes' of this *Love Message (Liebesbotschaft)* might well be mistaken for their companions in the *Maid of the Mill* cycle:

And if, in the first Rellstab song, Schubert gave us his last rippling brook, so in the next he wrote his last scenic ballad of several dramatic movements. This *Warrior's Foreboding* gives ample scope for poetic suggestion. A heavy opening section shows us the soldier, awake and heavy-hearted while his camp comrades lie in deep sleep; a fast-moving section then recalls the happy sleep and dream which were once enjoyed; the repeated quavers of *Erl King* are evoked as the words pass to 'Here by the flickering light, the weapons of war glint, and I would fain avoid them.' There follows an *agitato* section in which the soldier pulls himself together to face whatever fortune will bring, growing to a fateful stillness at the words 'Soon falls on me unbroken sleep.' He wishes his loved one good night and the music passes quietly to the heavy dactylic rhythm of its opening.

No song is more universally admired, and therefore badly sung, than the Rellstab *Serenade*; and none is more admired of musicians than the one which follows, *Resting-place (Aufenthalt)*. This song is a *locus classicus* of the direct impress of verbal stress on its composer's mind—one of the most clear examples, even in Schubert, of music which might more easily be called a translation than a setting:

We may be deeply thankful that Schubert lived long enough to set six of Heine's poems before his song-making was finished. After the tragic, portentous *Atlas,* with music that wonderfully expresses the burden of the proud heart condemned to bear the world's troubles, we have a gentle song which forces us at once to see the anticipation of Schumann's art, for we cannot help thinking of Schumann at the mention of Heine, and *Her Portrait* would seem Schumannesque even without our knowing its poet. *Fishermaiden* is a happy, lilting six-eight song, with an open-air melody that could have been written only by the composer of *Hark, hark, the lark.* Then, for the last three Heine songs, come three of Schubert's greatest songs in his serious, even sinister mood. *The Town* is a sombre vignette, which seeks to give us atmosphere rather than melody: the vocal line is a series of short phrases spoken with as close a recitation of the words as would occur in a monologue with pianoforte accompaniment. Some of these phrases are intoned to one note with its near neighbours, maybe as appoggiaturas. The impression of a city wrapped in chilly mist, the city in which the beholder lost his love, his all, is conveyed in this recitative-like voice part, whispered over low octave rumblings and vague diminished-seventh arpeggios. Only towards the end, in angry declamation, does the song rise to *forte.* *By the Sea,* like *Du bist die Ruh,* looks simplicity itself, but is a searching test for voice and hands. The picture evoked is like that of the Elgar 'Enigma' Variation which portrays the breadth, depth and utter level of the sea spreading to an evening horizon. Like the Elgar clarinet which quotes *Calm Sea and Prosperous Voyage,* Schubert's singer has to make gradation of tone from a basic *mezza voce,* yet suggest depths of feeling. It is as difficult for such a technique not to seem merely restrained and negative, as it is for the tremolo parts of the accompaniment to impart warmth to their *pianissimo* without spoiling the breadth of the seascape by undue agitation.

The atmosphere of the last Heine song, *Der Doppelgänger,* is as difficult to translate into words as the German title is difficult to translate into English. Schubert's use of chords in certain inversions, or with certain spacings of their component intervals—in this case his doubling of the treble notes by parallel notes two octaves lower— is not to be explained in terms of text-book harmony. Surely he did not think of a single chord just as the right one between other chords, or as the result of parts flowing from a previous chord. A chord to him suggested a certain atmosphere; he decided on his chord after he knew his poem. This particular poem, which one has seen translated under various titles—*The Wraith, The Shadow, The Spectral Self*—tells of a man who, at dead of night, looks at an empty house; like Scrooge, he sees the figure of himself in former days. 'Horrible! I can see my own face now the moon has emerged. Why does the figure mock the torments I endured there all those years ago?' The setting of these words, like that of another Heine poem, *The Town,* shows the use of a technique not perfected by Schubert before discovering Heine. Of the former song, Capell writes: 'Were unimaginable developments latent? Or is the new quality in this last music only an innocent reflection of the new-found, different poet?' We are not aware, till we look at the song after already playing or singing it several times, that the setting is strophic and in balanced phrases, so recitative-like and declamatory is the vocal line, so subtle the variation on the four hollow, tolling chords of the piano part, and so sombre and slow the pace of the music. Indeed, climax comes not from any purely musical movement, but from the intensity of the poem itself and the horrified outcry of the man speaking. Nobody will deny that this song is without rival as a musical clothing of its poem. It is not musically difficult. It just happens that not every musician is poet enough to sing it.

Schubert, being what he was, did not go from the world in a way dramatically sensational, leaving *Doppelgänger* as his last song. He had instead to leave us *Pigeon Post,* a playful countrified polka-song, from which we may suppose that, had he lived another year, the brook would have rippled again, the lover uttered sweet sadness in another barcarolle, the churchyard offered peace to another weary wanderer, the knight made chivalric love to his lady once more, the midnight wind blasted and roared in the forest to another ballad of terror or courage, and the fields and hedgerows smiled and blossomed into another spring.[1] Can we suppose that any Schubert song was to come that would not have expressed 'the rapture and poignancy of first sensations'?

[1] Despite his declared intention to compose no more songs.

APPENDICES

APPENDIX A

CALENDAR

Figures in brackets denote the age reached by the person mentioned during the year in question.)

Year	Age	Life	Contemporary Musicians
1797		Franz Peter Schubert born, Jan. 31, in Vienna, son of Franz Schubert (*c.* 33), a schoolmaster.	Donizetti born, Nov. 25. Albrechtsberger aged 61; Auber 15; Beethoven 27; Bishop 11; Boccherini 44; Boïeldieu 22; Catel 24; Cherubini 37; Cimarosa 48; Clementi 45; Czerny 6; Dittersdorf 58; Dussek 36; Eybler 32; Field 15; Gossec 63; Grétry 56; Gyrowetz 34; Haydn 65; Hérold 6; Hummel 19; Kozeluch 43; Lesueur 37; Loewe 1; Marschner 2; Méhul 34; Mercadante 2; Meyerbeer 6; Monsigny 68; Paer 26; Paisiello 56; Piccinni 69; Pleyel 40; Reichardt 45; Rossini 5; Salieri 47; Sarti 68; Schenk 36; Seyfried 21; Spohr 13; Spontini 23; Viotti 44; Vogler 48; Wanhal 58; Weber 11; Weigl 31; Winter 42; Zelter 39; Zumsteeg 37.
1798	1		
1799	2		Dittersdorf (60) dies, Oct. 24; Halévy born, May 27.
1800	3		Piccinni (72) dies, May 7.
1801	4		Bellini born, Nov. 1; Cimarosa (52) dies, Jan. 11; Lanner born, April 11.

Appendix A—Calendar

Year	Age	Life	Contemporary Musicians
1802	5		Sarti (73) dies, July 28; Zumsteeg (42) dies, Jan. 27.
1803	6	Begins to study alone at the piano.	Adam born, July 24; Berlioz born, Dec. 9; Glinka born, June 2; Lortzing born, Oct. 23.
1804	7	Receives his first regular instruction in music, but is found to have already mastered its elements.	Benedict born, Nov. 27; Strauss (J. i) born, March 14.
1805	8	Learns the violin from his father and the piano from his brother Ignaz (21).	Boccherini (62) dies, May 28.
1806	9	Receives singing lessons from Michael Holzer, who also teaches him piano, organ and counterpoint.	
1807	10	Studies under Holzer continued.	
1808	11	Sings soprano and plays the violin at the parish church of Liechtental, where Holzer is choirmaster. Having been examined by Salieri (58) and Eybler (43), he is admitted as chorister in the imperial chapel and as pupil at the Seminary, Oct.	Balfe born, May 15.
1809	12	Becomes first violinist in the school band at the Seminary, where he sometimes acts as deputy conductor.	Albrechtsberger (73) dies, March 7; Haydn (77) dies, May 31; Mendelssohn born, Feb. 3.
1810	13	Begins to sketch numerous compositions, which he discards. Fantasy for piano duet composed, April.	Chopin born, Feb. 22; Nicolai born, June 9; Schumann born, June 8.
1811	14	First song, *Hagars Klage*, composed, March 30. It attracts Salieri's (61) attention. Setting	Hiller born, Oct. 24; Liszt born, Oct. 22.

Year	Age	Life	Contemporary Musicians
		of Schiller's *Eine Leichenphantasie.*	
1812	15	Composes church and instrumental music. His quartets played at his father's house. Cantata for his father's nameday, Sept. 27. Death of his mother.	Dussek (51) dies, March 20.
1813	16	Composition of Kotzebue's (52) magic opera, *Des Teufels Lustschloss,* begun. Symphony No. 1, D major, Oct. S. leaves the Seminary, Oct. He studies under Salieri (63). Songs, partsongs, canons, chamber music and three Kyries composed. Second marriage of S.'s father, to Anna Kleyenböck.	Dargomizhsky born, Feb. 14; Grétry (72) dies, Sept. 24; Verdi born, Oct. 10; Wagner born, May 22; Wanhal (74) dies, Aug. 26.
1814	17	After some preliminary studies at the training-school of St. Anna, S. becomes assistant teacher at his father's school. *Des Teufels Lustschloss* finished, May 15, and revised version, Oct. 22. Mass in F major composed May 17–July 22. Meeting with Mayrhofer (27), and setting of his poem, *Am See,* Dec. Composition of three string quartets and many songs, including *Gretchen am Spinnrade.*	Reichardt (62) dies, June 17; Vogler (65) dies, May 16.
1815	18	A vast number of works composed, including songs (nearly 150), *Die Nonne, Heidenröslein, Erlkönig* and songs from Ossian; Mass in G major and other church music; Sym-	Franz born, June 20; Heller born, May 15.

Year	Age	Life	Contemporary Musicians
		phonies Nos. 2 and 3; and operettas and melodramas, *Der vierjährige Posten*, libretto by Körner (24), *Claudine von Villa Bella*, libretto by Goethe (66), *Die Freunde von Salamanka, Fernando, Adrast* and *Der Spiegelritter*.	
1816	19	Applies for the post of head teacher at the school of music at Laibach, but does not obtain it, April. Tired of teaching at his father's school, he goes to live with Schober (18), who admits him to his circle of cultivated friends. Cantatas for Salieri's (66) jubilee, June 16, and *Prometheus*; Symphonies Nos. 4 and 5; *Magnificat, Stabat Matar* and Mass in C major; unfinished opera, *Die Bürgschaft*; a large number of songs, including *Der Wanderer*, the Harper's and Mignon's songs in Goethe's (67) *Wilhelm Meister*.	Paisiello (75) dies, June 5.
1817	20	Meeting with Vogl (49), who recognizes S.'s importance as a song writer. Composition of songs to words by Mayrhofer (30) and Schober (19); two Overtures in the Italian style; seven piano sonatas.	Gade born, Feb. 22; Méhu (54) dies, Oct. 18; Monsigny (88) dies, Jan. 14.
1818	21	S. becomes music master to the Esterházy family and goes with them to Zseliz in the summer. They introduce him to Schönstein (22). Symphony No. 6 and songs composed.	Gounod born, June 17; Kozeluch (46) dies, May 7.

Year	Age	Life	Contemporary Musicians
		Through Vogl's (50) influence the operetta, *Die Zwillingsbrüder,* is commissioned.	
1819	22	Operetta, *Die Zwillingsbrüder,* finished, Jan. 19. Visit to Upper Austria with Vogl (51), summer. Piano Quintet (the 'Trout,' Op. 114).	Offenbach born, June 21.
1820	23	Oratorio, *Lazarus,* begun, Feb. *Die Zwillingsbrüder* produced at the Kärntnertor Theatre, June 14. Operetta, *Die Zauberharfe,* produced at the Theater an der Wien, Aug. 19. Opera, *Sakuntala,* begun. Composition of numerous songs; Psalm 23; Quartet Movement in C minor. Opera, *Alfonso und Estrella,* planned by S. and Schober (22).	Serov born, Jan. 23; Vieuxtemps born, Feb. 20.
1821	24	Vogl (53) sings *Erlkönig* for the first time in public, March 7, and S. at last begins to be known outside his circle of friends. Three songs (Op. 6) dedicated to Vogl. He makes the acquaintance of the Sonnleithner family, at whose house his music is frequently performed and thanks to whom twenty songs are published. Symphony in E minor sketched and a number of songs, including settings of Goethe's (72) *Suleika* (I and II) and *Mahomets Gesang,* composed, also a great deal of dance music, *Ländler, Deutsche,* etc. *Gesang der Geister über den*	

Year	Age	Life	Contemporary Musicians

Wassern for chorus and orchestra. During a visit to the castle of Ochsenburg, near St. Pölten, Schober (23) and S. complete the first two acts of *Alfonso und Estrella,* Sept.

1822　25　*Alfonso und Estrella* finished, Feb. 27. Meeting with Weber (36), who visits Vienna. S. calls at the house of Beethoven (52) with a set of Variations on a French song for piano duet (Op. 10), composed in 1818, which he has dedicated to him. Mass in A flat major, *Wanderer* Fantasy for piano (Op. 15), vocal quartets and numerous songs composed. The publishers become interested in S. and issue some of his works, especially songs, but he is too inexperienced in money matters to make an adequate living. Liszt (11) introduced to S. by Salieri (72). Symphony No. 8, B minor (unfinished), presented to the Musikverein of Graz, in return for his election as honorary member.

Franck born, Dec. 10; Raff born, May 27.

1823　26　Opera, *Fierabras,* finished, Oct. 2. Another meeting with Weber (37), whose *Euryanthe* S. criticizes unfavourably, Oct. Helmina von Chézy's (40) drama, *Rosamunde,* with music by S., produced at the Theater an der Wien, Dec. 20, without success. Operetta, *Die Verschworenen oder Der häusliche Krieg;*

Lalo born, Jan. 27; Steibelt (58) dies, Sept. 20.

Year	Age	Life	Contemporary Musicians
		song cycle, *Die schöne Müllerin*, and many other songs; piano Sonata, A minor (Op. 143).	
1824	27	Octet (Op. 166) finished, March 1. String Quartet, A minor (Op. 29), performed by Schuppanzigh (48), March 14. Second visit to Esterházy's estate at Zseliz, May–Oct. He falls in love (?) with Caroline Esterházy (17). Sonata (*Grand Duo*) for piano, 4 hands (Op. 140).	Bruckner born, Sept. 4; Cornelius born, Dec. 24; Reinecke born, June 23; Smetana born, March 2; Viotti (71) dies, March 3.
1825	28	Excursion to Upper Austria, including Salzburg and Gastein, spring. Return to Vienna, autumn. S. sends to Goethe (70) settings of three of his poems, *An Schwager Kronos*, *An Mignon* and *Ganymed*, with a dedication, June, but receives no answer. Songs from Scott's (54) *Lady of the Lake*, also *Die Allmacht*, *Die junge Nonne* and others. *Trauermarsch* on the death of Tsar Alexander I (48) for piano duet.	Salieri (75) dies, May 7; Strauss (J. ii) born, Oct 25; Winter (70) dies, Oct. 17.
1826	29	Applies for the post of vice musical director to the court, but Weigl (60) is appointed. *Marche héroïque* on the accession of Nicholas I (29), for piano duet; string Quartets, G major and D minor; *Rondo brillant* for violin and piano (Op. 70); songs including *Hark, hark, the lark* and *Who is Silvia?*	Weber (40) dies, June 4/5.
1827	30	First part of *Winterreise* com-	Beethoven (57) dies, March

Year	Age	Life	Contemporary Musicians

pleted, Feb. Visit to the dying 26.
Beethoven (57), March. Visit
to Dr. Karl Pachler and Marie
Pachler ⁄ Koschak at Graz,
Sept. Second part of *Winter⁄
reise*, Oct. Two piano Trios,
B flat major and E flat major
(Opp. 99 and 100); *Impromp⁄
tus* for piano (Op. 142); dance
music; songs. Three Italian
songs (Op. 83) dedicated to
Lablache (33).

1828 31 Suffers from attacks of head⁄
ache. The publishers become
more and more interested in
him, but still fail to offer satis⁄
factory terms. He is too poor
to accept another invitation to
Graz, July. Symphony No. 7,
C major; String Quintet in C
major; piano Sonatas in C
minor, A major and B flat
major; Mass in E flat major,
church music and songs, in⁄
cluding those in the *Schwanen⁄
gesang*. Excursion made to
Eisenstadt, but visits to Upper
Austria and to Pest postponed
owing to illness, Oct. Attacks
of giddiness and fatigue, end of
Oct. S. takes to his bed, Nov.
14. He is sleepless and de⁄
pressed, then develops typhus.
Schubert dies in Vienna,
Nov. 19.

Auber aged 46; Balfe 20;
Bellini 27; Benedict 24; Ber⁄
lioz 25; Bishop 42; Boïeldieu
53; Bruckner 4; Catel 55;
Cherubini 68; Chopin 18;
Clementi 76; Cornelius 4;
Czerny 37; Dargomizhsky 15;
Donizetti 31; Field 46; Franck
6; Glinka 25; Gossec 94;
Gounod 10; Halévy 29;
Hérold 37; Hummel 50;
Liszt 17; Loewe 32; Lortzing
35; Marschner 33; Mendels⁄
sohn 19; Meyerbeer 37; Paer
57; Rossini 36; Schenk 67;
Schumann 18; Smetana 4;
Spohr 44; Spontini 54; Verdi
15; Wagner 15; Weigl 62;
Zelter 70.

APPENDIX B

THIS list is based on Nottebohm's Thematic Catalogue of Schubert's printed works and on Breitkopf & Härtel's complete edition. It therefore does not contain lost or otherwise unpublished compositions, except in the case of the string Quartets, for particulars of which we are indebted to a list published by Otto Erich Deutsch in *Music & Letters,* January 1943. The piano Sonatas are listed according to a chronology published in *The Daily Telegraph.*

[In the earlier editions of this book the list appeared in the order of opus numbers; but as these have, in Schubert's case, not even the advantage of being chronological, I have regrouped the whole according to categories. I have also added a complete and detailed alphabetical list of the songs. The dates are those of composition, not of publication.—E. B.]

ORCHESTRAL WORKS

Concerto

Concertstück for violin and orchestra (1816).

Dances

5 *Deutsche,* with coda and 7 trios (1813).
Minuet.
5 Minuets with 6 trios (*Deutsche*) (1813).

Overtures

B flat major (1816).
C major (in Italian style) (1817).
D major (in Italian style) (1817).
D major (to the comedy *Der Teufel als Hydraulicus*) (1812).
D minor (1817).
E minor (1819).
2 Overtures (supplement).

Symphonies

No 1, D major (1813).
No. 2, B flat major (1815).

No. 3, D major (1815).
No. 4, C minor ('Tragic') (1816).
No. 5, B flat major (1816).
No. 6, C major (1818).
No. 7, C major (1828).
No. 8, B minor (unfinished) (1822).
E minor (sketch).

CHAMBER MUSIC

Nonet and Octets

Eine kleine Trauermusik, for 2 clarinets, 2 bassoons, double bassoon, 2 horns and 2 trombones (1813).

Minuet and Finale, for 2 oboes, 2 clarinets, 2 bassoons and 2 horns.

Octet, F major (Op. 166), for 2 violins, viola, cello, double bass, clarinet, bassoon and horn (1824).

Quintets

A major (the 'Trout,' Op. 114), for piano, violin, viola, cello and double bass (1819).

C major (Op. 163), for 2 violins, viola and 2 cellos (1828).

Rondo for violin and string quartet (1816).

Piano Quartet

Adagio and Rondo concertante, for piano, violin, viola and cello.

String Quartets

Mixed keys (1811, lost).
Mixed keys (No. 1 [1]) (1812).
Mixed keys (1812, lost).
C major (No. 2) (1812).
Overture in B flat major (1812, lost).
B flat major (No. 3) (1812–13).
E flat major (1813, lost).
C major (No. 4) (1813).
B flat major (No. 5) (1813).

---

[1] Numbers in brackets are those of the 'complete' edition.

D major (No. 6) (1813).
E flat major (No. 10) (Op. 125, No. 1) (1813).
5 Minuets and 6 Trios (1813).
5 Waltzes and 7 Trios (1813).
Minuet in D major (1813).
Grave in C minor (1814).
D major (No. 7) (1814).
B flat major (No. 8) (Op. 168) (1814).
G minor (No. 9) (1815).
E major (No. 11) (Op. 125, No. 2) (1816).
B flat major (? 1818, unfinished and unpublished).
Allegro in C minor (Quartet Movement) (No. 12) (1820).
A minor (No. 13) (Op. 29) (1824).
D minor (No. 14) (1824).
G major (No. 15 (Op. 161) (1826).

Piano Trios

B flat major (Op. 99) (1827).
E flat major (Op. 100) (1827).
Notturno (Op. 148).
Sonata, B flat major (1812).

String Trio

B flat major, for violin, viola and cello (1817).

Piano with One Instrument

Fantasy (Op. 159), for piano and violin (1827).
Introduction and Variations on *Trockne Blumen* from *Die schöne Müllerin*
    (Op. 160), for piano and flute (1824).
Rondo brillant (Op. 70), for piano and violin (1826).
Sonata, A major (Op. 162), for piano and violin (1817).
Sonatina, A minor (Op. 137, No. 2), for piano and violin (1816).
Sonatina, D major (Op. 137, No. 1), for piano and violin (1816).
Sonatina, G minor (Op. 137, No. 3), for piano and violin (1816).
Sonata for piano and arpeggione or cello (1824).

Appendix B—Catalogue of Works

PIANO MUSIC

Four Hands

Allegro moderato and Andante.
Andantino varié on French themes (Op. 84, No. 1).[1]
Children's March, G major (1827).
Divertissement on French themes (Op. 63).[1]
Divertissement à la hongroise (Op. 54) (1824).
3 Fantasies (1810–13).
Fantasy, F minor (Op. 103).
Fugue, E minor (Op. 152) (1828) (also for organ).
Introduction and Variations on an Original Theme (Op. 82, No. 2).
4 *Ländler* (1824).
Lebensstürme (Op. 144) (1828).
Marche héroïque for Nicholas I (Op. 66) (1826).
6 Marches (Op. 40).
2 *Marches caractéristiques* (Op. 121).
3 *Marches héroïques* (Op. 27).
3 *Marches militaires* (Op. 51).
Overture, C major.
Overture, D major.
Overture, F major (Op. 34) (1819).
Overture, G minor (1819).
2 Overtures (supplement).
6 Polonaises (Op. 61).
4 Polonaises (Op. 75).
Rondo, A major (Op. 107) (1828).
Rondo, D major (Op. 138).
Rondo brillant on French themes (Op. 84, No. 2).[1]
Sonata, B flat major (Op. 30) (1824).
Sonata (*Grand Duo*), C major (Op. 140) (1824).
Trauermarsch for Alexander I (Op. 55) (1825).
Variations on a French Song (Op. 10) (1818).
Variations on an Original Theme, A flat major (Op. 35) (1824).
Variations on a Theme from Hérold's *Marie* (Op. 82, No. 1) (1827).

---

[1] These three pieces were originally intended as one work, but were published separately.

Schubert

Two Hands

Abschied von der Erde, melodrama, with recitation (see under Songs).
Adagio and Rondo, E major (Op. 145) (1817).
Allegretto, C minor (1828).
Andante, C major (1812).
Damenländler und Ecossaisen (Op. 67).
Deutsche und Ecossaisen (Op. 33) (1824).
Erste Walzer (Op. 9).
Fantasy (*Wanderer*) (Op. 15) (1822).
Grätzer Galopp, etc. (1827).
Grätzer Walzer (Op. 91) (1827).
4 *Impromptus* (Op. 90) (1828).
4 *Impromptus* (Op. 142) (1827).
Klavierstück, A major.
3 *Klavierstücke* (1828).
12 *Ländler* (Op. 171).
March, E major.
Moments musicaux (Op. 94) (? 1828).
2 Scherzos (1817).

Sonatas:
   E major (3 movements only) (1815).
   C major (3 movements only) (1815).
   E major (5 movements, published as 5 *Klavierstücke*) (1816).
   A flat major (1817).
   E minor (2 movements only) (1817).
   E flat major (Op. 122, originally in D flat major) (1817).
   F sharp minor (unfinished) (1817).
   B major (Op. 147) (1817).
   A minor (Op. 164) (1817).
   C major (unfinished) (1818).
   F minor (unfinished) (1818).
   C sharp minor (unfinished) (1819).
   A major (Op. 120) (1819).
   A minor (Op. 143) (1823).
   C major ('Reliquie,' unfinished) (1825).
   A minor (Op. 42) (1825).
   D major (Op. 53) (1825).
   G major (Op. 78) (1826).
   C minor (1828).

Appendix B—Catalogue of Works

A major (1828).
B flat major (1828).

Valses nobles (Op. 77).
Valses sentimentales (Op. 50).
Variation on a Theme by Diabelli (1821).
10 Variations (1815).
Variations on a Theme by Anselm Hüttenbrenner (1817).
Walzer, Ländler und Ecossaisen (Op. 18) (1821).
20 Waltzes (Op. 127).
Numerous other sets of Dances.

CHURCH MUSIC

Accompanied

Auguste jam coelestium, soprano and tenor (1816).
Gradual, *Benedictus*, chorus (Op. 150).
3 *Kyrie*, chorus.
Magnificat, solo voices and chorus (1816).
Mass, F major (1814).
Mass, G major (1815).
Mass, B flat major (1815).
Mass, C major (1816).
Mass, A flat major (1819–22).
Mass (German), F major (1826).
Gesänge zur Feier des heiligen Opfers der Messe.
Mass, E flat major (1828).
Offertory (Op. 46), *Totus in corde*, soprano and tenor.
Offertory (Op. 47), *Salve Regina*, soprano.
Offertory, *Intende voci*, tenor and chorus (1828).
Offertory, *Tres sunt*, chorus.
Salve Regina, chorus (1816).
Salve Regina (Op. 153), soprano (1824).
Salve Regina, tenor (1814).
Stabat Mater, chorus (1816).
Stabat Mater (Klopstock), solo voices and chorus (1816).
Tantum ergo, chorus (1828).
Tantum ergo (Op. 45), chorus (1822).
Tantum ergo, solo voices and chorus (sketch).

Schubert

Unaccompanied

Antiphons for Palm Sunday, for mixed choir (Op. 113) (1820).
Kyrie, for mixed choir.
Salve Regina, for four male voices (1824).
Salve Regina, for mixed choir (1816).

CHORAL WORKS FOR MIXED VOICES

With Orchestra

Cantata in honour of Josef Spendou (Op. 128) (1816).
Cantata on the Emperor's Birthday, *Constitutionslied* (Op. 157).
Glaube, Hoffnung und Liebe (1828).
Lazarus, religious drama (unfinished) (1820).
Namensfeier Cantata (1812).
Schlacht, Die, Cantata (sketch).

With Piano

An die Sonne.
Begräbnislied.
Cantata for Irene Kiesewetter, *Der Tanz* (1828).
Frühlingsmorgen (Op. 158) (1819).[1]
Gebet (Op. 139) (1824).
Gott der Weltschöpfer.
Gott im Ungewitter.
Hochzeitsbraten, Der (Op. 104) (1827).
Hymne an den Unendlichen (Op. 112, No. 3) (1815).
Lebenslust.
Miriams Siegesgesang (Op. 136) (1828).
Osterlied.
Quartet, *Schicksalslenker* (Op. 146).

Unaccompanied

Christ ist erstanden.
Psalm 92 (1828).

---

[1] The music originally that of a Cantata for Vogl's birthday.

Appendix B—Catalogue of Works

CHORAL WORKS FOR MALE VOICES

With Orchestra

Gesang der Geister über den Wassern (Op. 167) (1820, revised 1821).
Hymne (Op. 154) (1828).
Nachtgesang im Walde (Op. 139B) (1827).

With Piano, etc.

Bergknappenlied.
Bootgesang (Op. 52, No. 3) (1825).
Dörfchen, Das (Op. 11, No. 1) with guitar (1822).
Frühlingsgesang (Op. 16, No. 1) (Schober) (1823).
Geist der Liebe (Op. 11, No. 3) with guitar (1822).
Gondelfahrer, Der (Op. 28) (1824).
Im Gegenwärtigen Vergangenes.
Nachthelle (Op. 134) (1826).
Nachtigall, Die (Op. 11, No. 2) with guitar (1822).
Naturgenuss (Op. 16, No. 2).
Pastorella, La.
Ständchen (Op. 135), first version (1827).
Trinklied ('Freunde, sammelt euch') with bass solo.
Trinklied ('Auf, Jeder sei . . .').
Widerspruch (Op. 105, No. 1) (1826–8).
Zur guten Nacht (Op. 81, No. 3) (1816).

Unaccompanied

An den Frühling.
Beitrag zur Jubelfeier Salieris (1816).
Dörfchen, Das.
Einsiedelei, Die.
Entfernten, Der.
Ewige Liebe (Op. 64, No. 2).
Flucht (Op. 64, No. 3).
Frühlingsgesang (1827).
Geistertanz, Der.
Gesang der Geister über den Wassern (2 versions) (1817).
Grab und Mond.
Hymne ('Komm', heil'ger Geist').
Jünglingswonne (Op. 17, No. 1).
Liebe (Op. 17, No. 2).
Lied im Freien.

Mondenschein (Op. 102).
Nacht, Die (Op. 17, No. 4).
Nachtmusik (Op. 156) (1822).
Ruhe, schönstes Glück der Erde (1819).
Schlachtlied (Op. 151) (1827).
Sehnsucht (1819).
Trinklied (Op. 155).
Wehmut (Op. 64, No. 1).
Wein und Liebe.
Wer ist gross ?
Zum Rundetanz (Op. 17, No. 3).

CHORAL WORKS FOR FEMALE VOICES

Coronach (Op. 52, No. 4) (1825).
Gott in der Natur (Op. 133) (1822).
Grosse Halleluja, Das (Klopstock) (1816).
Klage um Ali Bey.
Leben, Das.
Psalm 23 (Op. 132) (1820).
Ständchen (Op. 135), second version (1827).

WORKS FOR THE STAGE

Additions to Hérold's opera, *La Clochette* (1821).
Adrast, opera (fragment) (1815).
Alfonso und Estrella, opera (Op. 69) (1821–2).
Bürgschaft, Die, opera (fragment) (1816).
Claudine von Villa Bella, operetta (fragment) (1815).
Fernando, operetta (1815).
Fierabras, opera (Op. 76) (1823).
Freunde von Salamanka, Die, operetta (1815).
Häusliche Krieg, Der (see *Verschworenen, Die*).
Rosamunde von Cypern, incidental music (Op. 26) (1823).
Spiegelritter, Der, operetta (fragment) (1815).
Teufels Lustschloss, Des, opera (1813–14).
Verschworenen, Die, opera (1823).
Vierjährige Posten, Der, operetta (1815).
Zauberharfe, Die, melodrama (1820).
Zwillingsbrüder, Die, operetta (1818–19).

Appendix B—Catalogue of Works

SONGS [1]

Abend, Der (Kosegarten) (1815).
Abend, Der (Matthisson) (1814).
Abendbilder (Silbert) (1819).
Abendlied (?) (1816).
Abendlied (Claudius) (1816).
Abendlied (Stolberg) (1815).
Abendlied der Fürstin (Mayrhofer) (1816).
Abendlied für die Entfernte (Schlegel) (1825).
Abendrot, Das (Schreiber) (1818).
Abendröte (Schlegel) (1820).
Abendständchen (Baumberg) (1815).
Abendstern (Mayrhofer) (1824).
Abends unter der Linde (Kosegarten) (1815).
Abgeblühte Linde, Die (Széchényi) (1817).
Abschied (Mayrhofer) (1816).
Abschied (Rellstab) (S.G. 7) (1828).
Abschied (Schubert) (1817).
Abschied von der Erde, melodrama (Pratobevera) (1825).
Abschied von der Harfe (Salis) (1816).
Adelaïde (Matthisson) (1814).
Adelwold und Emma (Bertrand) (1815).
Alinde (Rochlitz) (1816).
Alles um Liebe (Kosegarten) (1815).
Allmacht, Die (Pyrker) (1825).
Alpenjäger, Der (Mayrhofer) (1817, 2 versions).
Alpenjäger, Der (Schiller) (1817).
Als ich sie erröten sah (Ehrlich) (1815).
Alte Liebe rostet nie (Mayrhofer) (1816).
Altschottische Ballade, Eine (*Edward*) (trans. Herder) (1827).
Am Bach im Frühling (Schober) (1816).

---

[1] List compiled from the complete edition. The songs in the cycles are
here given separately in the alphabet, which, though not altogether satisfactory, at least solves the question of the *Schwanengesang*, which was not
definitely designed as a cycle. The abbreviations given in brackets after
the songs in question are as follows: S.M.=*Die schöne Müllerin*; W.R.=
Winterreise; S.G.=*Schwanengesang*. The figure following indicates the
number of the song in the cycle.—E. B.

Am Feierabend (Müller) (S.M. 5) (1823).
Am Fenster (Seidl) (1826).
Am Flusse (Goethe) (1815 and 1822).
Am Grabe Anselmos (Claudius) (1816).
Am Meer (Heine) (S.G. 12) (1828).
Am See (Bruchmann) (1822).
Am See (Mayrhofer) (1814).
Am Strome (Mayrhofer) (1817).
Amalie (Schiller) (1815).
Ammenlied (Lubi) (1814).
Amphiaraos (Körner) (1815).
An Chloen (Jacobi) (1816).
An dem jungen Morgenhimmel (Fouqué) (1814).
An den Frühling (Schiller) (1815, 2 versions).
An den Mond (Goethe) (1815, 2 versions).
An den Mond (Geuss, lieber Mond) (Hölty) (1815).
An den Mond (*Was schauest du*) (Hölty) (1816).
An den Mond in einer Herbstnacht (Schreiber) (1818).
An den Schlaf (Uz) (1816).
An den Tod (Schubart) (1817).
An die Apfelbäume (Hölty) (1815).
An die Dioskuren (see *Lied eines Schiffers*).
An die Entfernte (Goethe) (1822).
An die Freude (Schiller) (1815).
An die Freunde (Mayrhofer) (1819).
An die Geliebte (Hell) (1815).
An die Laute (Rochlitz) (1816).
An die Leyer (Bruchmann) (1822).
An die Musik (Schober) (1817).
An die Nachtigall (Claudius) (1816).
An die Nachtigall (Hölty) (1815).
An die Natur (Stolberg) (1816).
An die Sonne (Baumberg) (1815).
An die Sonne (Tiedge) (1815).
An die Türen (see *Gesang des Harfners*).
An die untergehende Sonne (Kosegarten) (1816).
An eine Quelle (Claudius) (1816).
An Emma (Schiller) (1814).
An Laura (Matthisson) (1814).
An mein Clavier (Schubart) (1816).

Appendix B—Catalogue of Works

An mein Herz (Schulze) (1825).
An Mignon (Goethe) (1815).
An Rosa (Kosegarten) (1815, 2 versions).
An Schwager Kronos (Goethe) (1816).
An Sie (Klopstock) (1815).
An Silvia (see *Who is Silvia?*).
Andenken (Matthisson) (1814).
Annot Lyle's Song (Scott) (1827).
Antigone und Oedip (Mayrhofer) (1817).
Atlas, Der (Heine) (S.G. 8) (1828).
Atys (Mayrhofer) (1817).
Auf dem Flusse (Müller) (W.R. 7) (1827).
Auf dem See (Goethe) (1817).
Auf dem Strom (Rellstab), with horn obbligato (1828).
Auf dem Wasser zu singen (Stolberg) (1822).
Auf den Sieg der Deutschen (occasional song).
Auf den Tod einer Nachtigall (Hölty) (1816).
Auf der Bruck (Schulze) (1825).
Auf der Donau (Mayrhofer) (1817).
Auf der Riesenkoppe (Körner) (1818).
Auf einen Kirchhof (Schlechta) (1815).
Aufenthalt (Rellstab) (S.G. 5) (1828).
Auflösung (Mayrhofer) (1824).
Augenlied (Mayrhofer) (1815).
Aus 'Diego Manazares' (Schlechta) (1816).
Aus 'Heliopolis' (*Fels auf Felsen*) (Mayrhofer) (1822).
Aus 'Heliopolis' (*Im kalten, rauhen Norden*) (Mayrhofer) (1822).
Ave Maria (see *Ellen's Songs*).

Baches Wiegenlied, Des (Müller) (S.M. 20) (1823).
Ballade (Kenner) (1815).
Befreier Europas in Paris, Die (occasional song).
Bei dem Grabe meines Vaters (Claudius) (1816).
Bie dir allein! (Seidl) (1826). (4 refrain songs, No. 2.)
Beim Winde (Mayrhofer) (1819).
Berge, Die (Schlegel) (1815).
Bertas Lied in der Nacht (Grillparzer) (1819).
Betende, Die (Matthisson) (1814).
Bild, Das (?) (1815).
Blanka (Schlegel) (1818).
Blinde Knabe, Der (Cibber, trans. Craigher) (1825).

Blondel zu Marien (?) (1818).
Blumen Schmerz, Der (Mailath) (1821).
Blumenbrief, Der (Schreiber) (1818).
Blumenlied (Hölty) (1816).
Blumensprache, Die (Platner) (1817).
Böse Farbe, Die (Müller) (S.M. 17) (1823).
Brüder, schrecklich brennt (occasional song).
Bundeslied (Goethe) (1815).
Bürgschaft, Die (Schiller) (1815).

Come, thou monarch of the vine (Shakespeare) (1826).
Cora an die Sonne (Baumberg) (1815).
Cronnan (Ossian) (1816).
Crusader's Return, The (Scott) (1827).

Da quel sembiante appresi (Metastasio) (1820).
Danksagung an den Bach (Müller) (S.M. 4) (1823).
Daphne am Bach (Stolberg) (1816).
Das war ich (Körner) (1815).
Dass sie hier gewesen (Rückert) (1823).
Delphine (Schütz) (1825).
Didone (Metastasio) (1816).
Dithyrambe (Schiller) (1824).
Don Gayseros (Fouqué) (1814).
Doppelgänger, Der (Heine) (S.G. 13) (1828).
Drang in die Ferne (Leitner) (1822).
Drei Sänger, Die (fragments).
Du bist die Ruh' (Rückert) (1823).
Du liebst mich nicht (Platen) (1822).

Echo, Das (Castelli) (1827).
Edone (Klopstock) (1816).
Edward (see *Alstchottische Ballade*).
Eifersucht und Stolz (Müller) (S.M. 15) (1823).
Einsame, Der (Lappe) (1825).
Einsamkeit (Mayrhofer) (1818).
Einsamkeit (Müller) (W.R. 12) (1827).
Einsiedelei, Die (Salis) (1816 and 1817).
Ellen's Song (*Ave Maria*) (Scott) (1825).
Ellen's Song (*Huntsman, rest*) (Scott) (1825).
Ellen's Song (*Soldier, rest*) (Scott) (1825).
Elysium (Schiller) (1817).

Entfernten, Die (Salis) (1816).
Entsühnte Orest, Der (Mayrhofer) (1820).
Entzückung (Matthisson) (1816).
Entzückung an Laura (Schiller) (1816 and a fragment of 1817).
Epistel : Musikalischer Schwank (Collin), a musical letter addressed to Spaun (1822).
Erinnerungen (Matthisson) (1814).
Erlafsee (Mayrhofer) (1817).
Erlkönig (Goethe) (1815).
Erntelied (Hölty) (1816).
Erscheinung, Die (Kosegarten) (1815).
Erstarrung (Müller) (W.R. 4) (1827).
Erste Liebe, Die (Fellinger) (1815).
Erster Verlust (Goethe) (1815).
Erwartung, Die (Schiller) (1815).

Fahrt zum Hades (Mayrhofer) (1817).
Finden, Das (Kosegarten) (1815).
Fischer, Der (Goethe) (1815).
Fischerlied (Salis) (1816 and 1817).
Fischermädchen, Das (Heine) (S.G. 10) (1828).
Fischers Liebesglück, Des (Leitner) (1827).
Fischerweise (Schlechta) (1826).
Florio (Schütz) (1825).
Flüchtling, Der (Schiller) (1816).
Flug der Zeit, Der (Széchényi) (1817).
Fluss, Der (Schlegel) (1820).
For leagues along the watery way (see *Norna's Song*).
Forelle, Die (Schubart) (1817).
Fragment aus dem Aeschylus (Mayrhofer) (1816).
Freiwilliges Versinken (Mayrhofer) (1820).
Freude der Kinderjahre (Köpken) (1816).
Freudvoll und leidvoll (Goethe) (1815).
Fröhlichkeit, Die (Prandstetter) (1815).
Frohsinn (?) (1817).
Frühe Liebe, Die (Hölty) (1816).
Frühen Gräber, Die (Klopstock) (1815).
Frühlingsglaube (Uhland) (1820).
Frühlingslied (Hölty) (1816).
Frühlingssehnsucht (Rellstab) (S.G. 3) (1828).
Frühlingstraum (Müller) (W.R. 11) (1827).

Fülle der Liebe (Schlegel) (1825).
Furcht der Geliebten (Klopstock) (1815).

Ganymed (Goethe) (1817).
Gebet während der Schlacht (Körner) (1815).
Gebüsche, Die (Schlegel) (1819).
Gefangenen Sänger, Die (Schlegel) (1821).
Gefror'ne Tränen (Müller) (W.R. 3) (1827).
Geheimes (Goethe) (1821).
Geheimnis (Mayrhofer) (1816).
Geheimnis, Das (Schiller) (1815 and 1822).
Geist der Liebe (Kosegarten) (1815).
Geist der Liebe (Matthisson) (1816).
Geisternähe (Matthisson) (1814).
Geistertanz, Der (Matthisson) (1814, also a fragmentary setting).
Geistesgruss (Goethe) (1815).
Genügsamkeit (Schober) (1815).
Gesang an die Harmonie (Salis) (1816).
Gesang der Geister über den Wassern (Goethe, fragment) (1816).
Gesang der Norna (see *Norna's Song*).
Gesang des Harfners (*An die Türen*) (Goethe) (1816).
Gesang des Harfners (*Wer nie sein Brot*) (Goethe) (1816, 3 versions).
Gesang des Harfners (*Wer sich der Einsamkeit ergibt*) (Goethe) (1815 and 1816).
Gestirne, Die (Klopstock) (1816).
Gestörte Glück, Das (Körner) (1815).
Glaube, Hoffnung und Liebe (Kuffner) (1824).
Goldschmiedsgesell, Der (Goethe) (1815).
Gondelfahrer (Mayrhofer) (1824).
Götter Griechenlands, Die (Schiller) (1820).
Gott im Frühlinge (Uz) (1816).
Gott und die Bajadere, Der (Goethe) (1815).
Grab, Das (Salis) (1815, 1816 and 1817).
Grablied (Kenner) (1815).
Grablied auf einen Soldaten (Schubart) (1816).
Grablied für die Mutter (?) (1818).
Greise Kopf, Der (Müller) (W.R. 14) (1827).
Greisengesang (Rückert) (1823).
Grenzen der Menschheit (Goethe) (1821).
Gretchen (*Ach neige*) (Goethe, fragment) (1817).
Gretchen am Spinnrade (Goethe) (1814).
Grosse Halleluja, Das (Klopstock) (1816).

Gruppe aus dem Tartarus (Schiller) (1817).
Gruss an den Mai (Ermin) (1815).
Guarda che bianca luna (Vitorelli) (1820).
Gute Hirt, Der (Uz) (1816).
Gute Nacht (Müller) (W.R. 1) (1827).

Hagars Klage (Schücking) (1811).
Halt! (Müller) (S.M. 3) (1823).
Hänflings Liebeswerbung (Kind) (1817).
Hark, hark, the lark (Shakespeare) (1826).
Heath this night must be my bed, The (see *Norman's Song*).
Heidenröslein (Goethe) (1815).
Heimliches Lieben (Klenke) (1827).
Heimweh, Das (Hell) (1816).
Heimweh, Das (Pyrker) (1825).
Heiss mich nicht reden (see *Mignon's Songs*)
Hektors Abschied (Schiller) (1815).
Herbst (Rellstab) (1828).
Herbstabend, Der (Salis) (1816).
Herbstlied (Salis) (1816).
Hermann und Thusnelda (Klopstock) (1815).
Herrn Josef Spaun (Collin).
Himmelsfunken (Silbert) (1819).
Hippolyts Lied (Schopenhauer) (1826).
Hirt, Der (Mayrhofer) (1816).
Hirt auf dem Felsen, Der (Müller and Chézy), with clarinet obbligato (1828).
Hochzeitlied (Jacobi) (1816).
Hoffnung (Goethe) (1815).
Hoffnung (Schiller) (1815 and 1819).
Huldigung (Kosegarten) (1815).
Huntsman, rest (see *Ellen's Songs*).
Hymne (Ich sag' es jedem) (Novalis) (1819).
Hymne (Wenige wissen) (Novalis) (1819).
Hymne (Wenn alle untreu werden) (Novalis) (1819).
Hymne (Wem ich ihn nur) (Novalis) (1819).

Ich bin vergnügt (see *Lied*, Claudius).
Idens Nachtgesang (Kosegarten) (1815).
Idens Schwanenlied (Kosegarten) (1815).
Ihr Bild (Heine) (S.G. 9) (1828).
Ihr Grab (Roos) (1822).
Im Abendrot (Lappe) (1824).

Im Dorfe (Müller) (W.R. 17) (1827).
Im Freien (Seidl) (1826).
Im Frühling (Schulze) (1826).
Im Haine (Bruchmann) (1822).
Im Walde (Schlegel) (1820).
Im Walde (Schulze) (1825).
In der Ferne (Rellstab) (S.G. 6) (1828).
In der Mitternacht (Jacobi) (1816).
Incanto degli occhi, L' (Metastasio) (1827).
Iphigenia (Mayrhofer) (1817).
Irdisches Glück (Seidl) (1826).   (4 refrain songs, No. 4.)
Irrlicht (Müller) (W.R. 9) (1827).

Jagdlied (Werner) (1817).
Jäger, Der (Müller) (S.M. 14) (1823).
Jäger, ruhe (see *Ellen's Songs*).
Jägers Abendlied (Goethe) (1816).
Jägers Liebeslied (Schober) (1827).
Johanna Sebus (Goethe, fragment) (1821).
Julius an Theone (Matthisson) (1816).
Junge Nonne, Die (Craigher) (1825).
Jüngling am Bache, Der (Schiller) (1812, 1815 and 1819).
Jüngling an der Quelle, Der (Salis) (1821).
Jüngling auf dem Hügel, Der (Hüttenbrenner) (1820).
Jüngling und der Tod, Der (Spaun) (1817).

Kampf, Der (Schiller) (1817).
Kennst du das Land (see *Mignon's Songs*).
Klage (*Dein Silber schien*) (Hölty) (1816).
Klage (*Trauer umfliesst*) (?) (1816).
Klage (Matthisson) (1816).
Klage der Ceres (Schiller) (1815).
Klaglied (Rochlitz) (1812).
Knabe, Der (Schlegel) (1820).
Knabe in der Wiege, Der (Ottenwald) (1817).
Knabenzeit, Die (Hölty) (1816).
Kolmas Klage (Ossian) (1815).
König in Thule, Der (Goethe) (1816).
Krähe, Die (Müller) (W.R. 15) (1827).
Kreuzzug, Der (Leitner) (1827).
Kriegers Ahnung (Rellstab) (S.G. 2) (1828).
Labetrank der Liebe (Stoll) (1815).

Lachen und Weinen (Rückert) (1823).
Lambertine (Stoll) (1815).
Laube, Die (Hölty) (1815).
Laura am Clavier (Schiller) (1816).
Lay of the Imprisoned Huntsman (Scott) (1825).
Lebenslied (Matthisson) (1816).
Lebensmelodien (Schlegel) (1816).
Lebensmut (Rellstab, fragment) (1828).
Lebensmut (Schulze) (1826).
Leichenphantasie, Eine (Schiller) (1811).
Leiden der Trennung (Metastasio, trans. Collin) (1816).
Leidende, Der (Hölty) (1816).
Leiermann, Der (Müller) (W.R. 24) (1827).
Letzte Hoffnung (Müller) (W.R. 16) (1827).
Liane (Mayrhofer) (1815).
Licht und Liebe (Collin) (1816).
Lieb Minna (Stadler) (1815).
Liebe, Die (see *Freudvoll und leidvoll*).
Liebe, Die (Leon) (1817).
Liebe Farbe, Die (Müller) (S.M. 16) (1823).
Liebe hat gelogen, Die (Platen) (1822).
Liebende, Der (Hölty) (1815).
Liebende schreibt, Die (Goethe) (1819).
Liebesbotschaft (Rellstab) (S.G. 1) (1828).
Liebesgötter, Die (Uz) (1816).
Liebeslauschen (Schlechta) (1820).
Liebesrausch (Körner) (1815).
Liebeständelei (Körner) (1815).
Liebhaber in allen Gestalten (Goethe) (1815).
Liebliche Stern, Der (Schulze) (1825).
Lied (Claudius) (1816, 2 versions).
Lied (Fouqué) (1816).
Lied (Pichler) (1816).
Lied (Salis) (1816).
Lied (Schiller) (1815).
Lied (Stolberg) (1822).
Lied aus der Ferne (Matthisson) (1814).
Lied der Anne Lyle (see *Annot Lyle's Song*).
Lied der Liebe (Matthisson) (1814).
Lied des gefangenen Jägers (see *Lay of the Imprisoned Huntsman*).

Lied des Orpheus (Jacobi) (1816).
Lied eines Kindes (fragment).
Lied eines Kriegers (?) (1824).
Lied eines Schiffers an die Dioskuren (Mayrhofer) (1816).
Lied im Grünen, Das (Reil) (1827).
Lied vom Reifen, Das (Claudius) (1817).
Liedesend (Mayrhofer) (1816).
Liedler, Der (Kenner) (1815).
Lilla an die Morgenröte (?) (1815).
Lindenbaum, Der (Müller) (W.R. 5) (1827).
Litanei auf das Fest aller Seelen (Jacobi) (1818).
Lob der Tränen (Schlegel) (1817).
Lob der Tokayers (Baumberg) (1815).
Lodas Gespenst (Ossian) (1815).
Lorma (Ossian, fragment) (1816).
Luisens Antwort (Kosegarten) (1815).

Macht der Liebe, Die (Kalchberg) (1815).
Mädchen, Das (Schlegel) (1819).
Mädchen aus der Fremde, Das (Schiller) (1814 and 1815).
Mädchens Klage, Des (Schiller) (1811, 1815 and 1816).
Mädchen von Inistore, Das (Ossian) (1815).
Mahomets Gesang (Goethe, 2 fragments) (1817 and 1821).
Mainacht, Die (Hölty) (1815).
Männer sind méchant, Die (Seidl) (1826). (4 refain songs, No. 3.)
Marie (Novalis) (1819).
Marienbild, Das (Schreiber) (1818).
Meeresstille (Goethe) (1815).
Mein! (Müller) (S.M. 11) (1823).
Memnon (Mayrhofer) (1817).
Mignon's Song (*Heiss mich nicht reden*) (Goethe) (1821 and 1826).
Mignon's Song (*Kennst du das Land?*) (Goethe) (1815).
Mignon's Song (*Nur wer die Sehnsucht kennt*) (Goethe) (1815, 1816 and 1826, 5 versions).
Mignon's Song (*So lasst mich scheinen*) (Goethe) (1821 and 1826).
Minnelied (Hölty) (1816).
Minona (Bertrand) (1815).
Mio ben, ricordati (Metastasio) (1820).
Misero pargoletto (Metastasio) (1813).
Mit dem grünen Lautenbande (Müller) (S.M. 13) (1823).
Modo di prender moglie, Il (?) (1827).

Mondabend, Der (Ermin) (1815).
Mondnacht, Die (Kosegarten) (1815).
Morgengruss (Müller) (S.M. 8) (1823).
Morgenkuss nach einem Ball, Der (Baumberg) (1815).
Morgenlied (Stolberg) (1815).
Morgenlied (Werner) (1820).
Morgenlied (?) (1816).
Müller und der Bach, Der (Müller) (S.M. 19) (1823).
Müllers Blumen, Des (Müller) (S.M. 9) (1823).
Musensohn, Der (Goethe) (1822).
Mut (Müller) (W.R. 22) (1827).
My hawk is tired (see *Lay of the Imprisoned Huntsman*).

Nach einem Gewitter (Mayrhofer) (1817).
Nacht, Die (Ossian) (1817).
Nacht, Die (Uz) (1816).
Nächtens klang die süsse Laute (Fouqué) (1814).
Nachtgesang (Goethe) (1814).
Nachtgesang (Kosegarten) (1815).
Nachthymne (Novalis) (1820).
Nachtstück (Mayrhofer) (1819).
Nacht und Träume (Collin) (1825).
Nachtviolen (Mayrhofer) (1822).
Nähe des Geliebten (Goethe) (1815).
Namenstagslied (Stadler).
Naturgenuss (Matthisson) (1815).
Nebensonnen, Die (Müller) (W.R. 23) (1827).
Neugierige, Der (Müller) (S.M. 6) (1823).
Non t' accostar all' urna (Vitorelli) (1820).
Nonne, Die (Hölty) (1815).
Norman's Song (The heath this night) (Scott) (1825).
Norna's Song (For leagues along the watery way) (Scott) (1825).
Nur wer die Sehnsucht kennt (see *Mignon's Songs*).

Orest auf Tauris (Mayrhofer) (1820).
Orpheus (Jacobi) (1816).
Ossians Lied nach dem Falle Nathos' (1815).

Pastorella, La (Goldoni) (1817).
Pause (Müller) (S.M. 12) (1823).
Pax vobiscum (Schober) (1817).
Pensa, che questo istante (Metastasio) (1813).
Perle, Die (Jacobi) (1816).

Pflicht und Liebe (Gotter, fragment).
Pflügerlied (Salis) (1816).
Phidile (Claudius) (1816).
Philoktet (Mayrhofer) (1817).
Pilgerweise (Schober) (1822).
Pilgrim, Der (Schiller) (1822).
Post, Die (Müller) (W.R. 13) (1827).
Prometheus (Goethe) (1819).
Punschlied (Schiller) (1815).

Rast (Müller) (W.R. 10) (1827).
Raste, Krieger (see *Ellen's Songs*).
Rastlose Liebe (Goethe) (1815).
Rattenfänger, Der (Goethe) (1815).
Ritter Toggenburg (Schiller) (1816).
Romanze (Matthisson) (1814).
Romanze des Richard Löwenherz (see *Crusader's Return*).
Rose, Die (Schlegel) (1822).
Rosenband, Das (Klopstock) (1815).
Rückblick (Müller) (W.R. 8) (1827).
Rückweg (Mayrhofer) (1816).

Sänger, Der (Goethe) (1815).
Sänger am Felsen, Der (Pichler) (1816).
Sängers Habe, Des (Schlechta) (1825).
Sängers Morgenlied (Körner) (1815, 2 versions).
Scene aus Goethes 'Faust' (1814).
Schäfer und der Reiter, Der (Fouqué) (1817).
Schäfers Klagelied (Goethe) (1814).
Schatten, Die (Matthisson) (1813).
Schatzgräber, Der (Goethe) (1815).
Schatzgräbers Begehr (Schober) (1822).
Schiffer, Der (Mayrhofer) (1817).
Schiffer, Der (Schlegel) (1820).
Schiffers Scheidelied (Schober) (1827).
Schlachtgesang (Klopstock) (1816).
Schlaflied (Mayrhofer) (1817).
Schmetterling, Der (Schlegel) (1815).
Schöne Müllerin, Die (Müller), cycle of 20 songs (1823).
Schwanengesang (Heine, Rellstab and Seidl), cycle of 14 songs (1828).
Schwanengesang (Kosegarten) (1815).
Schwanengesang (Senn) (1822).

Schweizerlied (Goethe) (1815).
Schwertlied (Körner) (1815).
Schwestergruss (Bruchmann) (1822).
Sehnen, Das (Kosegarten) (1815).
Sehnsucht (Goethe) (1814).
Sehnsucht (Mayrhofer) (1820).
Sehnsucht (Schiller) (1813 and 1819).
Sehnsucht (Seidl) (1826).
Sehnsucht der Liebe (Körner) (1815).
Sei mir gegrüsst (Rückert) (1821).
Selige Welt (Senn) (1822).
Seligkeit (Hölty) (1816).
Selma und Selmar (Klopstock) (1815).
Seufzer (Hölty) (1815).
Shilrik und Vinvela (Ossian) (1815).
Sieg, Der (Mayrhofer) (1824).
Skolie (Deinhardstein) (1815).
Skolie (Matthisson) (1816).
Soldier, rest (see *Ellen's Songs*).
Sommernacht, Die (Klopstock) (1815).
Son fra l' onde (Metastasio) (1813).
Sonett (*Allein, nachdenklich*) (Petrarch, trans. Schlegel) (1818).
Sonett (*Apollo, lebet noch*) (Petrarch-Schlegel) (1818).
Sonett (*Nunmehr, da Himmel*) (Petrarch-Schlegel) (1818).
Spinnerin, Die (Goethe) (1815).
Sprache der Liebe (Schlegel) (1816).
Stadt, Die (Heine) (S.G. 11) (1828).
Ständchen (Rellstab) (S.G. 4) (1828).
Ständchen aus 'Cymbeline' (see *Hark, hark, the lark*).
Sterbende, Die (Matthisson) (1815).
Sterne, Die (Fellinger) (1815).
Sterne, Die (Kosegarten) (1815).
Sterne, Die (Leitner) (1828).
Sterne, Die (Schlegel) (1820).
Sternennächte, Die (Mayrhofer) (1819).
Sternewelten, Die (Fellinger) (1815).
Stimme der Liebe (Matthisson) (1815 and 1816).
Stimme der Liebe (Stolberg) (1816).
Strom, Der (Stadler) (1817).
Stürmische Morgen, Der (Müller) (W.R. 18) (1827).

Suleika I (Was bedeutet die Bewegung) (Goethe) (1821).
Suleika II (Ach, um deine feuchten Schwingen) (Goethe) (1821).
Täglich zu singen (Claudius) (1817).
Taubenpost, Die (Seidl) (S.G. 14) (1828).
Taucher, Der (Schiller) (1813–14).
Täuschung (Müller) (W.R. 19) (1827).
Täuschung, Die (Kosegarten) (1815).
Thekla : Eine Geisterstimme (Schiller) (1813 and 1817).
Tiefes Leid (Schulze) (1825).
Tischlerlied (?) (1815).
Tischlied (Goethe) (1815).
Tod Oscars, Der (Ossian) (1816).
Tod und das Mädchen, Der (Claudius) (1817).
Todesmusik (Schober) (1822).
Totengräberlied (Hölty) (1813).
Totengräbers Heimweh (Craigher) (1825).
Totengräberweise (Schlechta) (1826).
Totenkranz für ein Kind (Matthisson) (1815).
Totenopfer (Matthisson) (1814).
Traditor deluso, Il (Metastasio) (1827).
Tränenregen (Müller) (S.M. 10) (1823).
Trauer der Liebe (Jacobi) (1816).
Traum, Der (Hölty) (1815).
Trinklied (Zettler) (1815).
Trinklied, 'Bacchus' (see *Come, thou monarch of the vine*).
Trinklied vor der Schlacht (Körner) (1815).
Trockne Blumen (Müller) (S.M. 18) (1823).
Trost (Mayrhofer) (1819).
Trost (?) (1817).
Trost an Elisa (Matthisson) (1814).
Trost im Liede (Schober) (1817).
Trost in Tränen (Goethe) (1814).

Uber allen Zauber Liebe (Mayrhofer, fragment).
Über Wildemann (Schulze) (1826).
Um Mitternacht (Schulze) (1826).
Unendlichen, Dem (Klopstock) (1815).
Ungeduld (Müller) (S.M. 7) (1823).
Unglückliche, Der (Pichler) (1821).
Unglückliche, Der (see *Wanderer, Der* [Schmidt]).
Unterscheidung, Die (Seidl) (1826). (4 refrain songs, No. 1.)

Uraniens Flucht (Mayrhofer) (1817).
Vater mit dem Kind, Der (Bauernfeld) (1827).
Vaterlandslied (Klopstock) (1815).
Vatermörder, Der (Pfeffel) (1811).
Verfehlte Stunde, Die (Schlegel) (1816).
Vergebliche Liebe (Bernard) (1815).
Vergissmeinnicht (Schober) (1822).
Verklärung (see *Vital spark of heavenly flame*).
Versunken (Goethe) (1821).
Vier Weltalter, Die (Schiller) (1816).
Viola (Schober) (1822).
Vital spark of heavenly flame (Pope, trans. Herder) (1813).
Vögel, Die (Schlegel) (1820).
Vom Mitleiden Mariä (Schlegel) (1818).
Von Ida (Kosegarten) (1815).
Vor meiner Wiege (Leitner) (1827).

Wachtelschlag, Der (S. F. Sauter) (1822).
Waldesnacht (see *Im Walde*, Schlegel).
Wallensteiner Lanzknecht beim Trunk, Der (Leitner) (1827).
Wanderer, Der (Schlegel) (1819).
Wanderer, Der (Schmidt) (1816).
Wanderer an den Mond, Der (Seidl) (1826).
Wanderers Nachtlied (Goethe) (1815 and 1822).
Wandern, Das (Müller) (S.M. 1) (1823).
Wasserflut (Müller) (W.R. 6) (1827).
Wegweiser, Der (Müller) (W.R. 20) (1827).
Wehmut (Collin) (1822).
Wehmut (Salis) (1816).
Weiberfreund, Der (Cowley, trans. Ratschy) (1815).
Weinen, Das (Leitner) (1827).
Wer kauft Liebesgötter? (Goethe) (1815).
Wer nie sein Brot (see *Gesang des Harfners*).
Wer sich der Einsamkeit ergibt (see *Gesang des Harfners*).
Wetterfahne, Die (Müller) (W.R. 2) (1827).
Who is Silvia? (Shakespeare) (1826).
Widerschein (Schlechta) (1828).
Wie Ulfru fischt (Mayrhofer) (1817).
Wiedersehn (Schlegel) (1825).
Wiegenlied (Claudius) (1816).
Wiegenlied (Körner) (1815).

Schubert

Wiegenlied (Seidl) (1826).
Willkommen und Abschied (Goethe) (1822).
Winterabend, Der (Leitner) (1828).
Winterlied (Hölty) (1816).
Winterreise, Die (Müller), cycle of 24 songs (1827).
Wirtshaus, Das (Müller) (W.R. 21) (1827).
Wohin ? (Müller) (S.M. 2) (1823).
Wonne der Wehmut (Goethe) (1815).

Zufriedene, Der (Reissig) (1815).
Zügenglöcklein, Das (Seidl) (1826).
Zuleika (see *Suleika*).
Zum Punsche (Mayrhofer) (1816).
Zur Namensfeier des Herrn Andreas Siller (occasional song).
Zürnende Barde, Der (Bruchmann) (1822).
Zürnenden Diana, Der (Mayrhofer) (1820).
Zwerg, Der (Collin) (1822).

APPENDIX C

PERSONALIA

Barbaja, Domenico (1778–1841), Italian impresario, first a waiter, afterwards circus proprietor and finally the most popular of operatic managers. From 1821 to 1825, coming from the Teatro San Carlo in Naples, he was manager of the two chief houses in Vienna—the Kärntnertor Theatre and the Theater an der Wien.

Bauernfeld, Eduard von (1804–90), law student in Vienna, later civil servant and playwright.

Bocklet, Carl Maria von (1801–81), Bohemian pianist and violinist, settled in Vienna from 1820. Friend of Beethoven and Schubert.

Castelli, Ignaz Franz (1781–1862), Austrian dramatist, librettist and minor poet, editor of the *Allgemeiner musikalischer Anzeiger* (1829–40).

Chézy, Wilhelmine (or Helmina) Christine von, née von Klencke (born 1783), German dramatist and novelist, born in Berlin.

Collin, Heinrich von (1771–1811), and *Collin, Matthäus von* (1779–1824), brothers, Viennese poets. Heinrich wrote the drama of *Coriolan* for which Beethoven composed an overture.

Craigher, Jacob Nicolas von, Baron, Austrian nobleman, merchant and amateur poet.

Diabelli, Anton (1781–1858), Viennese music publisher, composer of piano and church music.

Eybler, Josef (1764–1846), Austrian composer and theorist, pupil of Albrechtsberger, was successively appointed *Regius Chori* at the Carmelite church in Vienna, imperial music teacher and, in 1825, *Capellmeister* to the court.

Fouqué, Friedrich Heinrich Karl, Baron de la Motte (1773–1843), German romantic poet.

Grillparzer, Franz (1791–1872), Austrian dramatist and poet in Vienna.

Grob, Therese (born 1800), Austrian soprano singer, daughter of a Viennese silk manufacturer, after whose death Schubert became a friend of the family.

Gyrowetz, Adalbert (1763–1850), Bohemian composer who first studied law in Prague, finished musical studies in Italy, visited Paris and London, became *Capellmeister* at the two court theatres in Vienna in 1804.

Haydn, Michael (1737–1806), Austrian composer, brother of Joseph Haydn, became musical director to the Bishop of Grosswardein in 1757 and to the Archbishop of Salzburg in 1762.

Herbeck, Johann (1831–77), court *Capellmeister* in Vienna, director of the court opera from 1871.

Herder, Johann Gottfried (1744–1803), German poet and translator, whose collection, *Stimmen der Völker,* contained folk poetry of various countries in his German versions.

Hölty, Ludwig Heinrich Christoph (1748–76), German romantic poet. One of the principal founders of the famous poetical brotherhood known as the *Hainbund.*

Hummel, Johann Nepomuk (1778–1837), Hungarian pianist and composer, pupil of Haydn and Salieri, *Capellmeister* to Prince Esterházy 1804–11.

Hüttenbrenner, Anselm (1794–1868), Austrian composer, pupil of Salieri (q.v.) and friend of Beethoven and Schubert.

Hüttenbrenner, Heinrich, brother of the preceding, amateur poet.

Hüttenbrenner, Josef, another brother, an amateur who served Schubert with great fidelity, making duet arrangements, correcting proofs and looking after his business arrangements.

Jacobi, Johann Georg (1740–1814), minor German poet.

Kind, Friedrich (1768–1843), German novelist and minor poet, author of the libretto of Weber's *Freischütz.*

Klopstock, Friedrich Gottlieb (1724–1803), German poet.

Körner, Karl Theodor (1791–1813), German patriotic poet of the Napoleonic wars, in which he fell as a member of Lützow's volunteer corps.

Kosegarten, Ludwig (1758–1818), German clergyman and minor poet.

Kotzebue, August Friedrich Ferdinand von (1761–1819), German dramatist, obtained an appointment at St. Petersburg, was arrested and sent to Siberia in 1800. A comedy secured his return, when he received the directorship of the German theatre at St. Petersburg.

Kreutzer, Conradin (1780–1849), German composer and conductor, pupil of Albrechtsberger in Vienna, where he was conductor at the Kärnt-nertor and Josefstadt Theatres 1825–40.

Kupelwieser, Josef, brother of Leopold Kupelwieser, compiler of Schubert's libretto for *Fierabras.*

Kupelwieser, Leopold (1796–1862), Austrian painter, became professor at the Kunstakademie, Vienna.

Lablache, Luigi (1794–1858), Italian bass singer of French and Irish descent.

Lachner, Franz (1803–90), Bavarian composer and conductor, studied in

Vienna and became conductor at the Kärntnertor Theatre in 1827. Later at Mannheim and Munich.

Lanner, Josef Franz Karl (1801–43), Austrian violinist and composer of dance music, colleague and later rival of Johann Strauss, sen.

Lappe, Carl (1773–1843), minor German romantic poet and schoolmaster, pupil of Kosegarten (q.v.).

Leitner, Carl Gottfried von (1800–90), minor Austrian poet.

Linke, Joseph (1783–1837), violoncellist and composer, member of Prince Rasumovsky's quartet in Vienna.

Loewe, Karl (1796–1869), German composer, especially of songs and narrative ballads carrying on the style of Reichardt, Zelter and Zumsteeg.

Matthisson, Friedrich von (1761–1831), minor German poet, remembered chiefly by Beethoven's setting of his *Adelaïde*.

Mayrhofer, Johann (1787–1836), Austrian civil servant, a close friend of Schubert's and a poet of classical leanings.

Méhul, Étienne Henri (1763–1817), French composer, produced twenty-four operas in seventeen years.

Metastasio (Pietro Trapassi) (1698–1782), Italian poet, librettist and trans-lator. He lived in Vienna for many years.

Milder-Hauptmann, Anna (1785–1838), German soprano singer, born at Constantinople.

Moscheles, Ignaz (1794–1870), Bohemian pianist and composer, living in Vienna in his early days and later mainly in London.

Mosel, Ignaz Franz von (1772–1844), Viennese diplomatist and amateur composer. In 1821 he was vice-director of the royal opera house.

Müller, Sophie (1803–30), actress and singer settled in Vienna from 1822.

Müller, Wilhelm (1794–1827), German poet who served as volunteer in the Prussian army. Father of the philologist Max Müller.

Novalis (Friedrich Leopold von Hardenberg) (1772–1801), German romantic poet and novelist.

Pachler-Koschak, Marie, Austrian pianist, wife of Dr. Karl Pachler, a barrister at Graz.

Pichler, Karoline (1769–1843), Austrian novelist and minor poetess.

Platen, August von, Count (1796–1835), German poet and dramatist, a classic in a romantic age.

Pyrker, Johann Ladislaus (1773–1847), Austrian prelate and poet, Bishop of Zips (1818), Patriarch of Venice (1820) and Archbishop of Erlau (1827).

Randhartinger, Benedikt (1802–93), Austrian tenor singer and conductor, pupil at the Seminary in Vienna after Schubert, sang in the court chapel from 1836 and became conductor there in 1862.

Reichardt, Johann Friedrich (1752–1814), German composer, critic and writer on music, appointed *Capellmeister* and court composer to Frederick the Great in 1776, dismissed from his Berlin appointment 1794. Important precursor of Schubert as a composer of songs.

Rellstab, Heinrich Friedrich Ludwig (1799–1860), German novelist, poet and music critic of the *Vossische Zeitung* in Berlin.

Rochlitz, Johann Friedrich (1769–1842), German music critic and founder of the *Allgemeine musikalische Zeitung* in Leipzig. An occasional poet.

Rückert, Friedrich (1788–1866), German poet and orientalist.

Ruczizka, Wenzel (1758–1823), composer and teacher in Vienna, violinist at the Hofburg Theatre, pianoforte master at the Seminary, court organist in 1793.

Salieri, Antonio (1750–1825), Italian composer and theorist settled in Vienna from 1766, appointed court *Capellmeister* and composer in 1788.

Salis-Seewis, Johann Georg von (1762–1834), Swiss poet.

Schechner, Nanette (1806–60), Bavarian singer, pupil of Weber, sang much in Italian opera, afterwards in German. Married in 1832 and left the stage in 1835.

Schlechta, Franz von, Baron, Austrian government official and amateur poet.

Schlegel, August Wilhelm von (1767–1845), and *Schlegel, Friedrich von* (1772–1829), brothers, German poets, literary critics and translators. The former began a translation of Shakespeare, afterwards revised and continued by Ludwig Tieck.

Schober, Franz von (1798–1883), a Swede of Austrian descent, settled in Vienna. One of Schubert's most intimate friends and an amateur poet.

Schopenhauer, Johanna (1766–1838), minor German poetess, mother of the philosopher.

Schreiber, Alois (1763–1841), historian, professor of aesthetics at Heidelberg and Karlsruhe, a minor poet.

Schröder-Devrient, Wilhelmine (1804–60), German dramatic soprano, made her first appearance in 1821, in Vienna.

Schubart, Christian (1739–91), German poet, musician and revolutionary.

Schulze, Ernst (1789–1817), minor German romantic poet.

Schuppanzigh, Ignaz (1776–1830), Austrian violinist in Vienna, director of the Augarten concerts, founder of a quartet of his own and that of Prince Rasumovsky.

Schwind, Moritz von (1804–71), Austrian painter of the romantic school.

Sechter, Simon (1788–1867), Bohemian theorist and composer in Vienna.

Seidl, Johann Gabriel (1804–75), Austrian schoolmaster, numismatist and poet.

Appendix C—Personalia

Senn, Johann Michael (1795–1857), Austrian soldier and poet, friend of Schubert's, who studied at the Seminary.

Spaun, Josef von, Freiherr (1788–1865), one of Schubert's earliest friends; civil servant in Vienna and the provinces.

Stolberg, Friedrich Leopold, Count (1750–1819), German poet, translator of Homer, Plato and Ossian.

Széchényi, Louis, Count, Hungarian nobleman and amateur poet.

Ubland, Ludwig (1787–1862), German poet.

Uz, Johann Peter (1720–96), minor German poet.

Vogl, Johann Michael (1768–1840), Austrian baritone singer at the court opera in Vienna, from which he retired with a pension in 1822, devoting himself to songs.

Weigl, Josef (1766–1846), Austrian composer, assistant conductor at the court opera in Vienna, 1790. Vice-*Capellmeister* to the court 1827.

Weiss, Franz (1788–1830), viola player in Vienna, member of Rasumovsky's quartet.

Zelter, Karl Friedrich (1758–1832), composer, conductor and teacher in Berlin, friend of Goethe, many of whose poems he set to music.

Zumsteeg, Johann Rudolf (1760–1802), German composer, educated at Stuttgart, where be became *Capellmeister* to the Duke of Württemberg in 1792. Friend of Schiller. Precursor of Schubert in vocal composition, especially of ballads.

APPENDIX D

BIBLIOGRAPHY

Abraham [Ed.], 'Schubert: A Symposium.' (London, 1946.)

Bauer, Moritz, 'Die Lieder Franz Schuberts.' Vol. i only. (Leipzig, 1915.)

Bie, Oscar, 'Das deutsche Lied.' (Berlin, 1926.)

—— 'Franz Schubert: sein Leben und sein Werk.' (Berlin, 1925.)

Biehle, H., 'Schuberts Lieder in Kritik und Literatur.' (Berlin, 1928.)

Bosch, H., 'Die Entwicklung des Romantischen in Schuberts Liedern.' (Borna⁄Leipzig, 1930.)

Brown, Maurice J. E., 'Schubert's Variations.' (London, 1954.)

—— 'Schubert: Discoveries of the Last Decade.' (*M.Q.,* xlvii, 1961.)

—— 'Essays on Schubert.' (London, 1966.)

—— 'Schubert Songs.' (London, 1967.)

—— 'Schubert: a Critical Biography.' (London, 1958.)

—— 'Schubert: Discoveries of the Last Decade.' (*M.Q.,* lvii, 1971.)

Buenzod, E., 'Franz Schubert' (in French). (Paris, 1937.)

Capell, Richard, 'Schubert's Songs.' (London, 1928; rev. 1973.)

Cuzon, Henri de, 'Les Lieder de Franz Schubert.' (Paris, 1899.)

Dahms, Walter, 'Schubert.' (Stuttgart, 1928.)

Deutsch, Otto Erich, 'Franz Schubert: die Dokumente seines Lebens und Schaffens.' 2 vols. (Munich, 1913–14.)

—— 'Schubert: a Documentary Biography,' enlarged English edition, translated by Eric Blom. (London, 1946.)

—— 'Schubert: Thematic Catalogue of all his Works.' (London, 1951.)

—— 'Die historischen Bildnisse Franz Schuberts in getreuen Nach⁄bildungen.' (Vienna, 1922.)

—— 'Schuberts Goethe⁄Lieder.' (Vienna, 1926.)

—— [Ed.], 'Schubert: die Erinnerung seiner Freunde.' (Leipzig, 1957, 3/1974; Eng. trans., 1958.)

Einstein, A., 'Schubert.' (London, 1951.)

Feigl, Rudolf, 'Klar um Schubert: Beseitigung von Irrmeinungen, Fehl⁄angaben, usw.' (Linz, 1938.)

Fischer⁄Dieskau, D., 'Auf den Spuren der Schubert⁄Lieder: Werden, Wesen, Wirkung. (Wiesbaden, 1971; Eng. trans., 1976.)

Flower, Newman, 'Franz Schubert: the Man and his Circle.' (London, 1928.)

216

Appendix D—Bibliography

Friedlaender, M., 'Beiträge zur Biographie Franz Schuberts.' (Berlin, 1887; Leipzig, 1928, as 'Franz Schubert: Skizze seines Lebens und Wirkens.')

Georgiades, T. G., 'Schubert: Musik und Lyrik.' (Göttingen, 1967.)

Gérold, Th., 'Schubert (in French). (Paris, 1923.)

Grove, George, 'Beethoven—Schubert—Mendelssohn,' reprint of articles from 'Dictionary of Music and Musicians,' 4th edition. (London, 1951.)

Günther, F., 'Schuberts Lied: eine ästhetische Monographie.' (Stuttgart, 1928.)

Heuberger, Richard, 'Franz Schubert.' (Third edition, Berlin, 1920.)

Hoorickx, van R., 'Thematic Catalogue of Schubert's Works: New Additions, Corrections and Notes.' (R. B. M., xxviii–xxx, 1974–6.)

Hutchings, A., 'Schubert.' (London, 1945, rev. 4/1973.)

Kahl, Willi, 'Verzeichnis des Schrifttums über Franz Schubert, 1828–1928.' (Ratisbon, 1938.)

Klein, R., 'Schubert-Stätten.' (Vienna, 1972.)

Kobald, Karl, 'Franz Schubert and his Times.' Translated from the German by Beatrice Marshall. (London, 1928.)

Költzsch, Hans, 'Franz Schubert in seinen Klaviersonaten.' (Leipzig, 1927.)

Laaff, Ernst, 'Franz Schuberts Sinfonien.' (Wiesbaden, 1933.)

Landormy, Paul, 'La Vie de Schubert.' (Paris, 1928.)

Le Masséna, C. E., and *Merx, Hans,* 'The Songs of Schubert: a Guide.' (New York, 1928.)

Mies, Paul, 'Schubert, der Meister des Liedes.' (Berlin, 1928.)

—— 'Franz Schubert.' (Leipzig, 1954.)

'*Music & Letters,*' Schubert Number, Vol. IX, No. 4. (London, 1928.)

Newman, W. S., 'Freedom of Tempo in Schubert's Instrumental Music.' (M.Q., lxi, 1975.)

Niggli, A., 'Franz Schuberts Leben und Werke.' (Leipzig, 1925.)

Nottebohm, Gustav, 'Thematisches Verzeichnis der im Druck erschienenen Werke von Franz Schubert.' (Vienna, 1874.)

Orel, A., 'Franz Schubert, 1797–1828: sein Leben in Bildern.' (Leipzig, 1938.)

—— 'Der junge Schubert: aus der Lernzeit des Künstlers.' (Vienna and Leipzig, 1940.)

Paumgartner, Bernhard, 'Die Schubertianer.' (Vienna, 1928.)

—— 'Franz Schubert.' (Zurich, 1943.)

Petzoldt, R., 'Franz Schubert: sein Leben in Bildern.' (Leipzig, 1953.)

Porter, E. G., 'The Songs of Schubert.' (London, 1937.)
—— 'Schubert's Harmonies.' (M.R., xviv, 1958.)
—— 'Schubert's Song technique.' (London, 1961.)
Prod'homme, G. J., 'Schubert raconté par ceux qui l'ont vu.' (Paris, 1928.)
Radcliffe, P., 'Schubert Piano Sonatas.' (London, 1967.)
Reed, J., 'Schubert: the Final Years.' (London, 1972.)
—— 'How the "Great" C major was written.' (M.L., lvi, 1975.)
Reissmann, A., 'Franz Schubert: sein Leben und seine Werke.' (Berlin, 1873.)
Riezler, W., 'Schuberts Instrumentalmusik.' (Zurich, 1967.)
Rogeri, E., 'Schubert: la vita, le opere.' (Turin, 1928.)
Schnapper, Edith, 'Die Gesänge des jungen Schubert, vor dem Durchbruch des romantischen Liedprinzipes.' (Berne, 1937.)
Schubert, Franz, 'Briefe und Schriften.' Edited by Otto Erich Deutsch. (Munich, 1919.)
—— 'Letters and other Writings.' Edited by Otto Erich Deutsch. Translated by Venetia Savile. (London, 1928.)
—— 'Tagebuch.' Facsimile of the Original MS. edited by Otto Erich Deutsch. (Vienna, 1928.)
Smith, Alexander Brent, 'Schubert: Quartet in D minor and Octet. (Oxford and London, 1927.)
—— 'Schubert: the Symphonies, C major and B minor.' (Oxford and London, 1926.)
Spaun, Josef von, 'Erinnerungen an Franz Schubert.' Edited by Georg Schünemann. (Zürich, 1936.)
Stefan, Paul, 'Franz Schubert.' (Berlin, 1928.)
Therstappen, H. J., 'Die Entwicklung der Form bei Schubert, dargestellt an den ersten Sätzen seiner Sinfonien.' (Leipzig, 1931.)
Tovey, Donald Francis, 'Franz Schubert,' in 'The Heritage of Music,' edited by Hubert J. Foss. (Oxford and London, 1927.)
Truscott, H., 'Franz Schubert' in 'The Symphony', ed. R. Simpson. (Harmondsworth, 1966-7.)
Vetter, Walther, 'Franz Schubert.' (Potsdam, 1934.)
—— 'Der Klassiker Schubert.' (Leipzig, 1953.)
Werle, H. [Ed.], 'Franz Schubert in seinen Briefen und Aufzeichnungen.' (Leipzig, 1948.)
Westrup, J. A., 'Schubert Chamber Music.' (London, 1969.)
Whitaker-Wilson, C., 'Franz Schubert: Man and Composer.' (London, 1928.)
Wiora, W., 'Das Deutsche Lied.' (Wolfenbüttel and Zurich, 1971.)

THE POETS OF SCHUBERT'S SONGS

THIS list shows the authors' names and the number of their poems set to music by Schubert, as published in Breitkopf & Härtel's complete edition. The number of each volume is indicated above the names. The figures in line with each name show how many poems were set, though it should be remembered that Schubert often used the same verses more than once. The 71 Goethe settings, for instance, include only 59 different poems.

B. & H.'s Edition	Vol. I	II	III	IV	V	VI	VII	VIII	IX	X	Total
Bauernfeld	—	—	—	—	—	—	—	1	—	—	1
Baumberg	—	—	5	—	—	—	—	—	—	—	5
Bernhardt	—	1	—	—	—	—	—	—	—	—	1
Bertrand	—	2	—	—	—	—	—	—	—	—	2
Bruchmann	—	—	—	—	—	—	5	—	—	—	5
Castelli	—	—	—	—	—	—	—	1	—	—	1
Chézy (see Müller, footnote)											
Cibber (trans. by Craigher)	—	—	—	—	—	—	—	1	—	—	1
Claudius	—	—	—	9	3	—	—	—	—	—	12
Collin, M.	—	—	—	1	—	—	2	1	—	1	5
Cowley (trans. Ratschzy)	—	—	1	—	—	—	—	—	—	—	1
Craigher	—	—	—	—	—	—	—	2	—	—	2
Deinhardstein	—	—	1	—	—	—	—	—	—	—	1
Ehrlich	—	1	—	—	—	—	—	—	—	—	1
Fellinger	—	2	1	—	—	—	—	—	—	—	3
Fouqué (de la Motte)	3	—	—	1	1	—	—	—	—	—	5
Goethe [1]	6	10	20	10	2	9	5	4	—	5	71
Goldoni	—	—	—	—	—	—	—	—	1	—	1
Gotter	—	—	—	—	—	—	—	—	1	—	1
Grillparzer	—	—	—	—	—	1	—	—	—	—	1
Hardenberg (see Novalis)											
Heine	—	—	—	—	—	—	—	—	6	—	6

[1] The two Suleika songs are actually by Marianne Willemer.

B. & H.'s Edition	Vol. I	II	III	IV	V	VI	VII	VIII	IX	X	Total
Hell	—	—	—	1	—	—	—	—	—	—	1
Herder	—	—	—	—	—	—	—	—	1	—	1
Hölty	1	9	—	11	—	—	—	—	—	—	21
Hüttenbrenner, H.	—	—	—	—	—	1	—	—	—	—	1
Jacobi	—	—	—	6	1	—	—	—	—	—	7
Kalchberg	—	—	1	—	—	—	—	—	—	—	1
Kenner	—	3	—	—	—	—	—	—	—	—	3
Kind	—	—	—	—	1	—	—	—	—	—	1
Klenke	—	—	—	—	—	—	—	—	1	—	1
Klopstock	—	—	9	4	—	—	—	—	—	—	13
Köpken	—	—	—	1	—	—	—	—	—	—	1
Körner	—	10	2	—	1	—	—	—	—	—	13
Kosegarten	—	13	7	1	—	—	—	—	—	—	21
Kuffner	—	—	—	—	—	—	—	1	—	—	1
Kumpf (Ermin)	—	1	1	—	—	—	—	—	—	—	2
Lappe	—	—	—	—	—	—	—	2	—	—	2
Leitner	—	—	—	—	—	—	1	—	7	—	8
Leon	—	—	—	1	—	—	—	—	—	—	1
Lubi	1	—	—	—	—	—	—	—	—	—	1
Mailath	—	—	—	—	—	1	—	—	—	—	1
Matthisson	14	3	1	7	—	—	—	—	—	1	26
Mayrhofer	1	—	2	10	16	10	3	4	—	1	47
Metastasio	—	—	—	1 [1]	—	—	—	—	—	9	10
Müller	—	—	—	—	—	—	20	—	24	1 [2]	45
Novalis (Hardenberg)	—	—	—	—	—	6	—	—	—	—	6
Ossian (trans. Harold, etc.)	—	2	3	2	1	—	—	—	—	1	9
Ottenwalt	—	—	—	—	1	—	—	—	—	—	1
Petrarch [3] (trans. A. W. Schlegel, etc.)	—	—	—	3	—	—	—	—	—	—	3

[1] Translated by Heinrich von Collin.

[2] Part of the words of the Müller song in this volume, *Der Hirt auf dem Felsen,* are by Helmina von Chézy.—E. B.

[3] One of the three Petrarch sonnets was formerly attributed to Dante, an old error. (See Capell, *Schubert's Songs,* page 147.)—E. B.

Appendix E—The Poets of Schubert's Songs

B. & H.'s Edition	Vol. I	II	III	IV	V	VI	VII	VIII	IX	X	Total
Pfeffel	1	—	—	—	—	—	—	—	—	—	1
Pichler	—	—	—	2	—	1	—	—	—	—	3
Platen	—	—	—	—	—	—	2	—	—	—	2
Platner	—	—	—	—	1	—	—	—	—	—	1
Pope (trans. Herder)	1	—	—	—	—	—	—	—	—	—	1
Prandstetter	—	—	1	—	—	—	—	—	—	—	1
Pratobevera	—	—	—	—	—	—	—	—	1	—	1
Pyrker	—	—	—	—	—	—	—	2	—	—	2
Reil	—	—	—	—	—	—	—	—	1	—	1
Reissig	—	—	1	—	—	—	—	—	—	—	1
Rellstab	—	—	—	—	—	—	—	—	7	3	10
Rochlitz	1	—	—	2	—	—	—	—	—	—	3
Roos	—	—	—	—	—	1	—	—	—	—	1
Rückert	—	—	—	—	—	1	—	4	—	—	5
Salis-Seewis	—	—	1	11	3	1	—	—	—	—	16
Sauter, S. F.	—	—	—	—	—	—	—	—	—	1	1
Schiller	8	5	10	6	5	4	2	1	—	1	42
Schlechta	—	1	—	1	—	1	—	3	1	—	7
Schlegel, A. W.	—	—	—	3	1	1	—	2	—	—	7
Schlegel, Fr.	—	—	2	—	2	10	1	1	—	—	16
Schmidt, G. P.	—	—	—	1	—	—	—	—	—	—	1
Schober	—	—	1	1	3	—	5	2	—	—	12
Schopenhauer, Johanna	—	—	—	—	—	—	—	1	—	—	1
Schreiber	—	—	—	4	—	—	—	—	—	—	4
Schubart	—	—	—	2	2	—	—	—	—	—	4
Schubert (Ferd.)	—	—	—	—	—	—	—	—	—	1	1
Schücking	1	—	—	—	—	—	—	—	—	—	1
Schulze	—	—	—	—	—	—	—	9	—	—	9
Schütz	—	—	—	—	—	—	—	2	—	—	2
Scott (trans. Storck, etc.)	—	—	—	—	—	—	—	6	2	—	8
Seidl	—	—	—	—	—	—	—	10	1	—	11
Senn	—	—	—	—	—	—	2	—	—	—	2
Shakespeare (trans. Mayer-hofer, A. W. Schlegel and Bauernfeld)	—	—	—	—	—	—	—	3	—	—	3

Schubert

B. & H.'s Edition	Vol. I	II	III	IV	V	VI	VII	VIII	IX	X	Total
Silbert	—	—	—	—	—	2	—	—	—	—	2
Spaun	—	—	—	—	I	—	—	—	—	—	I
Stadler	—	I	—	—	I	—	—	—	—	I	3
Stolberg	—	—	2	3	—	—	2	—	—	—	7
Stoll	—	—	3	—	—	—	—	—	—	—	3
Széchényi	—	—	—	—	2	—	—	—	—	—	2
Tiedge	—	—	I	—	—	—	—	—	—	—	I
Uhland	—	—	—	—	—	I	—	—	—	—	I
Uz	—	—	—	5	—	—	—	—	—	—	5
Vitorelli	—	—	—	—	—	—	—	—	—	2	2
Werner	—	—	—	—	I	I	—	—	—	—	2
Zettler	—	I	—	—	—	—	—	—	—	—	I
Anonymous	—	I	2	4	4	—	—	I	—	6	18

INDEX

Index

Index